STONE COUNTRY

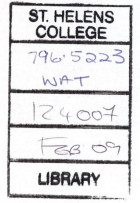
© *Stone Country Press 2008*

www.stonecountry.co.uk

ISBN 978-0-9548779-2-7

British Library Cataloguing-in-Publication Data
A catalogue record for this book is available from the British Library

The Stone Country Guide to

Bouldering in Scotland

Edited by John Watson

Foreword

'Stone Country' was published in 2005 in a bid to encourage people to explore Scotland's bouldering potential. It seemed unjust that Scotland's vast geology was given little more than lip-service by the climbing community and assumed not to have the same density of bouldering as other countries. This is changing rapidly as the vogue for pure bouldering continues... Scotland has plenty of stones and boulder fields which in recent years have attracted a little more focus, despite their relative diaspora and remoteness.

Hence the need for a proper Scottish bouldering guidebook. We have updated many areas, added a host of new venues and cleaned up the realities and descriptions of many problems…hopefully this will provide the travelling boulderer with a book they can reliably use to find good bouldering wherever they are in Scotland. It is a selective guide, choosing only the best problems in each area, concentrating on the classic lines and most popular problems, with a nod to both the specialist 'project' boulderer as well as the traditional 'circuit' boulderer...

...whichever you are, happy bouldering!

John Watson

SCOTTISH BOULDERING VENUES

1 ABERDEENSHIRE p.8
2 INVERNESS & STRATHSPEY p.24
3 EAST COAST p.45
4 TROSSACHS p.61
5 CLYDE p.76
6 THE SOUTHWEST p.93
7 ARROCHAR p.103
8 LOCHABER p.124
9 WEST COAST p.140
10 THE NORTHWEST p.156
11 THE ISLANDS p.172

www.stonecountry.co.uk

Harold Raeburn testing the 'limits of adhesion' at Salisbury Crags in the early 1900's..

Testing the limits of adhesion on Glencoe granite in 2007

'Bloc to the Future' - A Brief History of Scottish Bouldering

There is an unprecedented gold-rush on world bouldering, with young (and older) climbers seeking new gravities on untouched rock; from the glowing boulders of Hampi in India to the ancient 'stanes' and 'clachs' of Scotland… it is maybe the last undrawn map for the climber in a modern age of fading heroes: Murray, Smith, Cunningham, Patey et al 'diminishing into the west' in a sunset of epic stories and golden era rock climbing! Maybe bouldering is just the open-ended extension of limits in rock climbing, a natural continuation to this history? Whatever your opinion, most young climbers have as large a portfolio of 'want to do' bouldering problems as they have routes, and this includes venues that they want to visit: Fontainebleau, Hampi, Castle Hill, Bishop, Hueco Tanks, Albarracin… for the dedicated boulderer, stony landscapes are addictive playgrounds and future climbing heritage sites. Bouldering itself has become a climbing lifestyle, an approach - a thing on to itself and we should maybe invite it into the mountaineering pantheon as soon as we can.

In Scotland it is no different and exploration really is only limited by the weather, imagination, will-power and the almighty midge! Dumbarton is the heartland of Scottish bouldering but new and more remote venues have been opened in the last two decades allowing the sport to flourish and experiment on some of the most varied geology on the planet, and maybe that is the strongest attraction of Scottish stones. But what of the historical context of bouldering? Even in Scotland, it is not a recent phenomenon.

In Harold Raeburn's instructional Mountaineering Art published in 1920 (curiously dedicated to 'the solution of some severe problems of mountaineering art'), his sister Ruth Raeburn wrote the section on 'Climbing for the Novice' and introduces us to the art of bouldering:

Bouldering is of great use in teaching what small holds can be employed with safety – at a pinch – on great climbs. It has also a wonderful effect in improving the balance, and in teaching the correct attitudes to assume, and efforts to make, on various kinds of holds. On a single fifteen foot boulder one may find a series of climbs containing all the characteristic difficulties one will encounter in a whole day's climb on a great rock-peak.

Of course, for the modern day boulderer, we have just removed the great rock peak and are happy with a boulder, finding the 'correct attitude' to conquer a sequence of moves; all that has changed is the scenery for the pantomime. From Raeburn's day through to the late 20th century, bouldering continued with this philosophy that it was all practice for something grander. If bouldering, in a modern sense, is just an extension of rock climbing standards and technique, then we can see why it maybe wasn't so much in the consciousness of the golden era climbers. Here is W.H.Murray on what lay before Scottish climbers in the 1930's (taken from his autobiography *The Evidence of Things Not Seen*):

With so much ground inviting exploration, easier routes were naturally taken first. We felt no pressures, no interest in the aid climbing starting in Germany, other than the natural urge shared by all to climb harder as skills are won.

John Cunningham demonstrating the Narnain classic 'Crucifix' to a bemused post-war Creagh Dhu party.

Sixty years of Ben Ledi bouldering...

Murray's statement isn't so different to the modern boulderer decrying dry tooling! In Murray's time, there were plenty of other standards to be pushed, both technically and technologically (especially in ice climbing), so bouldering was yet to be seen as significant. It only became significant when rock climbing standards, in terms of sheer physical difficulty, became an issue… so maybe not until the likes of Robin Smith, Jimmy Marshall and John Cunningham (for example) started pushing grades in the 50's and 60's that we saw Scotland's 'first' boulder problems (it will be even longer before the 'philosophy' of bouldering as an aesthetic thing in itself takes over from mere grade-bumping).

Probably Scotland's most significant 'first' boulder problem was on the Narnain boulders, under the craggy shadow of the Cobbler - that working-class mountain overlooking the distant industry of the Clyde, where Creagh Dhu members 'bust their chops' on weekend excursions from the shipyards and factories of Glasgow. One such climber was John Cunningham, who in an early photograph is seen in strenuous mid-bouldering on the north arête of the Narnain boulder, surrounded by no fewer than eight bemused onlookers with their hands shoved meekly in their pockets while Cunningham stretches to the top of the problem. It was such a significant climbing moment it merited a photograph to itself, and the hunch-backed deep-pocketing of the other climbers suggests Cunningham was gifted with more futuristic abilities than they. These days Crucifix would be given British 6a, which is an E4 crux move - impressive when you think this was only a few years after the Second World War had just kidney-punched the soul and sugar out of Scotland.

Elsewhere, others were 'keeping their hand in' on the boulders - Kevin Howett discovered that the Ben Ledi boulders and their problems had been demonstrated to members of the Ochils mountaineering club by a Falkirk cobbler named Ferguson in the 1940's. Subsequently the SMC Southern Highlands described these problems in a 1949 edition, such as the classic highball 5a arête on the 'Corpse' boulder that was called simply Bernie's Climb - bouldering was beginning to be taken seriously, the first signs of which are the colonisation of names and grades.

In the 50's and 60's, Robin Smith was pushing rock grades into Extreme levels (British 5a moves and above). Indeed, while naturally onsighting routes, he had a boulderer's eye for lines that exhibited sheer problem-solving and technical difficulty - in May 1957 he climbed the diversionary slab of the Rosetta Stone on the top of the Cir Mhor pinnacle on Arran, just for the hell of it, and a boulder problem was born. This is a highball friction problem at British 5a (given HVS at the time) but shows that in attempting such short lines, Robin Smith was keen to 'train' his body to use fewer holds, to problem solve or to seek steeper ground. Like Raeburn he used the Salisbury crags in Edinburgh to do just such training and 'limits' exploration and two years later he did Shibboleth, the first multi-pitch E2 in Scotland with its notorious bouldery (and wet) crux sequence.

3

The highball tradition at Dumbarton Rock...

Mal Smith on BNI Direct at Dumbarton Rock

It wasn't until the 1970's that bouldering began to become a sociable and common activity amongst climbers attempting to break physical climbing boundaries. Naturally it was Dumbarton rock which led the vanguard of rock standards, maybe because the rock here is so athletic in character and 'modernistic' (Dave Cuthbertson's words in the 'E11' film). The routes themselves all have a high entry level of at least HVS 5a, many significantly harder, so it was logical that climbers would practise on the giant boulders below the crag and attempt to winkle out the secrets of this faceted and bemusing geology. In the early sixties Neil MacNiven and Brian Shields had climbed most of the early classic boulder problems such as the terrifying hanging slab of *BNI*, but again with an eye on training for the routes. Later in the sixties and into the 70's, there was a more concentrated focus and specific 'problems' were solved such as Pete Greenwell's now classic *Gorilla* (a first 6b in 1978). In the 1980's, Gary Latter added some new classic 6a's such as *Mestizo, Toto*, the butch 6b that is *Pongo* and the highball 6b that is *Physical Graffiti*. Dave Cuthbertson also added hard problems such as *Mugsy*, touching the Brit 6c grade. Then the 90's was ushered in with the dedicated bouldering of Andy Gallagher. Andy's dynamic power and industrial finger strength opened the eyes to what was possible at Dumbarton and brought it in line with bouldering grades elsewhere in Britain and Europe, especially in relation to the new bouldering addiction to traversing (*Consolidated, 90's Traverse, Mugsy Traverse*), which was reflective of the need for endurance for the new sports routes popping up at 'the Rock' and on the continent. Andy also added hard problems such as *Slap Happy, Shadow* and *Trick of the Vale*, still considered testpieces to today's indoor-trained bouldering specialist.

Then in 1994 a young Malcolm Smith nonchalantly cranked out the first Brit 7a problem *The Shield* and then stunned everyone with the sit start to the classic *Pongo* crack in 1998, the first boulder problem in Scotland to break the elusive Fontainebleau 8th grade and link the frustratingly distant holds at the bottom of the crack. Also in the late 90's and continuing to the present, Dave MacLeod or 'Dumby Dave' raised the bar even further with ascents of high 7th and 8th grade problems such as *In Bloom, Firestarter, Sabotage, King Kong* and the recent Font 8b's of *Pressure* and *Sanction*. So Dumbarton is an example of the generational excitement of world bouldering and the constant game with physical climbing limits... Dumby will probably continue to produce jaw-dropping boulder problems well into the future.

With the acceleration of bouldering standards at Dumbarton, the rest of Scotland seemed a curiously ignored backwater, especially by a strong English bouldering scene which rarely if ever travelled north of Dumbarton, but that balance is now being redressed and it is now not uncommon to see strong climbers from all round Europe visiting the remote boulders of Coire Lagan in Skye, the red Torridonian sandstone blocs of Applecross and Coigach, or the wave-washed schist boulders at Portlethen in Aberdeen, home to hard modern testpieces such as Tim Rankin's *Kayla*.

Richie Betts on 'Match & Snatch' at Cummingston

'The evidence of things not seen...'

With the amount of geology in the country, it is no surprise that boulderers are scouring the glens and coastlines looking for superb natural bouldering lines. This has led to a bonanza of fresh exploration, though in many cases it is wise to note many climbers will have been here before. Popular crag areas always had notable bouldering asides, such as Cummingston and Reiff, where Brian Lawrie climbed the highball 6a *Earthshaker* (named and climbed well before boulder mats muffled the sound of falling climbers). Glen Nevis too was a natural bouldering venue, with the Sky Pilot wall producing classic hard lines around the Millenium, such as Dave Cuthbertson's 7c problems *Beatleback* and *Catch 22*. The trend for naming and grading boulder problems is a comparatively recent event, aided and abetted by the Internet, so a natural humility must be maintained when 'claiming' a problem... unless it is a significant cutting edge line, it is impossible to tell who may have climbed this before. Naming, grading and mapping a problem is just a sign of a healthy climbing community finding a 'new vein', and in generational terms of Scottish climbing, bouldering may be seen as the natural legacy of rock climbing and sport climbing, or it may mutate further into the likes of urban 'buildering', *Parkour* and indoor climbing that we see exhibited by the younger generation, who knows?

Bouldering in Scotland has a healthy ethic, fed from a deep historical source of traditionalism, competition and humility within a bigger landscape, and it is good to see these sources being reflected online and in the climbing magazines: bouldering is a naturally open forum and the fruits of everyone's quiet exploration or online enthusiasm all adds to the dynamic weave of Scottish climbing. It is vital as individuals we accept responsibility for our bouldering and leave projects to others if we find them too hard or feel the urge to 'improve holds' or even submit false claims. The explosion of interest in bouldering shows a new archaeology of climbing happening right in front of us. It is a fascinating time for climbing in general - the evolution of websites, blogs and forums adds to 'the evidence of things not seen' in our vertical world. Suitable overseeing words from W.H.Murray, which we can also take to mean that in the long run our climbing will be seen in true and proper context.

Bloc Notes for Scotland

Weather

Scotland is notorious for changeable weather. One day can be sunny and crisp, the next foul and 'dreich'. Though you should always be emotionally prepared to be rained off, you can always find steep bouldering somewhere that can stay dry in the rain (venues such as Dumbarton, Cullen Caves, Ardmair). The summer (June, July, August) is a poor time to boulder due to humidity, heat, rampant vegetation (bracken and boulder mats at war!) and of course insects (midges, which should need no introduction, and ticks, which can carry pathogens), so coastal venues are best then (Garheugh, Thirlstane, Portlethen, Sandwood Bay etc). Dry spells during high pressure weather in autumn, winter and spring provide cool dry conditions perfect for bouldering. Bouldering in this country needs careful selection with all these factors in mind, so keep your plans as flexible as possible and move around. The weather can be perfect in Aberdeen one day, for example, yet be downright biblical in the West (that's the usual case!).

Not injured... just sleeping it off!

Emergencies

Bouldering can be as dangerous as any other climbing activity and accidents do happen (you don't have ropes after all). Remember, all decisions made are the climber's individual responsibility, so take care! The culture in Scotland is to accept you are responsible for your own welfare, so don't go blaming (or suing) others - it's bad form and won't stick. It is wise to take bouldering mats and friends who know the art of 'spotting' (not just fag-in-mouth, hands out beggar-bowl spotting), and always check your landings. Scotland has many remote areas where mobiles don't work, so think twice about highball problems and bad landings… you may be a long way from succour with a sprained ankle or worse. Telephone 999 or 112 on your mobile to access all emergency services.

Access

Like our Scandinavian neighbours, Scotland now has an enlightened attitude to freedom of access, thanks to the statutes of the Scottish Parliament. You are free to access and explore most areas, but this comes with a responsibility to be sensitive to others whose livelihood depends on the land. It's always the best option to talk to farmers over difficult access, and explain your bouldering rights patiently. During stalking time, please use the hill-phone facilities to check for activity. Also, please take note of bird bans and do not disturb the flora and fauna. If you come across a nesting bird, move on, there's plenty of bouldering elsewhere. Also, car-parking can be limited, so always be considerate or park further away and walk. It's always polite just to ask private landowners or farmers where it's best to park… they're often more helpful than you think.

Ethics

An increasing awareness of ethics comes with experience and love of the hills, but there are a few things to be school-masterly about: do not wilfully disturb the flora and fauna, don't clean over-vegetated problems (it grows back), leave no litter (that includes fingertape, chalk balls, rags, drinks cans and carpets etc). Most Scottish bouldering venues will naturally lead you to feel part of the landscape, so don't act as if you own it. Online ethics are another thing entirely… false claims will lead you only to ignominy and public shame, so be humble and if you fail on a problem, just take the medicine and train harder!

Geology

Thankfully Scotland has a rich geology and options for choosing rock specific for conditions is one of the bonuses of bouldering in Scotland: sandstone, gritstone, limestone, granites, schists, conglomerate, quartzites, gabbros, basalts, dolerites, greywackes, gneiss… all have differing characteristics. If you like grit-stone bouldering for example, try the Torridonian sandstone of the North West venues – it is a red pebbled sandstone that behaves just like some classic Peak venues. The landscape in Scotland is also dramatic due to the mix of glaciation and geology, so whichever glen you decide to explore, it is likely to be spectacular. In Scotland, bouldering isn't just about the numbers…

www...

www.stonecountry.co.uk
www.scottishclimbs.com
www.transition-extreme.com
www.cubbyimages.com
www.mountaineering-scotland.org.uk

www.smc.org.uk
www.ukclimbing.com
www.betaguides.com
www.alphamountaineering.co.uk
www.davemacleod.com

Web Sources

The web is a fantastic place to banter about bouldering, provide new information and source many differing opinions as well as topos and maps and other paraphernalia. In Scotland, the most useful information site is www.scottishclimbs.com where new problems can be reported on their own 'wiki' where you can edit and update information. Bouldering news and updates can also be found on various blogs, as well as at www.stonecountry.co.uk. If all else fails, a Google search usually reveals something. Listed on the left are other useful sites.

Classic Grade Breakers

Font 4	Steptoe - Dumbarton	Font 7a	Malcolm's Arête - Torridon
Font 5	Blue Meanie - Dumbarton	Font 7b	Mother Farquhar - Aberdeen
Font 6a	Red 22 - Glen Lednock	Font 7c	Precious - Arrochar
Font 6b	Spank the Ramp - Brin	Font 8a	Deep Breath - Glen Nevis
Font 6c	Fight Club - Trossachs	Font 8b	Sanction - Dumbarton

Grading

This guide uses the standard European 'Fontainebleau' grading system, mainly due to its familiarity in Europe and its wide range of grades to express difficulty (which also just means controversy). No system is perfect, and be prepared to find a problem easier or harder than the grade suggested – this is due to lack of repeats, conditions on the day, your personal fitness, author integrity (or lack of!) and dozens of other factors (sheer outrageousness, sandbagging etc.). We have tried to keep the grades fair to Fontainebleau standards and have taken note of repeat ascensionists' opinions – remember, a Font 5 can feel very hard and some 7b's may be easier than you think, or the other way round… so just have fun.

1 **ABERDEENSHIRE**

*Ali Coull on his own
Boltsheugh Eliminate*

ABERDEEN

The Aberdeen bouldering scene is vibrant, prolific and republican when once it was a backwater area of secluded 'training' areas overshadowed maybe by the proximity of traditional climbing in the Cairngorms and on the sea-cliffs. The bouldering has been developed over recent years on the excellent sea-washed schists and granites of the Aberdeen sea-cliffs, specifically the areas south of Portlethen, around Berrymuir Head and down as far as Muchalls. These secluded coves and bays have all provided fruitful territory for the local bouldering community to develop some very hard and technically notable problems on steep calved boulders and wave-washed walls. Inland, areas such as the Luath Stones at Alford and Pannannich Hill near Ballater have provided excellent circuit areas for a summer's evening escape from work. Of course, giant stones reside everywhere in the Cairngorms and the slow diaspora of the mat-backed boulderer is beginning to penetrate even these remote corries and glens, so future bouldering development is guaranteed for the adventurous.

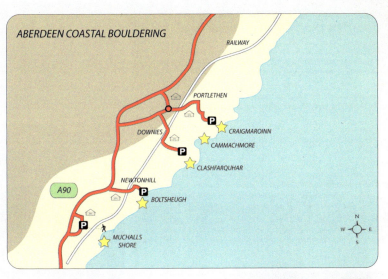

Luath Stones - mainly short problems up to Font 7a on excellent quartzy schist, good for family days out and the kids.

Craig Corn Arn - numerous granite stones on Pannannich Hill near Ballater. Lots of bouldering potential.

Portlethen - or 'Craigmaroinn'. Powerful short bouldering on steep schist. Some tidal problems. Excellent rock.

Cammachmore - large bay with some good shore-line bouldering and wildlife. Take a few mats though and spotters!

Clashfarquhar - some good sunny easier bouldering, but mainly a hardcore heaven for the local powerhouses.

Boltsheugh - originally a sports venue and a popular stamina training area. Very sunny aspect and pleasant even in winter.

Muchalls Shore - lots of easier grades on a variety of tidal rocks and walls. Good for a little exploring and seclusion.

9

BOLTSHEUGH   NO 914 933

Originally a short sports venue, many of the sport climbs can now be bouldered with a few mats. Although straight-up problems are limited, there are many excellent traverses, including Wilson Moir's F8a+ and fun can be had with imaginative eliminate problems, though beware: eliminate rules apply! The rock is a lovely wave-cleaned schist but behaves like granite, so chalk up and brush the slopers and quartz nubbins. It faces south east and catches the sun for most of the day and is especially good on a still winter day. A great place for working power and stamina together, or for simply getting a suntan.

Approach: The steep walls can be accessed via Newtonhill. This is a picturesque fishing village on the coast half way between Stonehaven and Aberdeen. From the A90 turn off at signposts for Newtonhill, drive into the village via a roundabout and follow the road past the playing fields and over a railway bridge, turn left then sharp right down Skateraw Road. Continue downhill to a small parking area at the clifftops. To the left (north) is the Craig Stirling area. Take a path on the right (south) downhill for 200m to a cement outflow tank, from here skirt round the base of the crags to the bolted bouldering cliffs. 2 minutes walk.

10

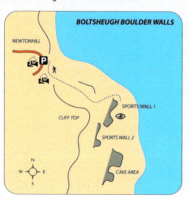

BOLTSHEUGH BOULDER WALLS

NEWTONHILL

CLIFF TOP

SPORTS WALL 1

SPORTS WALL 2

CAVE AREA

'The Enemy Within' Boltsheugh

BOLTSHEUGH SPORTS WALL BOULDERING

1. *The Traverse* Font 7a **
Climbing the base of the crag from far left to far right using any holds is a good work-out. Eliminating all possible jugs and staying as low as possible is Wilson Moir's F8a+

2. *The Wall* Font 5
Sit start the right vertical wall, gain ledges and crank through smaller holds straight up.

3. *The Corner Crack* Font 6a
Sit start right of the corner on edges, move into the corner to a good slot then crank up through the crack.

4. *Arête* Font 6a *
Sit start and gain quartz nubbins through the hard pinch hold, boom up for jug, finish left or right.

5. *Johnny's Dangler* Font 6c **
The excellent lip left of the corner. Sit start at big jugs, reach backwards to a large flat hold, traverse along the lip, boost up to a poor sloper left of the arête, match and finish at high jugs.

6. *Deadheads Direct* Font 7b ***
Sit start and gain the hanging ramp, then a small crimp and throw for the small sloping corner, finish up the sports route if you dare!

7. *The Overhang* Font 6a *
Sit start on big jugs and crank through a RH pocket to more jugs, jump off.

8. *The Enemy Within* Font 4 *
The HVS traditional crack can be climbed up and down for a good warm-up.

CAVE AREA

1. *The Lip* Font 6b+ *
The low lip left of the second sports wall can be climbed from far left to far right to a mantel finish.

Climb down and right of the second sports wall along tidal platforms, watch for waves!

2. *The Cave Traverse* Font 5+ *
Traverse round the tidal platforms to the big cave. From good holds on right of the cave, traverse right along the graffiti wall to finish at jugs. Back and forth at will for training.

3. *Ali's Eliminate* Font 7a+ **
Sit start under graffiti at slots, heel hook up to a LH sidepull, lock off right to a RH crimp and cross over LH to far right slots, match and boost high left for a sloping nubbin, then gain break.

4. *The Floestone Wall* Font 7a*
Left of the cave is a low undercut wall, traverse round to this on crimps on the far left 'floestone' wall, match a very low pale sloper, boost up to crimps on wall and finish at jugs.

11

Guy Robertson pulling on 'Johnny's Dangler'

PORTLETHEN

'Old Portlethen is a faded north eastern fishing village just south of Aberdeen, blurred by the haar that seeps in off the North Sea and bleached by sunny rain-shadow days when the west is cursed with south-westerlies. The residents' gardens are decked with the dead memorabilia of the sea and everything feels like the detritus of time. It is easy to sit here and soak up the sun on a good day, listening to the seagulls squabble, feeling the boulder mat warm in the heat. You can wait for the Turtle boulder to rise bubbling out of the tide to dry its flanks. The shoreline itself is littered with scratched fishing floats, cloudy glass and plastic bottles and sleeping boulders. The schist boulders, squat and rubbed by the sea, have delightful textures, like chocolate sweets rubbed down to the hard toffee underneath. They suggest shapes to the mind, like clouds which have solidified and dropped to the ground. The Sea Turtle sits in a rock-pool and its tidal belly is veined and smooth as a turtle's shell, whereas the Sea Pig is a snouty little gem you feel floated in with the jetsam one day. Portlethen is a sea-salt's exotic collection of rock animals with strange and contorted features.'

12

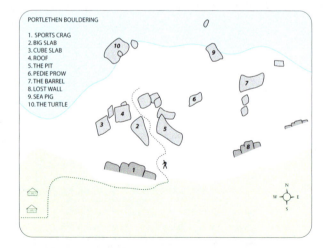

PORTLETHEN BOULDERING

1. SPORTS CRAG
2. BIG SLAB
3. CUBE SLAB
4. ROOF
5. THE PIT
6. PEDIE PROW
7. THE BARREL
8. LOST WALL
9. SEA PIG
10. THE TURTLE

Tim Rankin powering up 'Georgie Boy'

Approach: Portlethen, or 'Craigmaroinn', is situated midway between Stonehaven and Aberdeen off the A90. At the motorway flyover for Portlethen, make your way into the main village, then at a roundabout turn off over the railway bridge and follow a country road down to the old village, where careful parking must be found. The last cul de sac on the right has a small access path between the houses which swings left down through a field and right over a fence by the cliff-top. A bit further on there is access to the shore, where the boulders lie under a small sports crag.

'The Pit'

1. **Pendulum** Font 6c+ **
Step off the left-hand spike and monkey rightwards along the lip, drop into the notch and crank out the right-hand groove. Font 7b if you add *The Pit*.

2. **The Buzz** Font 7a+ ***
From an undercut flake at the left roof, smear and pull hard to climb out left and up. Clever footwork makes this a little easier!

3. **The Pit** Font 7a ***
Same start as *The Buzz*, but undercut right and straight up. Can be finished left or right at the same grade.

4. **The Pain** Font 7a *
Sit start on flat boulder, climb the very crimpy flake crack from small undercuts, finish straight over. Ouch!

5. **Georgie Boy** Font 7c ***
The Pit Boulder central roof undercuts. Power up and back, smearing on nothing, to gain the crack of *The Pain*. High body tension classic. Finishing up *Pit Left Hand* is *Shameless* Font 7c+.

6. **Kayla** Font 7c+ ***
The Pit Boulder central roof, right from the back at brushed crimps, torque back to a good hold on the lip, travel left, heel hook and finish up the wall above using holds on *The Pain*.

Luke Fairweather on 'Pendulum'

13

The Turtle

1. Fat Slapper Font 6c *
Turtle Boulder. Sit start at the seaward lip sloper with feet on the jammed boulder, aim left to a good hold and pull over.

2. Shell Shock Font 6a+ **
From the jug on the arête, trend left to rock over.

3. Turning the Turtle Font 6a **
From the jammed block under the boulder, climb out to jug on lip over the rock pool and straight up.

4. Turtle Traverse Font 7b ***
The Turtle boulder. A smooth wave-worn delight, start at the seaward groove, pull on and traverse round the corner (crux) to finish up *Turning the Turtle* or at the left edge for more of a pump.

The Broccoli Garden/Barrel

1. Broccoli Garden Font 6a+ *
Broccoli Garden. Under the middle of the roof, sit start at a sidepull and gain the jug above to pull over onto slab.

2. Secret Garden Font 6a **
Sit start right of the above at a break, crank for a sidepull on the lip and over.

3. The Barrel Font 7a+ ***
Sit start on north wall, travel left round under the arête and continue under the lip to finish up the left edge.

4. Slap 'n Tickle Font 6b+ **
Sit start under the right arête and launch up this to rock over onto the slab.

The Seapig

1. The Prow Font 6c ***
Sea Pig boulder. From a sitting start at the pocket climb the prow to its top.

1b. True Prow Font 7a+ ***
As for the Prow, but use only handholds for your feet. Eliminate but excellent.

1c. Super Prow Font 7b **
Full eliminate is a power-piece. From the pinch on the prow, launch for the top. Weird, short and desperate!

2. The Ramp Font 5+ *
Climb the obvious seaward ramp from the jug right of the Prow pocket.

'The Turtle'

'The Barrel'

Tim Rankin on his own 'Superprow' eliminate

Slabs Area

1. The Long Fall Font 5 ***
The slab under the sports crag provides tricky climbing up the vague scoop to the apex of the slab.

2. Kama Sutra 5
Various techniques take the right hand thin slab in the corridor under the Sports Crag..

3. Ruff and Ready Font 5 ***
The Cube slab facing the sea. The left arête is best on the slabby side.

4. Slim and Thin Font 5+ *
The middle of the slab is technically engrossing.

5. Right Angle Font 4 ***
As the name suggests, take the right arête.

6. Beyond the Edge of Reason Font 7b+ **
The roof left of the slabs. Needs a few mats. From a cramped start on the prop boulder, reach back to lip, then cut loose and slap right to finish up the wee groove.

SLABS AREA

Tim Rankin starting up 'Beyond the Edge of Reason'

Tim Rankin on 'Kayla'
Portlethen

CAMMACHMORE   NO 927 952

'Chilled out bouldering venue, just south of Craigmaroinn. The Bay gets all the sun going and nesting puffins can be seen on the cliffs above and seals and porpoises in the water below. The climbing is on a variety of large and small blocs and walls on beautiful water washed schist. A good spread of grades is available. The only draw back is that mats and good spotters are definitely required!'

Tom Kirkpatrick

'Mad Mac the Muscle Man'

Approach Notes

The small village of Downies lies south of Portlethen. Follow signs to Downies and continue to the parking spot on the cliff-top. At low tide head straight down the path towards the sea, turning left at first col on the ridge to 'Gorilla's Head', walk round to the boulders on the far side of the bay. Alternatively, walk along the cliff top north to scramble straight down a vague path in the centre of the bay 5-10 minutes. A full guide is available on *www.scottishclimbs.com*. The best bouldering (and landings!) lies on *The Nose* boulder. The local testpiece is the very obvious prow, known as **Optimus Prime** at Font 7b+.

'The Nose Boulder'

1. **Lethal Layback** Font 6c+ *
SS at crimps, straight up wall to obvious knob, layback/mantel this up slab.

2. **Fools Gold** Font 6b *
SS left arête, finishing by fin of rock on top of arête.

3. **Eliminate** Font 6c
SS eliminate up groove to right of arête.

4. **Wish You Were Here** Font 6c ***
SS at left arête, traverse break on lip, round nose and up jugs on front wall.

5. **Crazy Diamond** Font 6a+ **
Start at quartz diamond, use slopers to climb wall direct.

6. **Go For It** Font 5 *
Groove to left of main arête.

7. **Red Baron** Font 4
Climb arête from standing.

8. **Mad Mac Muscle Man** Font 5+ *
SS using flakes and footlock to climb over lip.

Tom Kirkpatrick on 'Fool's Gold'

CLASHFARQUHAR   NO 932 957

Probably the finest hard bouldering in the Portlethen area - 'a notch above anything Porty has to offer', in the words of Tim Rankin. The only drawback is a complex and tidal approach and occasional damp rock. However, the sunnier walls on the more northerly rock platforms are excellent as well (and have easier problems). The area is great in the winter sun.

Approach Notes

From Downies village. The boulders are in bays south of Portlethen and Craigmaroinn. Once in Portlethen, follow signs for Downies at the school sports pitches. Follow the road down to limited parking at the clifftop warning signs at the bottom of Downies. Continue south along the headland, tracking the fences for 300m, until a small heather moor. Cross this to its southern end where two small bays can be seen and the boulder clusters on a rock platform.

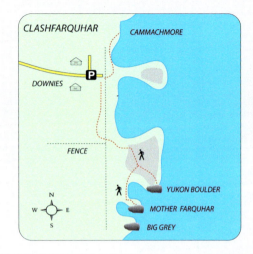

The Yukon boulder can be accessed immediately down and left of the bay, hidden from view by the headland - either scramble down rocky platforms on the east, or take the first easy sloping grass gully and turn left. The 'Big Grey' boulder cluster is obvious across the bay on a rock platform and requires a careful approach down the central grassy ridge - veering right at the bottom to a large boulder where *Mother Farquhar* is located. Around the bay it is an easy scramble at low tide to the Big Grey cluster.

Tim Rankin on 'Clash Arete'

18

Clashfarquhar Bay

Big Grey Area

1. Clash Arête Font 7a+ ***
Sit start the blunt arête and climb through the slanting undercuts and crimps. A superb technical problem and one of the best in the area. The standing start pulling on from the undercut is a good 6b.

2. Slab Man Font 7a+ **
Hand traverse the overhang lip of the boulder from the north groove to finish up *Clash Arête*. Starts sitting at the obvious big boss on the arête below the easy slab.

3. Magic Flump Font 7a+ **
Use the sloping shelf just right of the capping groove and struggle to reach the slanting hold, match this and climb left of the arête. No bridging!

4. Sweet Cheeks Font 7b+ ***
Climb the impressive overhanging arête right of the capping groove. Sit start at a vague break, slap desperately up the blunt nose to the better holds of the stand-up start (which is an excellent Font 6a).

5. Candy Man Font 7b ***
Start from holds either side of the thin seam crack just right of the arête, stand on and slap your way up small slopers and crimps either side of the seam crack until a good quartz crimp and rock up onto the slab. The arête and scoop are out, eliminate but obvious. The sit start link from *Sweet Cheeks* is the excellent *Central Belt Mafia* 7c.

6. Tastes Like Candy Font 6c ***
A superb problem exported from Font! Slap up the bulbous wall left of the rock shelf to a hard pull onto the slab. Sloping holds and easy to fail on!

7. Nip Chuck Font 6b+ **
Prop boulder wall to the right. Sit start from a sloping quartz shelf, gain two quartz crimps and climb over via the notch high left.

8. Swift Undercut Font 7a+ *
Prop boulder. The crimpy hanging wall aiming for a superb jug at the highest part of the wall. No feet allowed on the jammed boulder and no left arête.

9. Suppression Font 7c **
Climb *Swift Undercut* from a hanging start from the lip of the roof off two poor slopers.

10. Mother Farquhar Font 7b ***
Opposite the Big Grey cluster at botttom of the descent ridge is a boulder cluster perched on wet slabs under cliffs. This takes the underside of a small boulder leaning against another on the tide-line, hard to find! Sit start over a slimy stream, undercut the crack, feet on small jammed boulders, power up the 50 degree wall on crimps and pinches. A classic when dry.

'Sweet Cheeks'

'Nip Chuck' Pic Neil Morrison

19

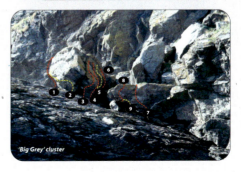

'Big Grey' cluster

'Yukon Boulder'

An excellent roofed boulder on a good platform facing due south, easily accessed. Been climbed on for years - problems are not given first ascents and are merely descriptive. Some good walls and slabs aroundabout as well.

1. *Yukon Afternoon* Font 6c ***
Sit start under the roof, swing round on flatties, crank up to finger edge and climb through the tan rock above the nose.

2. *The Crack* Font 4+ *
Obvious. Climb it!

3. *Gold Rush* Font 7a ***
The obvious and excellent left to right lip traverse from the central jugs at the bottom of the crack. Big cross through on jugs, travel along to slopers, gain jug above and finish up 5. From SS to 4 and staying low on lip is Font 7b.

4. *Golden Brown* Font 6c ***
The wall to the right of the crack is excellent if eliminate, started by a hanging crouch from the rail, 7a from the cave sitter.

5. *Gold Roof* Font 6b *
The wee roof of the right arête - sit start one hand at back, one on lip, again harder from sitting right in at the wall from an undercling and RH finger edge.

6. *Yukon Left Lip* Font 7a **
The obvious lip traverse round left of the described problems at Yukon wall. A topping traverse which gets the last rays of sun, either direction is good.

Gold Rush

MUCHALLS SHORE   NO 903 920

'The bouldering is spread out around a beautiful large bay, full of sea stacks, arches and caves, and is an enjoyable place to picnic and chill out between attempts on problems.'

Stuart Stronach

Bloc Notes

From the A90, take the first turning into Muchalls (1km south of the Newtonhill flyover if coming from Aberdeen, or a few miles north of Stonehaven if coming from the south). Drive into the village and take a sharp turn at the phone box. Continue down the hill to the old hotel, park considerably. Walk down the lane and under the railway line towards the sea until a bay with a prominent sea stack is visible on the right. Before a metal seat, steps lead down right towards the bay, a wooden bridge and more steps leads onto the pebble beach.

For those seeking specific descriptions of problems, an excellent full-colour guide is available online at *www.scottishclimbs.com* written by Staurt Stronach and Chris Fryer, who helped develop the area. Check the tide-tables online before you go… the best bouldering is probably in the secluded 'third bay' south, specifically on pebble-washed walls and on the tidal boulder known as 'The Grond'.

The Grond

1. **Perverse Traverse** Font 6a **
Traverse lip slopers to the horizontal break on the overhanging prow. Continue across this to finish Problem 4.

2. **South Side Story** Font 6a+ **
A 'classy' problem up the shallow groove in the overhanging prow. A harder variation uses the peapod sidepull out left to gain the pocket at the top of the groove (Font 6c).

3. **Flying Pig** Font 5+ *
Climb the edge between the south and landward faces from a sitting start.

4. **Thank You, Mr Limpet** Font 4+
From a sitting start at a small groove left again, make a hard pull onto the wall and proceed to the top.

5. **Weathertop** Font 4
Tiptoe delicately from left to right along the overhanging lip/wave on the landward side of the boulder.

Chris Fryer at Muchalls Shore
Pic by Matthew Bernstein

'The Grond'

CRAIG CORN ARN   NO 405 964

'The superb boulders beneath Craig Corn Arn are not often frequented which is a crying shame as they offer undoubtedly the best natural lines in the area. The surroundings are vintage Deeside but without the bustle and tranquillity is guaranteed.'

Tim Rankin

Situated on the the flanks of Pannannich hill east of Ballater, this outcrop (marked as Bellamore Craig on the map) has some excellent bouldering on numerous granite boulders above and below the crags. Some problems need brushed and cleaned, but there are over 50 problems currently, with projects for all.

Approach: Gain the A93 west out of Aberdeen. From Ballater, cross the river south and take the South Deeside road east on the B976 for a few kilometres or take the eastern river crossing at Dinnet and go west…either way, park at the entrance to a restored mill at a forested loop in the road and river. Take the forest track for about 500m and just before a gate, take the right turn up another forest track which leads you through a deer fence onto the hill. The boulders lie around and above the crags. 20 minutes.

Classic Problems

1. **Golden Brown** Font 6b ***

Half way up the boulder field on its left edge is a deceptively high slab. Climb the shallow rib up the centre of the slab. Superb moves on excellent rock leads with pulse racing to a friction finish. It doesn't get better than this.

2. **The Funk** Font 6b ***

The Summit boulders are the real place to clear your head after a hectic week at work. If you continue up pass the crag to the top of the hill and head left along the crest you will stumble upon this collection of angular blocks. Although the rock is never as good as below the crag the lines and landing more than make up for it. *The Funk* climbs the leaning arête of the highest boulder up the hill, harder from a sit start.

22

Craig Corn Arn, Deeside
Pic: Tim Rankin

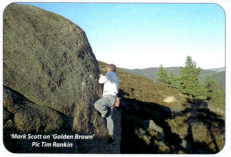

'Mark Scott on 'Golden Brown'
Pic Tim Rankin

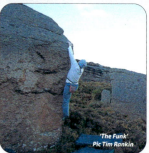

'The Funk'
Pic Tim Rankin

LUATH STONES   NJ 634 148

Bloc Notes

High on Green Hill above Alford in Aberdeenshire, a large prow of rock keeps sentinel over the Don valley. Surrounding this are numerous schist boulders providing playful bouldering problems and a fine area to picnic in the summer. They were developed by Stuart Stronach and Jo MacLeod in 2002 and now provide a pleasant diversion for the itinerant boulderer. The bouldering has good flat landings, is never too highball and the smaller oddly-shaped boulders such as the 'Sherman Tank' boulder provide quality traverses and friction problems.

Approach

The A944 leads to the town of Alford. Just before this is the village of Whitehouse, before the junction of the A944 and B992. Please park considerately a short way south of Whitehouse at a gatehouse by the entrance to the estate. On the track, take a left fork, continue for a few hundred metres, then take a right turn along the back of a walled garden, then a left turn uphill past ruined cottages to the obvious boulders on the hillside. 20 minutes.

The Sentinel

Sherman Tank Boulder - distinctive low boulder on the far left

1. **The Boar-Hound's Leash** Font 6b ***
A superb traverse along the steeper lip of this boulder from left to right to finish up the right arête.

2. **Cuchulainn** Font 7a+ *
Climbs the left side of the wee prow from a sitting start. The right side is Fingal Font 6a+ **

The Arch Boulder - distinctive arch-shaped boulder lower tier

1. **Archbishop** Font 4+ **
Bridges up the obvious left scoop finishing right at the arête.

2. **Archangel** Font 5 *
Takes the arête on its right side.

3. **Archdeacon** Font 5 *
Takes the flake in the central wall.

4. **Architect** Font 6c **
The difficult right arête from a sitting start.

5. **Archenemy** Font 6a **
The puzzling arête slab on the east face which can be climbed statically with technique and faith.

The Sentinel - obvious high tier wall, beautifully tiger-striped schist.

1. **North for a Day** Font 7a ***
A tip-bursting excursion up the tiger-striped face from the seam, traveling slightly right, then back into the high scoop to finish direct.

2. **Jo's Arête** Font 5 *
The right arête on the left side. Finishing direct in the scoop is Font 6a.

3. **A Little Less Conversation** Font 6b+ **
The left arête is an excellent sloper exercise.

The Mouse - the offwidth-split hump of rock to the right of The Sentinel.

1. **Five Days Till Heaven** Font 6a **
Climbs the hanging crack just right of the main offwidth.

2. **Slim Shady** Font 5+ *
Takes the groove on the far right of the wall.

3. **Broken Rib** Font 5 *
The arête at the far left end of the face with a high and exciting crux.

23

INVERNESS & STRATHSPEY

This is the hub of the Scottish Highlands - with the Cairngorms National Park on its doorstep, it is no surprise that Inverness and Aviemore ('Capital of the Outdoors') have a rapidly growing selection of bouldering venues. Aside from the accessible venues of Strathspey, Nairn Valley and the Moray Coast, the remote corries of the Northern Cairngorms are also full of potential development. This continues apace and new testpieces are being found all the time.

Strathconon - the crags of this glen have revealed some good bouldering venues, such as at Meig Crag and Scatwell. Esoteric but some good testpieces.

Brin Rock - a fabulous forested crag with hundreds of mossy boulders, giving a Fontaine-bleau feeling in the autumn. Fantastic bouldering outside of the high summer on excellent gneiss..

Duntelchaig - hundreds of erratic boulders around Loch Duntelchaig provides scope for endless development. The gneiss can be excellent but is often dirty.

Ruthven Stane - the 'Hulk' of Scottish bouldering. Muscular and contorted problems on immaculate Gneiss with perfect landings. The best stone in Scotland?

Tom Riach - a good low-grade stone hidden in the forest. Great climbing on a solid red conglomerate giant! Can be combined with a visit to Culloden and the bizarre Clava Cairns.

Cummingston - some of the best sandstone bouldering in Scotland. Caves and crag walls with pockets, crimps and slopers provides super-technical bouldering.

Cullen - large quartzite caves with some sport climbing and also some excellent steep bouldering - stays dry even in heavy rain.

Cuca Boulder - Aviemore's local power boulder. Limited but with very accessible problems from Font 6c-7b.

The Link Boulder - beautiful pink granite boulder overlooking Loch Morlich and Glenmore. Limited, but a great situation and some classic problems.

Shelterstone - remote collection of giant boulders under the eponymous crag. Excellent for a weekend's bivi and circuit bouldering on perfect granite.

26

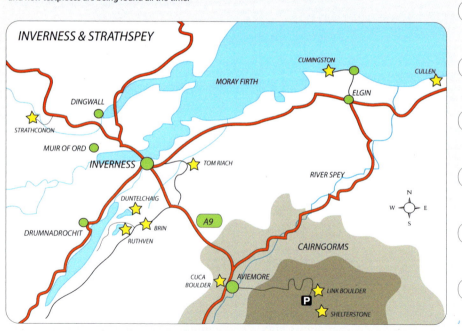

INVERNESS & STRATHSPEY

CUMINGSTON
CULLEN
MORAY FIRTH
ELGIN
DINGWALL
STRATHCONON
MUIR OF ORD
INVERNESS
TOM RIACH
RIVER SPEY
DUNTELCHAIG
A9
DRUMNADROCHIT
BRIN
RUTHVEN
CAIRNGORMS
N
W — E
S
CUCA BOULDER
AVIEMORE
LINK BOULDER
P
SHELTERSTONE

*Richie Betts on 'The Big Lebowski',
Ruthven Boulder*

BRIN ROCK NH 663 293

This is an atmospheric place to boulder, especially good in spring time or during a sunny late autumn when the mossy old pine forest resembles something out of *Lord of the Rings*. The rock is a rasping gneiss and conditions need to be cool and crisp for good skin care, also note that it can be a little flakey and vegetated on undeveloped boulders. That said, the best problems are all now clean and well-chalked, so you should not go wrong. Please clean any new problems sensitively as the whole area is a delicate habitat and many problems will never justify the destruction. Do not visit in summer as the midges, flies, bracken and humidity will not encourage a further return! Originally developed by Dave Wheeler and now one of the best Inverness venues next to the nearby Ruthven boulder.

Approach Notes

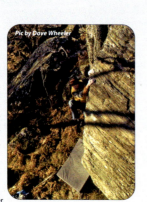

Pic by Dave Wheeler

From Inverness or Aviemore, drive along the A9 to Daviot and take the B851 exit signposted for Fort Augustus. Drive for 10 miles along a single track road with care, passing through the small villages of Inverarnie and Farr, until the sheer crags of Brin Rock can be seen on the right. Turn right towards Brin House and park on the left just after crossing the river (space for 2 cars, so be considerate). Cross the field towards the crag and enter the boulder field by the third gate. The first good boulder is 'the Block', just up the slope ahead.

28

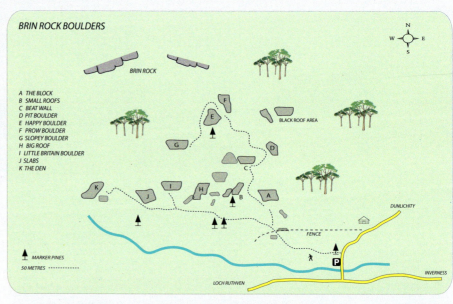

BRIN ROCK BOULDERS

BRIN ROCK

A THE BLOCK
B SMALL ROOFS
C BEAT WALL
D PIT BOULDER
E HAPPY BOULDER
F PROW BOULDER
G SLOPEY BOULDER
H BIG ROOF
I LITTLE BRITAIN BOULDER
J SLABS
K THE DEN

BLACK ROOF AREA

DUNLICHITY

FENCE

INVERNESS

MARKER PINES

50 METRES

LOCH RUTHVEN

Ben Litster clamping the slopers of 'Put My New Shoes On' - Slopey Boulder - Font 7c

Brin Testpieces

Pit Bull Font 7b+ *
The sit start to Ingrid Pit has some very hard crimp moves to get established on the original. FA Dave Redpath 2005

Put My New Shoes On Font 7c **
The impossibly slopey traverse on immaculate gneiss… from a standing start at the left arête, connive to gain a contorted finishing sequence at the right arête. FA Ben Litster 2007.

The Susurrus Font 7c ***
The huge roof at the bottom of the boulder jumble. Sit start in the depths of the cave and climb out right through slopers to good roof holds by a shelf, then campus left to the nose and surmount this! FA Mike Lee 2007

Crocabot Font 7b+ **
10m further along from the Den and about 10m uphill is a big horizontal roof feature, this problem takes the right hand side, from opposing crimps under the roof to holds on the lip and then good holds on the front face. FA Mike Lee 2007.

Old Love Font 7a **
8 metres uphill and right from *Crocabot*. The boulder sit starts an undercut blunt arête. FA Ben Litster 2007.

The Scientist Font 7b **
The technical and brutal sharp arête above the *New Shoes* problem. Highball but classic. FA Richie Betts 2008.

'Hit Me'

'Brin Done Before'

Brin Circuit

1. **Hit Me** Font 6b *
The Block boulder is the first good bloc over perfect grass landings. Warm up, then climb the problem just right of the arête to a dynamic slap up and right to a sloper, finish by a rockover.

2. **Preppy** Font 6a *
The wee roof boulder to the left of the Block. Sit start left to right to finish up jugs. Known as 'The Campus' for obvious reasons.

3. **Up Beat** Font 7a+ *
The 'Beat' boulder beside the larger blocks. Traverse from left to right on all holds. The lower eliminate is **Down Beat** Font 7b.

4. **Ingrid Pit** Font 5 *
The wall above the pit is climbed direct through crimps to better holds, don't fall into the pit!

5. **Spirited** Font 6c *
The 'Happy Boulder' lies on a good surface above a large pine higher up the hill. Climb the front arête from a sit start.

6. **Brin Done Before** Font 6c ***
The obvious Prow boulder behind the Happy boulder. Pull into the prow, heel-hook backwards to match a finger ledge, then cut loose… one of the best problems at Brin.

7. **Little Britain** Font 6c *
Adjacent left (west) to the *Susurrus* roof boulder is a weepy wall. Just right of the left arête is a layaway, now gain & surmount the lip. Pad the landing.

8. **The Scoop** Font 5 *
Further left are the obvious 'swamp wall' slabs. Climb scoop 4m left of the easy arête.

9. **Spank the Ramp** Font 6b ***
'The Den' lies over a perfect sandy landing to the far left of the boulder field near the river. Sit start and climb the obvious sloping ramp to jugs at the top of the ramp, finish up and left.

10. **Graeme's Pinch** Font 6c **
Sit start as for *Spank the Ramp* and gain the big jug, then go direct up to a RH pinch, cunning moves through a crimp gain the highest jugs on the arête (no jug gives an eliminate Font 7a).

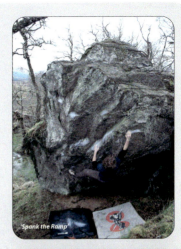

'Spank the Ramp'

'The Susurrus'

Trevor Woods on 'Barry Manilow'

RUTHVEN BOULDER   NH 636 277

The Ruthven boulder, or the 'Bunnet Stane', is the Hulk of Scottish boulders, a steroid-pumped glacial erratic packed with bulging gneiss veins. The bouldering is amongst the best in Scotland, and the moves are delicate despite the muscularity required. Save your skin for a good day and give it all you've got - the problems are all excellent.

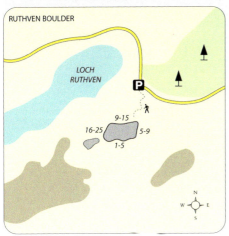

Approach Notes

The 'stane' itself is easy to find. It sits quite visibly on a grassy knoll overlooking Loch Ruthven, south of Inverness. The B851 should be taken about 10k south-westwards from the Daviot turn-off on the A9 (signed Fort Augustus), through Farr, past the crags of Brin Rock to a right turn before East Croachy. The road crosses the River Nairn and winds through a forest to a car-park beside Loch Ruthven, from where it is a short walk uphill through the heather to the stone. The problems are described anti-clockwise from the arête opposite the 'Baby Bonnet' boulder.

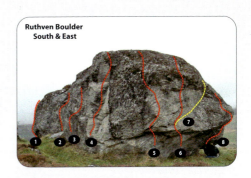

Ruthven Boulder
South & East

1. **Cheese Grater** Font 6b *
Opposite the 'Baby Bonnet'. Start on jugs under the lip pull over onto rounded holds on the arête and climb the right side of the arête. Named for a reason…

2. **The Descent of Man** Font 4
A layback gains the shelf and easier moves to the top. Also the descent…

3. **The Cheeky Girls (R)** Font 6a **
Just right again there is a sloping ledge just out of reach. Start on two edges just below this, gain the ledge, reach again for another rounded hold to an elegant finish. There is also a left hand version.

4. **Austin Powers** Font 5 **
The obvious groove, baby.

5. **The Razor's Edge** Font 7a *
SS small roof edges to a blind move to sharp edges (intermediate crimp), another crimp up and left leads to a direct flake top out.

6. **The Slippery Slope** Font 6c **
Two good edges to the big lip sloper, then sharp holds in the scoop allow better holds to be gained and a direct finish over the bulge.

7. **Sloping Off** Font 6c+ *
Break right from the lip sloper with a desperate move to get onto the ramp to finish out right over bulge.

8. **Barry Manilow** Font 7a+ ***
Start on small incut hold under roof travel right to a good hold under the nose (but no jugs!), break left through the prominent slopey nose and beg your way up to a high quartz hold. A classic struggle.

31

Ruthven Boulder
Front Face Problems

Ruthven Boulder Front Face

9. **Builders Butt** Font 5
Start on the jugs right of the nose and pull into the groove and tough moves gain the slab.

10. **Nefertiti** Font 6b **
Start on two small edges middle of left wall and gain the good hold, RH incut then a long Egyptian up and left to a good edge, up to a layaway flake and finish direct.

11. **Pinch Punch** Font 7a *
SS on small edge, gain shallow scoop, hang this and lunge for a good hold out left, a RH pinch to a LH edge then up to layaway and trend left to finish.

12. **The Groove** Font 5+ *
Start on small holds at the bottom of the groove, some nice moves lead to beter holds all the way up the groove.

13. **Outstanding** Font 6a+ ***
SS under roof up to juggy incuts then throw left for a hidden quartz hold, then a long reach for jugs and left on crystals to finish. Definitely outstanding.

14. **The Dude** Font 7a ***
SS as above but a long lunge up and right to sharp holds allows a tricky sequence straight over the bulge into a hanging mossy groove and slopey layaways. Finish slightly right. An outstanding counter-diagonal7. FA Ben Litster 2007.

15. **The Big Lebowski** Font 7a ***
The chilled out traverse from the lowest handrail, gain the higher sloping handrail and a heel-hook sequence allows the bulging corner to be turned to reach for a sidepull, then up left to a crescent crimp and over sharp holds to a tricky finish.

15a **Mike's Problem** Font 7a+ *
A direct line diverting straight up from the sloping shelf through a long move to a right hand pinch to a thin top-out. FA Mike Lee 2007.

Mike Lee on 'The Big Lebowski'

Trev Woods on 'Nefertiti'

Ruthven Boulder
West Face
& Baby Bunnet

The Dude Sit Start

*Ben Litster on first ascent of
'The Dude'*

33

16. Shreddies Font 6c
The west wall round the corner from the front face. As it suggests, a sharp solution to the undercut arête, finish directly up the painful wall!

17. The Big Tease Font 6b *
Start on two flat holds just right of the arête, long move up and right to obvious quartz holds finish direct.

18. Neil Armstrong Font 5 *
Start at a shallow horizontal crack and climb the wall on quartz holds.

19. Crystal Maze Font 6c *
SS flat hold traverse left then use sharp holds to gain the slabby wall. Harder if finished further left up The Big Lebowski.

20. Sylvester Font 6a+ *
From a low flat hold, travel left on good holds to smaller holds on the lip, then crank through the slab crack. Tweeky Pie Font 6c
is the more cunning and direct version.

21. Rock 'n Roll Baby Font 5 **
Start on jugs under the right edge traverse round to the crack, continue until you can rock up onto the slab.

Baby Bonnet – the small boulder on the right.

22. Bitch Slap Font 6c **
SS on a small shelf on the front right. Follow the holds left along the fault to a jug, take a slappy sequence left to finish up the blunt arête.

23. Turn The Other Cheek Font 6b+ *
Starts the same as above to the good hold then head right to rounded holds, struggle onto the slab.

DUNTELCHAIG   NH 641 315

Southwest of Inverness, Loch Duntelchaig is surrounded by craggy gneiss hills offering the boulderer a pleasant day's adventure discovering new lines and areas. The bouldering is extensive, and in the summer the higher hill areas provide relief from the flies and midges in the more wooded areas round the loch. The rock is a sharp gneiss which is superb on some boulders and awfully vegetated on others. The circuit here shown is accessible and the rock is excellent. If you can't manage *The Untrained Ear*, try it from a jumping start at the crimps!

Approach: On the A9, about five kilometres south of Inverness, take the Daviot B851 exit signposted for Fort Augustus. Drive for 4 kilometres to Inverarnie and take a right turn on to the B861, cross over the river and take a left turn onto a B road at a crossroads. Continue along this for four kilometres to Dunlichity church, stay on the road as it winds past the shores of Loch A' Clachain ('Loch of the Stones') until you arrive at a big layby by the shores of Loch Duntelchaig. Park here, take the good shore path over a weir and continue along the path by the shores for 10 minutes, passing crags and mossy boulders. The circuit is found in the pine woods, where it rises uphill. Turn left into the woods at a forestry layby, the boulders are obvious under the orange crag ('seventy foot wall').

The Untrained Ear area

1. ***River Crack*** Font 4
Gain the high hanging crack on the slab just above stream. Tricky start.

2. ***Streamline*** Font 6b *
Climb the bulging slopey arête from a sit start.

3. ***The Groove*** Font 6b *
Sit start the wee groove in the small boulder and climb it with difficulty.

4. ***Cave Flake*** Font 4
Climb out of the wee cave and up the juggy flake to top.

5. ***The Wall*** Font 6a *
From undercling and LH sidepull on wall, climb direct over the top of the orange wall.

6. ***Cave 2*** Font 6b *
From left side of cave, sit start at underclings, gain sharp crimps and crank up right to flake.

7. ***The All Seeing Eye*** Font 6c **
The main wall left of the arête, through the obvious flake feature at the top of the wall using a small backhand crimp.

8. ***The Untrained Ear*** Font 7a ***
From hanging jugs at the cave lip, crank up and right through crimps to the arête.

9. ***On My Way*** Font 5+ **
The boulder by the pine tree with a stone plinth. Climb the highball slab.

10. ***People That's Why*** Font 6a **
Sit start up the right arête to the top.

11. ***Harlem Rumble*** Font 6a+ **
From left side of overhanging bulge, climb to slopers on the nose and surmount on to slab.

12. ***The Jam Slab*** Font5+ *
Climb up the slab using all holds available.

13. ***Butterfly Collector*** Font 6c ***
Sit start holds right of arête and climb up and left onto slab, no left arête hold.

14. ***Dreams of Children*** Font 6a+ ***
Use right arête to bounce and grab the hold on the slab and rock up.

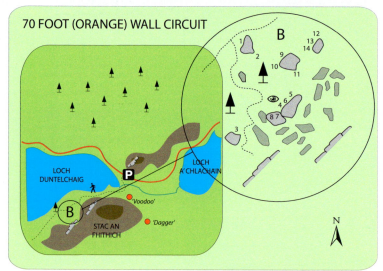

70 FOOT (ORANGE) WALL CIRCUIT

34

'The Butterfly Collector' Pic: Dave Wheeler

Duntelchaig Off-Circuit Classics

The Dagger Font 6c+ ***

Immediately after crossing the outflow from the lake, go through a gap in the fence and head eastwards across the moor aiming for an obvious large crooked pine tree on the skyline about 200 metres away. Pass to the right of the tree, drop down to a small stream, turn right and follow the stream up to the Dagger boulder - 10 mins. The problem takes the obvious steep blade of rock from a low start on the left. Gain the crimps in the roof and make a big move to the lip. Make another long reach again to pull over.

'The Dagger
Pic: Richie Betts

Voodoo Working Font 7a ***

Approach: follow the main track until the first boulders appear in the trees on the left. Take a small path between these boulders (various warm up problems) and hop over a small wire fence to reach a boulder at the far edge of the trees. From a standing start, rock over onto the slab using the tiny layback flake and obvious cluster of quartz crystals - sharp!

'Voodoo Working'
Pic: Richie Betts

35

Colin Lambton on the Link Boulder Right Lip

LINK BOULDER NH 988 069

Known in Gaelic as *Clach Bharraig*, this beautifully isolated pink granite erratic is easily found on the approach to Cairngorm Car Park. On ascending the 'link' road up to the car park, the boulder comes into view on the left hillside as the road rejoins the descent road. Park underneath the boulder and walk uphill to it in two minutes. The problems are not numerous, but they are quite hard and sit-starts can provide desperate sloping testpieces for colder days. The outlook over Loch Morlich, the Cairngorms and Aviemore is truly stunning – it's worth taking your boulder mat, if only to sit on and admire the view.

Angus Murray on Loch Morlich Arete

Link Boulder North

Link Boulder South

The Problems

1. **The Left Lip** Font 6c+ **
The left lip is a little tougher but finishes at the same apex sequence once you get into position.

2. **The Right Lip** Font 6c ***
The obvious right arête lip facing Aviemore. Slap along the edge to pull into groove just right of the apex. Little for the feet, so use your heels as much as possible.

3. **Loch Morlich Arête** Font 4 *
Climb the blunt arête rib facing Loch Morlich from a tough pull on at a good high hold in the groove.

4. **Morlich Slab** Font 4+ *
From crimps just right of the blunt arête, gain the slab and wobble across it up and right.

5. **Cairngorm Arête** Font 6b **
The steep undercut arête facing the Cairngorms. Gain good sidepulls on the arête and press on upwards. Tougher for the short. The sit start will be the hardest in Aviemore.

6. **Cairngorm Slab** Font 5+ *
The Cairngorm side has an undercut slab. Start on the right and pull on to the wall via a low RH crimp and LH crimp on slab. Gain the big sidepull and step gently to the top.

CUCA BOULDER NH 888 121

The Cuca Boulder is Aviemore's local outdoor power boulder, only five minutes walk from the town. At the south end of the village, park in a layby and walk up the road sign-posted to the youth hostel and church. Continue along the path leading to Craigellachie nature reserve on the right side of the hostel. Once through the pipe-bridge under the motorway follow the nature reserve path for 2 minutes until a large boulder on the left side of the path. From here, strike uphill towards the cliff. About 20 metres up the grass bank hides the Cuca boulder. The boulder was cleaned and developed by Andy Marshall and friends. Project link-ups can be combined at will for harder variations.

1. **Polyfase Deformation** Font 7a **
SS start on the lowest hold move up to the wobbly pinch and climb the arête.

2. **Plate Tectonics** Font 7a+ ***
SS climb first two moves of *Polyfase Deformation* before powerfully heading out left.

3. **Rock Mass Strength** Font 7a **
SS on the wobbly jug in middle of the wall and climb *Plate Tectonics*.

4. **Rise and Shine in the Babylon** Font 6b+ *
SS swing from side pull to sharp crimp and up the wall.

5. **The Quest for Knowledge** Font 6b+ *
SS on rail move up and left before joining *Rise and Shine in the Babylon*

6. **Rage** Font 7b ***
The traverse from far right to finish up *Plate Tectonics*. Hard link.

'Plate Tectonics'

'Polyfase Deformation'

TOM RIACH   NH 778 455

Tom Riach is a conglomerate erratic hidden in the woods above Culloden on the northern fringe of Drummossie Muir. From Inverness, take the sign-posted roads to Culloden Battlefield. Just past the visitor centre, take a right onto a B road. Go straight over the wee crossroads and dip down to the river and under the railway viaduct. At the top of the hill, take a left at the junction and park at a layby about a mile along this road, by a cycle-route signpost. From the west end of the layby go downhill (north) on a hidden forest track and after 30 metres fork left until you come across a fallen tree on the path, pass this on the right and continue on to the boulder after about 3 minutes.

Conglomerate

North Faces

North & East Face Problems

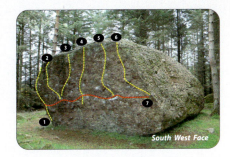

South West Face

South & West Face Problems

1. **Eclipse** Font 5+ *
The steepness of the North East face via a sharp hold.

2. **The Dark Side** Font 4+
The north wall just left of the arête.

3. **North Buttress** Font 4
North arête from the right.

4. **Grapeshot** Font 5 *
The wall just right of the arête, trending right.

5. **The Long Riach** Font 5+ **
The highest line on the face.

6. **Appin Colours** Font 5+ *
From the embedded boulder and go straight up.

7. **Drainpipe Scoop** Font 4
Big holds left of The Bulge.

8. **The Bulge** Font 6a *
Climb the bulging arête on its left side.

1. **West Arête** Font 5+ **
Sit start the arête and climb it.

2. **Butcher Left Hand** Font 6b **
Large pocket at chest height, aim for a sloper on top of a large inset block then straight up.

3. **The Butcher** Font 6a+ *
Same pocket to layaway and higher pocket.

4. **Rathole** Font 5+ *
Climb through the left of two holes at 3m.

5. **Mousehole** Font 6a+ *
The problem using the right of the two holes.

6. **Rabbit Run** Font 5+ *
Climb the wall left of the arête using arête to start.

7. **South West Face Traverse** Font 6c+ **
From south arête, finish up west arête. Or reverse it.

39

CUMMINGSTON   NJ 131 692

Some boulderers swear by the sandstone of Cummingston as the best bouldering in Scotland. Others find it impossibly fierce on the fingers and like 'Kyloe-In', conditions can be fickle, though a cool onshore breeze on a sunny day at low tide is perfect. The bouldering offers technical walls, fierce crimping and butch pocket-pulling on a hard orange sandstone of the Triassic era. The crags have been climbed on for years, the bouldering kicked off by Nick Clement (off-duty from the RAF) and an original guide was done by Pete Hill. The new bouldering has recently been developed by Charlie Hornsby, Iain MacDonald, Liam Johnston, Dave Wheeler and others. Most of the problems are on the crags and finish at juggy downclimbs or jump-offs, but on most problems, reaching these will feel like a just accomplishment.

Enjoying the slabs at Cummingston

CUMMINGSTON

'This problem epitomizes everything great about sandstone bouldering. Small holds, friction and technicality… brilliant!'
Tim Rankin on 'Masonic Finger-Shake'

SLABS
SEA STACK
JERKER
CAVE AREA
POCKETS WALL
SEA STACK
BALAMORY BOULDER
DOUBT WALL
NEST WALL
CAVE
PROPHET WALLS
CAVE
CAVE
CAVE
TUNNEL AREA
PIPE WALL

OLD RAILWAYTRACK

N W E S

CUMMINGSTON VILLAGE

P

41

Approach: 30 miles east of Inverness, between Lossiemouth and Burghead on the B9040 north of Elgin, the crags and associated bouldering are easily found once in the linear village of Cummingston. Take a seawards turn into Seaview Road, just east of a white memorial cross, turn left, then right and park beside the play park. The Tunnel area is straight below the car park, whereas the Seastack areas are a short walk westwards along the old railway cutting. The Tunnel Area is a good place to warm up.

The Balamory Boulder

CUMMINGSTON CIRCUIT

1. **Pipe Slab** Font 6a+ *
Pipe Wall. Climb the slab direct one metre right of the pipe.

2. **Pipe Overhang** Font 6a **
Pipe Wall. 5m left of the pipe, pull on to slab through roof using undercut for right hand.

3. **Tunnel Vision** Font 6a+ **
Tunnel. Starts in the east entrance on the north wall bulge and traverses right along the obvious break to a jug undercut which gains the central roof-flake, then lock up to a pocketed wall and rock over to finish. The Darkness Font 6b starts further west and traverse the whole cave.

4. **Bulgy** Font 6b *
Tunnel. On the south wall of the cave, this climbs the west end of the cave from a sit start at pockets. Crimp and pocket up to a jug, then climb a chicken-headed wall with a long reach right to finish.

5. **Jaws** Font 7a **
Prophet Area. The small boulder at the east end of the crags has a short prow, three moves long, from a low sit start on pinches to a mantel finish.

6. **Surf Nazis** Font 6c **
Prophet Walls. On the crag to the west Jaws, this climbs the wall below the peg, cranking up on underclings to a ferned slot, gain another undercling, move up to thin break and jump off.

7. **The Shield** Font 6c *
Prophet Walls. Climbs the obvious shield of rock round the corner to the right - from holds on the left slap desperately rightwards, aiming for crimps up and right, then stand on the wee ledge to finish.

8. **Masonic Finger-Shake** Font 6c+ ***
Prophet Walls. Best-named problem in the country, and you'll find out why! Situated on the right wall of the cave, it climbs the smooth wall from the shallow finger-pocket and finishes at the horizontal break. Step on with difficulty, (no good holds out right or left!) aim for a high right sidepull, hold the barndoor and reach up left to a break.

9. **Highball** Font 6c *
Prophet Walls. Takes the leaning wall right of the first corner opposite the Balamory boulder. Use slopers left of thin crack (out) to gain pinch on arête, then head up and left to finish.

10. **Balamory Traverse** Font 6a *
On the isolated Balamory boulder, the best problem is the full traverse, starting on the descent ramp, then anti-clockwise round the boulder to finish up the seaward east arête.

11. **The Nest** Font 6a *
Nest wall. Climbs the awkward square-cut corner to the jump-off jug at 'the nest' ledge. Has been climbed face-out!

12. **Bird Man** Font 7a ***
Nest Wall. A superb technical, fingery puzzle! From holds left of the thin crack, gain the slot, then traverse thinly up and right to the nest. Hard for the grade, but do-able once you know the secrets.

42

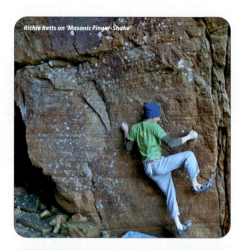
Richie Betts on 'Masonic Finger-Shake'

Dave Wheeler cruising 'Birdman'

13. *Bat Man* Font 6b *
Doubt Wall. Climbs out of the wee cave on the left, pulling up on pinches to the left wall to finish at a jug up and right.

14. *Cave Man* Font 6c ***
Cave Area. From the left arête, pull up to the lower line of pockets and monkey rightwards to midway jugs, then drop down to edges and stretch to the right arête to finish, or reverse until you drop. The lower line of holds R-L is *Sine Wave* Font 7a+.

15. *Gorilla* Font 7a **
Cave Area. Sit start low in the cave and work back to the right arête using an undercut and pinch to gain jugs at end of the Cave Man traverse.

16. *The Jerker* Font 6a ***
The front face of the cave has the classic bulging arête. Just opposite the stack, climb the prow from holds on the left and pull up the arête to finishing jugs.

17. *Fingerlicker* Font 7a ***
Inside the cave, traverse the north wall, climbing from the 'gap' up and right to a finishing jug up and left of the roof. Takes a complex sequence of punishing little holds, often wet, but superb when dry.

18. *The Crucifix* Font 6b *
Inside Cave. Sit start just left of the arête at a wee corner, gain a crucifix position and slap for a finishing jug.

19. *Match and Snatch* Font 7a+ ***
One of the best problems at Cummingston. Left of the *Jerker*, climb the crack to a cross-under to a high crimp, drop down to poor sloping holds and traverse left to snatch for a better LH hold, continue up and left to the top of the cave arête, turn the corner for another half grade.

20. *Ginger Rides Again* Font 7b **
The steep arête right of Fingerlicker and underneath *Match and Snatch*. Sit start with both hands lay-backing the wide crack on the left, slap right to a pinch, then gain the arête sloper, continue á cheval to the jugs. Direct maybe easier.

21. *Cave Beast* Font 6a **
The deep cave wall on the west, from a squarecut corner, left hand to slot and up to a layback, work feet along, bump right hand up the layback, get a pocket with the left hand and right hand to the jugs. SS will be the hardest at Cummy…

21. *Cave Arête* Font 6a+ *
West Cave. The R-L rising traverse left of the wee through-cave shelf. A hard bum start allows better holds to be gained on the arête continue up to jugs.

22. *Buddha's Choice* Font 6b **
Sit start the shelf at the through-hole on a large sidepull, gain slopers up on the hanging shelf, then a sloping square edge and snatch high and right, finish up left to horizontal jug flakes.

23. *Through-hole Wonder* Font 5+ *
Just opposite the above. Sit start and up to a rounded smooth hold, match this and crossover up the blunt arête to a jump-off.

24. *The Buddha of Brodie* Font 6b **
The excellent sunny wall west of the cave at its thinnest, LH on small pocket, rock up right to a flattie and finish on slopers.

'Cave Arete'

Pockets Wall and Cave Area

43

'Buddha's Choice'

CULLEN CAVES   NJ 495 681

2. St. Stephen's Cave

CULLEN CAVES

PORTKNOCKIE

CULLEN BAY

A98

TO ELGIN

CULLEN

'The coast-line, 1¼ mile long, presents a bold rocky front to the Bay of Cullen, which is 2½ miles wide across a chord drawn from Scar Nose to Logie Head, and which from that chord measures 7 furlongs to its innermost recess. Three singular masses of rock here have been named the Three Kings of Cullen, most likely after the Magi, or Three Kings of Cologne: Caspar, Melchior, and Balthazar - whose skulls are shown in the cathedral there.'

Ordnance Gazetteer of Scotland, 1882

St. Duane's Den

1. **Layback Crack** Font 6a *
Climb the left-hand flared crack from a sit start to jump-off jugs.

2. **Double-Pinch Traverse** Font 6b+ ***
Climb into the *Layback Crack*, then continue right along the powerful and excellent ramp via two crossover pinch moves to finish at high shattered jugs, jump off before they break on you!

3. **Duane's World** Font 7a+ *
The straight-up to the ramp from two obvious sidepull crimps at chest-height. Match these and make an infuriating lunge to the ramp... if you can hold this, further foot trickery and a crimp allows the high jugs to be gained.

1. **Kill All Hippies** Font 6b *

The left arête is climbed from a sit start with feet on the plinth. A blind slap round the corner and a hard cross through to a triangular hold gains the jump-off crack.

2. **Flower Power** Font 6c+ ***

Sit start as for *Hippies* but slap right to the obvious V hold jugs. Hook the left arête and gain a high left sidepull, heel hook by your right hand and throw for a high right jug. Superb and tricky to latch.

3. **The Thorn** Font 7a *

A frustrating dyno. From the handrail by the V hold and a LH pinch sidepull on the lip, dyno up and right to an edge and then a higher break.

4. **The Rose** Font 7b **

Sit start at the first cave corner, gain the handrail with difficulty and walk left upside down through the V hold to finish up *Flower Power*. Sustained and powerful.

5. **Welcome!** Font 6b

The arête under the *Welcome* graffiti. Sit start and gain big RH undercut flake, then small edges lead to a higher jump-off slot.

6. **Protected by Roses** Font 6c

The second corner arête has a tough sit start into undercuts to finish at the higher break. Use lower break.

44

Bloc Notes

From Cullen Beach walk to the west end of the shore past the Three Kings. The first large quartzite cave has a smaller north cave called 'St.Duane's Den', the next cave is further north along the shore and is known as 'St. Stephen's Cave'.

These caves can also be quickly reached from Portknockie. Park at the playpark and cross the fields to a signpost on the headland walk, where concrete steps lead down past the sea-arch to Jenny's Well and the bouldering caves. The rock is quartzite and plenty of chalk is needed to keep the haar off the holds. You can climb here even in torrential rain.

1. St. Duane's Den

3 EAST COAST

'Left Wall' at Wolfcrag

EAST COAST

This is the Forth and Tay catchment area, with bouldering areas within reach of Dundee, St. Andrews, Perth, Stirling and Edinburgh. Though the bouldering may not be the first to come to mind, the venues have some esoteric gems and if you are in the area and you are short of time, these areas are good options. All are within an hour and a half of Edinburgh, with some venues in the capital itself. The most extensive bouldering is undoubtedly at the Perthsire venue of Glen Lednock.

Glen Lednock

Glen Clova - the Red Craigs area is a good cragging spot, but also provides some steep bouldering on fine-grained Granodiorite. A glen for exploring and further development.

Weem - a beautiful forested sports venue north of Aberfeldy, this also has some bouldering on good pocketed schist walls. Idyllic in spring and autumn.

Glen Lednock - accessible bouldering from Perth, this beautiful area under the Lednock dam above Comrie is excellent for kids and superb in spring and autumn. Good rock and some hard testpieces.

Wolfcrag - a greenstone quarry used by local students for training over the years. An excellent fingery circuit and extremely accessible. Technical.

Ravenscraig - Fife has little bouldering apart from some loose sandstone around St. Andrews. This area in Kirkcaldy has an interesting overhang with sandy landings.

Salisbury Crags - Edinburgh's traditional city bouldering venue, perfect for an evening's escape. Eliminate by nature, and once the playground of Harold Raeburn.

Agassiz Rock - also of geological interest, this overhang under Edinburgh's Royal Observatory provides some fun eliminate bouldering, climb at will.

46

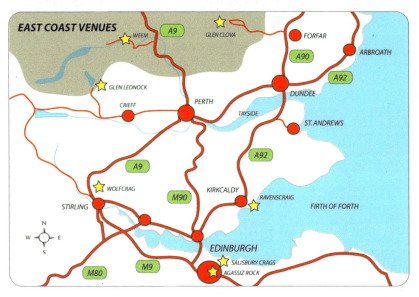

EAST COAST VENUES

WEEM A9 GLEN CLOVA FORFAR ARBROATH
A90 A92
GLEN LEDNOCK DUNDEE
CRIEFF PERTH TAYSIDE ST. ANDREWS
A9 A92
WOLFCRAG KIRKCALDY RAVENSCRAIG
M90 FIRTH OF FORTH
STIRLING
N
W   E
S
EDINBURGH
M80 M9 SALISBURY CRAGS
AGASSIZ ROCK

Dave Redpath on his own Agassiz 8a traverse

GLEN CLOVA   NO 292 756

The Red Craigs in Glen Clova have for years provided traditional testpieces on the excellent diorite (granite) crags. The bouldering has gradually been unearthed below the crags in the complex scree, with the best lines on the bigger stones between the Hotel and the Quarry, such as the high 'Sentinel' boulder on an alp above the 'hollow' parking space before the main Red Craigs jumble.

Many problems may have been done before by visiting craggers, but recent development is due to the enthusiasm of Chris Fryer and friends - a good circuit is now possible on cleaned rock. There are projects in the area and hundreds of easy and enjoyable lines, though the rock needs to be well cleaned in places. The roof circuit at the Red Craigs provides a short powerful circuit on the best rock. There are easier lines, but many bad landings, so mats are useful. This circuit is accessible and, due to the steeper aspect, provides better quality granodiorite.

For the adventurous, there are large boulders on the hills above the South Esk. Follow the river north from the Glen Doll car park for a few kilometres, then west for another 1k until the boulders can be found on the southern slopes of a crag called 'Juanjorge' (NO 265 793 GB Grid). There are also granite stones in and around the woods on the path north to this before Moulzie farm (around NO 284 774).

Approach Notes

From the A90 bypass of Forfar between Dundee and Aberdeen, take the Kirriemuir exit (A926) just after the MacDonalds. Travelling from the North, most people turn off at Peggy Scott's diner, then travel through Tannadice and Memus. Drive into Kirriemuir and follow the brown tourist signs to Glen Clova along the B955... it is a long glen and has a loop road. As long as you follow signs for 'Clova' you will find yourself at the Clova hotel. Cross the bridge here and continue west along the single-track road past a white cottage until the crags come into view up and right. There are three parking spaces, the first by a hollow full of boulders (the Sentinel boulder etc.), the second near the large Peel Boulder (NO 292 754) and the third at a small quarry if all places are filled. The rock is a fine-grained granodiorite, often sharp and crimpy, tape is useful for the odd finger-injury!

'The Peel Sessions'

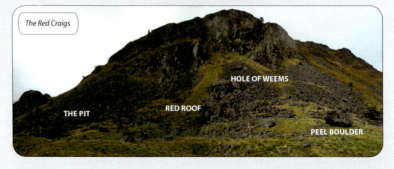

The Red Craigs

HOLE OF WEEMS

RED ROOF

THE PIT

PEEL BOULDER

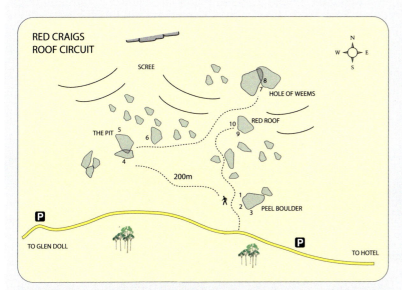

RED CRAIGS
ROOF CIRCUIT

SCREE

HOLE OF WEEMS

RED ROOF

THE PIT

200m

TO GLEN DOLL

PEEL BOULDER

TO HOTEL

Adrian Crofton gains daylight on
'The Hole of Weems'

Red Craigs Roof Circuit

1. *Groove Traverse* Font 6a
Sit start at the left arête and climb into the juggy crack, then traverse hard left through pink pockets to a crimpy flake to finish direct in a hanging groove. Pad the landing!

2. *The Peel Sessions* Font 6c+ ***
The west face of the roadside 'Peel boulder' is a classic. Sit start awkwardly and climb the central wall directly. No escaping early!

3. *The Peel Traverse* Font 7a *
Sit start at the left side of the roadside lip of the Peel boulder at jugs and follow the roof rightwards as low as possible to drop down and finish as far right as possible. Pumpy and good, but a bit grubby.

4. *Short Roof* Font 6a+
The south side of the pit has a low sheep-shelter roof. Climb it from flat holds on the right to pull out left on jugs.

5. *Pit Boy* Font 7a+ ***
Located on the north side of a large boulder about the same level as the Peel boulder but 200m west. Sit start at the obvious flake and climb up and right on perfect edges into the daylight. Permadry! FA Tim Rankin 2005.

6. *West Wall* Font 6c
Just right of the Pit cluster is a west wall with cleaned holds. Sit start at a flattie/sidepull and crank up right to the flake crack.

7. *Weems Arête* Font 6a+ *
The obvious through-cave high above the Peel boulder. From a plinth at the entrance to the cave, sit start and boost up to a sloping shelf pinch, then crank up to a high sloping edge to the right of the chockstone.

8. *Hole of Weems* Font 7a *
Step on inside the caves at pockets and crank right through the obvious sloper, then escape the cave via arête onto easier ground.

9. *The Ramp* Font 6c **
Above the Peel boulder right of the uphill path is a red roof. From a low start at a RH sidepull and LH crimp on arête, travel left through jugs to climb the ramp then slap back out right to the blunt nose.

10. *Rudolf* Font 6c ***
The red nose direct. From the low sit start, gain a high right slopey pinch, then a good sequence through slopers allows a rock-out right.

49

WEEM   *NN 844 500*

The leafy Perthshire village of Weem sleeps on the north bank of the Tay just west of Aberfeldy and provides sunny and pleasant bouldering on a couple of quartzy schist walls. The wooded hill is a sport-climbing mecca, but the walls provide good warm-up bouldering as well as a few testpieces. Bouldering can be found elsewhere, below the walls and around the crags... explore at will. The problems have been bouldered on for years, but Kev Howett worked out most of the harder lines including 'The Chop'. The right hand 'tyreswing' wall has easier slabbier lines while the left hand wall provides the harder highball lines.

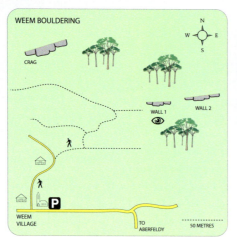

WEEM BOULDERING

CRAG

WALL 1   WALL 2

N W E S

WEEM VILLAGE

P

TO ABERFELDY

50 METRES

Approach Notes

The main road through Aberfeldy is the A827. If coming from the east, take the A9 to signposts for Aberfeldy 10 miles north of Dunkeld. Drive to the village and at the main crossroads follow the signs for Weem, crossing the River Tay. The road swings round into the village. Park at the church car-park on the right and walk uphill along a residential road beside the church. A hundred metres uphill is a path into the woods on the right. Follow this past a small hut then turn up into the woods. Take the first right junction, then at the next switchback break immediately right towards large beech trees, where you will find the walls and a tyre-swing rope for the kids.

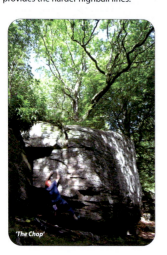

'The Chop'

Adrian Crofton on 'Too Hard too High'

WEEM LEFT WALL PROBLEMS

1. **The Chop** Font 7a **
The left hand wall is very crimpy and dynamic. Sit start at a rounded spike under roof and climb the walls above direct through small crimps. A fingery testpiece from Kev Howett.

2. **Jungle Formula** Font 5
Climb the rib to the right of *The Chop* from a sit start into a scoop then a rounded finish.

3. **In A Flap** Font 5+
From low jugs, climb the wall through a pocket aiming right to good holds, finish left.

4. **Lead On** Font 5+ *
Climb the main wall right of the arête from low holds, through a flat hold to horizontal pockets in the wall, finish direct on better holds.

5. **Cracked Knot** Font 6b *
Climb the thin central crack from a sit start under the roof. Finish to the left of the bigger crack through a large quartz hold.

6. **Palm Life** Font 6b *
Climb through the roof rightwards then left through vague scoops up to the small left-facing flake and a rounded finish.

7. **Too Hard Too High** Font 6c+ ***
The obvious groove just left of the right arête. From a sit start, pull into the groove with difficulty using a hard pinch. Finish up the wall direct.

8. **The Rest & Be Thankful** Font 5 *
From a sit start under the arête, climb the side wall via a diagonal crack to a ledge. Finish up the right arête.

9. **Green Fingers** Font 6a
Sit start as for Problem 8 but climb the overhanging wall to a flake on the lip. Finish up the wall through ledges.

10. **Getting Lippy** Font 6c+ *
A low level traverse from right to left along the lip of the roof. Start at right arête and stay as low as possible to the flat hold on *Lead On*, go round the arête and finish up the flat holds of *The Chop*.

GLEN LEDNOCK   *NN 726 286*

Glen Lednock is a collection of excellent boulders in a perfect situation. The huge dam that dominates the grassy alp of the Sput Rolla is paradoxically a picturesque viewpoint and a real playground for the boulderer. The rock is a very compact schist, crimpy and solid, behaving a little like granite. The bouldering was mostly developed by Kev Howett and friends, with additions from visiting raiders such as Tim Carruthers, Mike Tweedley and Tim Palmer amongst others. Many problems are easy in nature and provide great entertainment for the kids, especially the slabby blocks low down on the grassy swathes. Mats and spotters are required for some of the clustered boulders, but the circuit problems are mostly above good landings.

Approach

The Glen winds up north out of Comrie on the A85 west of Crieff. Comrie can be easily gained from Lochearnhead to the west, Perth to the east, or from the A9 to the south. If approaching from the A9 between Stirling and Perth, take the A822 Greenloaning exit, go through Braco and then shortly after take a left onto the B827 which is a fun road to drive to Comrie. Once in Comrie, go to the west end of the village and follow a small forested road north up into Glen Lednock proper. Drive carefully to the end of the public road, continuing uphill to the dam through some gates, where there are a few parking spaces on hairpins above the dam. The main area is across the river on the west. About 40 minutes drive from Stirling.

Lednock Dam Boulders

'Sneak By Night'

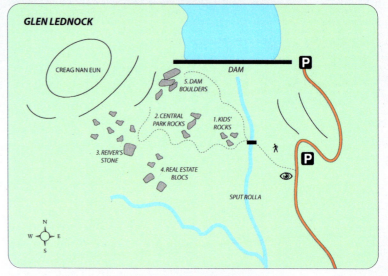

GLEN LEDNOCK

CREAG NAN EUN

DAM

5. DAM BOULDERS

2. CENTRAL PARK ROCKS

1. KIDS' ROCKS

3. REIVER'S STONE

4. REAL ESTATE BLOCS

SPUT ROLLA

N W E S

GLEN LEDNOCK CIRCUIT

The Reiver's Stone

The best stone at Glen Lednock, perched on a little mezzanine of flat stone and turf, this is seen below the high jumble of towers and boulders on the left flank of Creag nan Eun. At the third bend of the landrover track, it is hidden down and left. The north face has good slabby problems, the south face steeper problems and the east face good vertical crimpers. All in all, the perfect boulder!

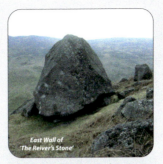

East Wall of 'The Reiver's Stone'

1. Sneak By Night Font 6b **
The excellent blunt left arête of the east wall. From a head-height flat hold climb the arête trending right using blind sloping crimps and gain a standing position on the slabbier wall. Truck up the slab.

2. Reiver's Logic Font 7a ***
An absolute belter and hard… from the obvious flat sidepull and ramp at the base of the *Sneak by Night* arête, clever footwork and sheer grunt gains the flat hold, now creep up the arête a bit until a crossover left hand gains a painful crimp, hold your position and snap right across the wall to good holds, finish direct up the wall.

3. Billy No Clan Font 6a *
The slabby north wall has a couple of good cracks on it which are fun from standing, but best combined with the sit start at the roofed base of the diagonal crack, push off a low ramp to good finger locks and rock over onto the right foot ledge. First ascent by Rory Howett 2003.

4. Night Walker Font 6a *
The south face flake on the left. From a sit start at the obvious ledge, crank left to layaways and throw up for the juggy lip and flake to finish.

5. Red 22 Font 6a+ ***
Easy when you get it all right, this superb problem climbs the steep south face and bulge direct. From the ledge, gain layaways in the centre of the wall, reach up and left for a blind sloper, hook and reach for hidden holds over the bulge lip, gain jug on right then rock out high left. Escaping out right early is *Blood Breakfast*, a good Font 4.

'Red 22' on the Reiver's Stone

Kev Howett on 'Reiver's Logic'

GLEN LEDNOCK CIRCUIT

The Central Park Rocks are three good large boulders by the track half-way up the hill, easily seen from the parking. The 'Eiffel Tower' is the split rock over the road, 'Canary Wharf' is the leaning prow with the horizontal crack and the 'Big Lamp' is the central boulder with a good landing on its front wall.

6. *Feathering the Penthouse* Font 6a+ **
The 'Eiffel' bloc leaning over the road. From the fist-jam crack gain the hanging crack and slab on the right. Blind and excellent.

7. *Eiffel Arête* Font 5
The blunt arête split by a very thin crack up to slabby rib.

8. *Bondage* Font 6c *
'Canary Wharf' bloc. The horizontal crack can be traversed from a sit start all the way left to right round the corner to a flake mantel.

9. *Best In Toon* Font 6b+ *
The flat featured wall above the good landing on the 'Big Lamp'. Various combinations here, but the best is from the flat hold on the left, up and right past a good hold to the vertical crack.

10. *Delicatessence* Font 6a+ *
The 'Upright' Boulder is below the Reiver Stone and has a high west face. The central slab by two diagonal cracks. From a low flake, snap for the first break then technique gains the second and then easy pulling to the top.

11. *Elizabethan Chorus* Font 6a **
The 'Real Estate' blocs lie down in the hollow below the Reiver Stone and 'Upright' boulder. It appears low but has a hidden higher wall. Climb the highest section of the south wall just right of the left arête. Sit start from below the arête up right to overlap and through direct to jugs. Going direct up the arête is Tim Carruthers' *Keep It Unreal* Font 7a+.

12. *Rock Around the Bloc* Font 7a **
The traverse of the Real Estate Bloc round the east and north walls, with the crux turning arête between the walls. FA Lawrence Hughes 2004.

13. *Breaking Wave* Font 7a ***
Dam Boulders. The pock-marked horizontally broken wall left of a pointed slab. Sit start in the break and go up to a thin crimp with your right hand, foot in break and then commit! Top out right through the dimpled glacis. FA Kev Howett 2003.

14. *Manic Stupor* Font 7b ***
Dam Boulders. The impressive central roof and best of the hard problems. From a crouch start at crimps, gain a layaway undercut, then snap up through a series of dynamic holds with increasing difficulty to throw for the lip with the right hand. If you stick it, traverse the lip to far left to finish. Powerful, technical and brutally good. FA Tim Palmer 2006.

54

'Manic Stupor'

'The move to the lip was at the very limit of my span and you sort of fall on to the top hold with your right hand… matching isn't a path either but I will leave u to work how to do that ha ha ha…'

Tim Palmer describing Manic Stupor

Kev Howett on 'Elizabethan Chorus'

RAVENSCRAIG NT 296 923

Kirkcaldy tries hard to have a 'Riviera' feel, with a long seafront and the picturesque park of Ravenscraig Castle at the east end of the town, its shore-front fortressed with sea-walls with hidden entrances and exits, all quite exciting as you hunt for bouldering on the sandstone bluffs. By far the best bouldering is the long roof hidden between the fortress walls under Ravenscraig Park. It is at first an impressive feature, with some hard-looking lines, but the rock is coarse and sandy, though that said, the established problems are all 'big' moves between generous features, so a little sandiness doesn't detract from the monkeying fun. The landings are terrific – very sandy, though the wall is tidal and Kirkcaldy tides should be Googled. Also watch out for poisonous jetsam and keep a wary eye out for needles and other things beneath your problem of choice. Most problems may vary even in our own limited geological timespan, so don't use wire brushes and don't even consider getting dry tools out – the locals will have you! The best problems have been climbed and named by Magnus Johnson and Mark Jarvie. There are plenty of slabby problems and small roofs elsewhere on the shore if you wish to explore further.

Approach

Drive to the east end of Kirkcaldy, following signs for Ravenscraig Castle – there is an obvious large car-park by the football fields with public toilets and burger shack. Follow the coastal path signs down to the shore and if the tide is out walk along the shore to the main roof. Alternatively, skirt along the red-chip paths and duck down under the walls when you spot the obvious red, black and tan roof.

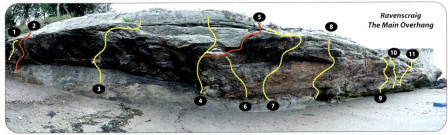

Ravenscraig
The Main Overhang

1. **No Rest for the Wicked** Font 5+ *
The furthest left line above the graffiti left of the giant flake. Move up and right to a rail and dyno right to the corner, finish up next problem.

2. **Flakosaurus Rex** Font 5
The obvious lateral flake, difficult mantel finish.

3. **Dynosaur** Font 6b *
5m right of the flake: from left-facing jugs dyno up to a big pocket, traverse right and mantel.

4. **Orion** Font 4+ *
Start below the ledge, from two left-facing pockets.

5. **Ursa** Font 5
Same start as Orion but traverse right at first ledge round sloping corner and mantel.

6. **Fury** Font 6c *
1m right of Orion, shallow LH pocket and RH undercling, up through edge to pair of slopers and mantel as for Ursa.

7. **Rage** Font 6c *
LH on half-moon hold, RH sloping ledge, up to pockets by the corner, then jump for jugs.

8. **Cave Route** Font 6c+ *
Sit start by the cave, head left then right to good holds in centre of wall, straight up to jugs.

9. **Seized Glory** Font 6b *
LH on lateral pocket, RH on left-facing hold, up to two-finger pocket to top.

10. **Crossroads** Font 6a
1m right of above, start on sloping pockets, up to left-facing slopey hold, through crimp to top.

11. **Meds** Font 6a
From eye-shaped protrusion aim right, then LH pocket, dyno for lip sloper, then right again to ledge.

12. **Come Fly With Me** Font 6c
Traverse. Start up flake, traverse sloping lip all the way to Orion.

55

WOLFCRAG   NS 789 980

Bloc Notes

This fine-grained greenstone quarry in the leafy Stirling suburb of Bridge of Allan provides the best bouldering circuit in the area. It is fingery and technical, with many manufactured holds – that said, don't add any more, as there are enough to get you up with dedication without resorting to frustration. The problems can be combined and eliminated ad infinitum, traverses can be linked and new variations always available due to the many chipped holds, not all of which are as positive as you think from below! Described are the classic lines, most of which can be jumped off at the first break or jugs – heading higher leads into solo territory, but always at about the same grade, so it's up to you how high you want to go. The main walls stay dry even in heavy rain – take a big mat and some carpet to dry toes: the jump-offs save energy but are hard on the legs. Most problems can be escaped by heading left or right along the breaks to ledges, or downclimbed. Sit starts make the problems harder, but are often awkward and dissatisfying.

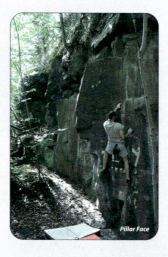

Pillar Face

Pockets Wall

Approach Notes

Best from the M9 Junction 11 roundabout to Dunblane, a few miles north of Stirling. Head back into Bridge of Allan and turn left just after the Allan Water bridge, up Blairforkie Drive. This winds uphill for a few hundred meters or so, take a sudden steep lane up to the right (Ferniebank Brae), signposted to the Golf Course. At the top of the hill at a T-junction turn right and park carefully. The quarry is just in the trees, 20 seconds approach! There is a good chip-shop, café and deli in Bridge of Allan, just by the river.

Waterfront

Pockets 3

Pillar Topo

56

WOLFCRAG CIRCUIT

1. *Arête* Font 4+
Start on left side pillar, via slot – jump off at jugs.
2. *Wolf Arête* Font 6a ***
Start on sidepulls, up to crimps, regain arête of pillar.
3. *Wolf Wall* Font 5 *
Same start as 2, veer right to better holds.
4. *Arête* Font 3+
Pillar. Right arête to long reach, jump off.
5. *Corner* Font 3+
Pillar. Via large jug to small hold then roof jugs.
6. *Crack* Font 5
Fingerlock crack from low hold.
7. *Wall* Font 5+
Pocket to crimp to top, two moves.
8. *The Outsider* Font 3
Hand-jam the crack!
9. *Wolfie* Font 6b **
Two-handed crimps and dyno to break.
10. *Pockets* 1 Font 6a *
Chipped holds trending left to break.
11. *Pockets 2* Font 5 *
Right trending pockets, via vertical, to break.
12. *Pockets 3* Font 5 *
Right set of slots to break.
13. *Tribal Look* Font 5 **
To left edge of niche, climb the crack to break, jump off.

14. *Dyno* Font 6b **
From shield hold dyno to niche flatties.
15. *The Pod* Font 5+ *
Gain shield, then pocket to niche.
16. *Pod Crack* Font 6a *
Climb crack and lunge to niche.
17. *Lock It* Font 6a+ ***
Technical crack, escape left at niche.
18. *Experiments in Incest* Font 6b ***
Mantelshelf the ledged corner to jug. Classic.
19. *Left Wall* Font 6b ***
Pockets and tiny crimps up wall to slot.
20. *Right Wall* Font 6a **
Right side of wall via pockets. Downclimb right.
21. *Slab* Font 5+
Edges and sidepulls to ledges.
22. *Slab* Font 4
Use flake holds to ledges.
23. *Undercut Wall* Font 5+ ***
Undercuts, left side of wall to slot.
24. *Ian's Wa'* Font 6a ***
Gain shield, veer left to slot.
25. *Waterfront* Font 6a+ ***
Undercut to pinch to high right crimps.
26. *Arête* Font 5 **
Mantle up to arête and ledges.

Cameron McIlwham on the Pod dyno,
Pic by Fraser Harle

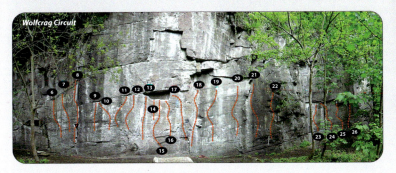

Wolfcrag Circuit

SALISBURY CRAGS   NT 270 729

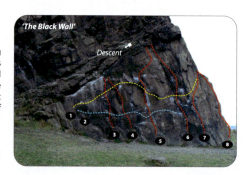

'The Black Wall'

Descent

Though roped climbing is forbidden on the Salisbury Crags, bouldering seems to be tolerated on some areas. The best place to boulder is undoubtedly the 'south quarry' area under *Arthur's Seat*. The rock is a hard angular basalt and was used by Harold Raeburn to practise his technique and take some pictures for his book *Mountaineering Art* which was first published in 1920, and which advocated bouldering as a means of general improvement in the mountains.

1. **The Black Wall Traverse** Font 7a ***
The classic slopey and crimpy traverse of the Black Wall from left to right, a bit polished but still excellently technical.

2. **The Low Traverse** Font 7b *
Start at the big flat hold left of 6, straight across down to 5, up to chalky hold just down and left of 5, across to chalky pocket then to chalky layback, diagonally down to top of long chalky right-facing layaway at bottom of 3, then to left-facing hold below start of 2, then reverse, with the crux matching the initial big flat starting hold. The strong version of this misses out the pocket.

3. **Left Wall Direct** Font 5 *
The far left line leading to the ledges. Downclimb Problem 1 to descend.

4. **Layback Problem** Font 6a *
Start at a layback, up to layback the slopey left-hand side of the chalky hold above, then jump or lock to finish as for 3.

5. **'M'** Font 6b *
Up the wall on laybacks to veer right to the hold that looks something like an 'M' just left of 6 then finish as for 6.

6. **Highball** Font 6b *
Up the highest part of the wall left of the arête.

7. **Arête Wall** Font 6a *
Climb the wall left of the arête to gain the arête and downclimb.

8. **The Arête** Font 4 *
Layback up the arête to the ledges.

Harold Raeburn bouldering on the Salisbury Crags

58

Approach: It really is best not to bring the car, parking charges are extortionate in Edinburgh! Catch the train to Edinburgh and see the Parliament at the same time if you are visiting. The crags are obvious from anywhere in the city, just look east. A path (the 'Radical Road') leads up under the crags from Holyrood to Arthur's Seat and the south quarry is found after the path turns a corner. It can also be accessed from Holyrood Park Road beside the Commonwealth Pool, go east over two wee roundabouts onto Queen's Drive, follow the path north from here.

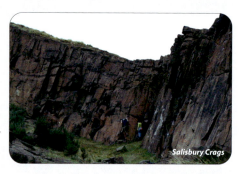

Salisbury Crags

'A knowledge of geology is of no small use to all climbers, and is absolutely essential to the exploring mountaineer. the great difference in the constitution, lie, and behaviour of different rock formations will soon force itself upon the attention of the climber. He soon finds he can take liberties with certain kinds of rocks which it would be criminal folly to attempt, if not impossible, with others...'

Harold Raeburn

AGASSIZ ROCK   NT 259 702

Agassiz Rock is as much known to the geologist as it is to the boulderer, having been the site of a special visit from the naturalist Louis Agassiz in 1840, when he confirmed striations on the andesite rock here were the acts of large glaciers moving past, thus reaffirming the local Enlightenment understanding that geological time was a little longer than some books suggested.

The bouldering lies on a well-polished overhang near the Blackford Hill quarry, underneath the Royal Observatory at the top of Blackford Glen. The overhang has the best rock and faces south, so climbing is possible in winter and even in rain. The main lines are quite juggy and polished, but for those who like steep eliminate climbing, and with a little imagination, it almost feels like the Bowder-stone in the Lakes! It is a great place to build stamina and create new eliminate problems. Some very hard traverses and eliminates up to 7c have been contrived, courtesy of the dedication of Ian Pitcairn, Paul Thorburn and Dave Redpath.

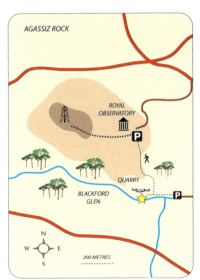

Approach Notes

If driving from elsewhere, gain the A720 Edinburgh bypass and take the Straiton junction north into the city. Continue for a few kilometres over two crossroads and at the bottom of a hill, at the third main junction, veer left and uphill past Edinburgh University buildings on West Mains road. At the next crossroads, take a left and follow signs to the Royal Observatory at the top of Blackford Hill.

From the Observatory car park, take the path at right angles to the mobile mast. Veer off left on a dirt path (blue marker post) and follow this downhill by a fence, through gorse to a hole in the fence by a distinctive stone wall. Drop down the hill here and swing right at the bottom through another hole in the fence, shortly after you will come across the south-facing bulging wall at the bottom of Blackford Quarry. For those who live in Edinburgh, the rock can also be gained from Blackford Glen Road end from the depot, walk along the glen to the quarry in about 2 minutes.

Stewart Brown on the Pocket Slopers

Agassiz Classic Problems

1. Pocket Slopers Font 6c+ **
Sit start at a bulging shelf, hook your right heel, left hand to dimple sloper, right up to sloper ledges, then crank up past the large pockets to a flat sloper then lunge right to jug. Eliminate all good pocket holds! (see main pic).

2. The Dyno Font 6c **
From the same start, cross your left hand to a sloper at the bottom of juggy layaway, then snatch right for the high pocket sloper on the wall, steady yourself and dyno straight up for high jugs to finish. No large jugs allowed!

3. The Lock Font 7a **
From the Pockets bulge sit start, traverse right along polished holds to gain the wobbly jug finger-lock under the roof, sort your feet and lunge up to the jug above near the crack, finish easily left.

4. Murder By Numbers Font 7b+ **
From a sit start under the bulge, gain the twin 'pinch crimps', then the cemented two-finger pocket, then snatch over the lip to slopers and gain finishing jugs by the *Crack*.

5. The Crack Font 4+ * (Var. Font 6b **)
Sit start under the crack and gain it with a tough move, romp up layaway polished crack jugs to slap up for more jugs, traverse left to finish. *Var:* Sit start under the Crack and gain a wobbly jug in the groove, then cross through another layaway up to a blunt undercling, a butch move allows the higher slot to be gained in the groove crack, traverse left to finish.

6. Groove Crack Font 5 *
Sit start the groove, a couple of juggy pulls gains the crack jugs to the right of the main crack, finish left.

7. Procrastination Font 7a+ **
The eliminate just right of the *Crack* and *Groove*. Sit start at a slot sidepull, pull up to crimps on the tan lip of the nose, then gain a blind two-finger pocket to finish right at jugs.

Agassiz Classics

Agassiz Traverses

Traverses

1. High Traverse Font 6b **
From the far left, traverse high right to the crack, drop down a little then turn the sharp nose by the second crack, drop down to jugs near the right flake.

2. Low Traverse Font 7b ***
From the low layaway jugs on the right, climb the nose of *Procrastination* to drop down to jugs by the *Crack*, traverse low along the polished rail sequence under the roof, then finish up the eliminate *Pockets Sloper* problem.

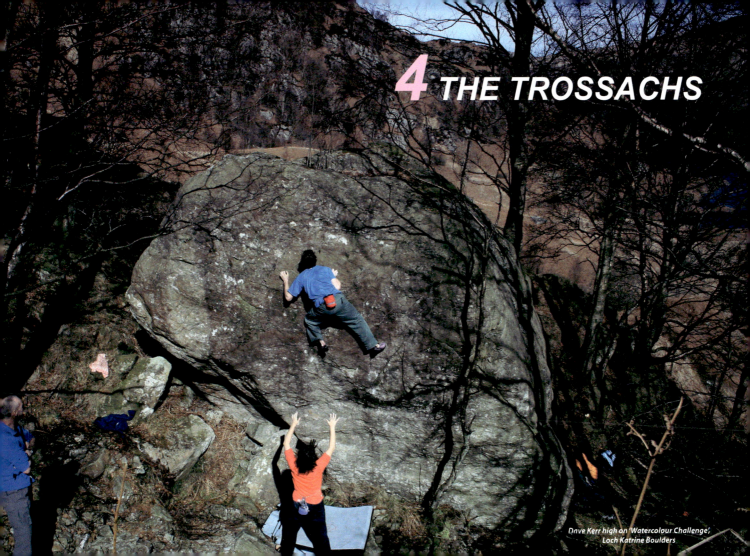

4 *THE TROSSACHS*

Dave Kerr high on 'Watercolour Challenge',
Loch Katrine Boulders

THE TROSSACHS

This is Mica Schist bouldering at its best! The main venues range from the East bank of Loch Lomond to the flanks of Ben Ledi and Glen Ogle, providing all the delights of schist, including gnarly quartz, sharp crimps, flying roofs, technical walls and delightful slopers! The best of the bouldering lies on more compact schist, such as at Loch Katrine. The finest time to visit these boulders is in a dry spring or settled autumn...in summer the bracken and insects are too vibrant and in winter, the ground can become a mire. Multiple mats, brushes, midge-cream, towels, finger-tape, chalk and Wellington boots can prove useful! That said, this must be one of the most picturesque areas to boulder in the whole of Britain...some special days can be had hidden away in these highlands.

Loch Katrine

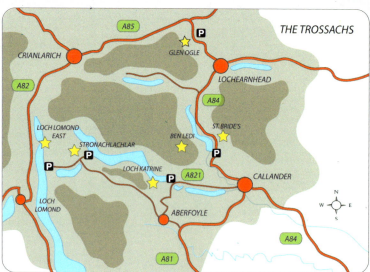

62

Glen Ogle - a sports crag venue, this short glen has hundreds of underdeveloped boulders. the best bouldering lies on the stones below the viaduct. Grades Font 3 to 7b.

St. Bride's Wall - a very accessible and excellent little wall. Limited bouldering, but the problems are good and the rock superb.

Ben Ledi - remote mountain boulders, but in a terrific situation and some classic hard testpieces. 40 minutes steep walk, but well worth the effort. Grades Font 3 to 7b.

Loch Katrine - the classic 'Trossachs' venue, good rock, varied boulders and problems. Stunning situation. Grades Font 3 to 7c.

Stronachlachlar - a fine circuit on schist stones at the north end of Loch Katrine. Excellent traverse problems. Font 3 to 7b.

Loch Lomond East - a diaspora of attractive boulders, mostly on the gravel shores of Loch Lomond. Good venue for a family visit and some hard testpieces. Font 3 to Font 7c+.

GLEN OGLE NN 577 258

Glen Ogle lies to the north of Lochearnhead and is littered with the bouldery remnants of shattered crags. The glen became popular as a sport-climbing mecca in the 1990's. Gradually the crags became worked and new routes drifted further and higher than before. Then the boulderers arrived, naturally lazy and burdened with mats and occasional stereos… from around 2000 Iain Beveridge and friends cleaned a batch of problems including the classic *Zorro* traverse on the High boulders, a 6c crimp-rail above a cracked slab. Kev Howett developed some highball crimp-fests, and some Glasgow-based climbers added some roof problems. There is now a good circuit of classic mid-grade problems allowing a fine day out in late spring when the sun climbs high enough to light the dark side of this glen. There are many easy lines and really you can boulder at will, but described here is a 'Font Red' circuit with a few harder 'bis' problems. There are many projects left to do, dependent on the often breakable nature of the schist, but that said, the glen is excellent for exploring and anyone can brush up a new problem fairly quickly. There are some truly highball problems and some super-steep roofs.

Glen Ogle is best in a dry spell in spring before the bracken and midges of high summer. It is dark and dank in winter so really March, April and May are the best months. Take as many mats as you can, especially for projects and try not to disturb the flora and fauna. Be careful with some holds, especially on highball problems.

Approach: North of Stirling, the A84 winds through Callander, along Loch Lubnaig and through the picturesque Strathyre and unpronounceable Balquhidder to Lochearnhead, which can also be approached from the east via Perth and Crieff along the A85. From the north take the A85 through Crianlarich towards Killin and over the pass.

To access the lower boulders, park at the downhill layby just above the stand of pines and cross the road (careful, the traffic is fast!), turn right into the trees immediately and find an old bridge over the burn from the east bank. Continue up and over a knoll to the obvious 'Split' boulder, where there are some good warm-up slabs. The circuit can be continued north from here. The higher laybys at the top of the glen allow access to Pylon Wall (which is sunny and excellent for good juggy problems and traverses), as well as the Viaduct boulders (underdeveloped).

Glen Ogle Bouldering Areas

ZORRO AREA
BEANFEAST
SPLIT ROCK
THE HOLLOW
THE PYRAMID
KING TUT'S

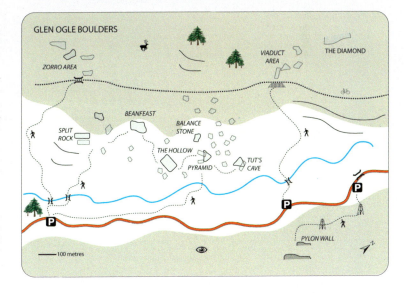

GLEN OGLE BOULDERS

ZORRO AREA
VIADUCT AREA
THE DIAMOND
BEANFEAST
BALANCE STONE
SPLIT ROCK
THE HOLLOW
PYRAMID
TUT'S CAVE
P
P
P
PYLON WALL
100 metres

63

The Low Boulders Circuit

1. Indian Sign Font 6b *
Split Rock. Warm up, then go for this short power problem on the steep back wall above the plinth on the far left. Crimps and pockets lead to a lunge to the top. Watch your back!

2. The Bulge Font 6b *
Past the Split Rock is a bulging low boulder with an undercut front face. Sit start and climb the bulge lunging left through a slot to escape up the arête.

3. 3 Bean Soup Font 6b+ **
The giant Beanfeast boulder lies further right. Sit start left wall from cave shelf on right, pull left into grey groove and crimp to highest point. Highball, mats comforting - an escape right is possible at half height.

4. A Real Munger Font 6a+ *
Beanfeast Boulder. The right hand wall can be climbed through the bulge before easing right.

5. Vorsprung Durch Technik Font 7a *
Beanfeast Boulder. From a sit-start on north face crimps, press up to a LH quartz slot, rotate and press out to sloper and jugs.

'Beanfeast Boulder'.

'Sleepy Hollow'

James Sutton on the 'Pyramid Lip'

6. Pickpocket Font 6b *
Downhill lies the giant Hollow boulder. This takes the short uphill roof from a crimpy crossover start to a pocket, then right to jugs and a final throw for lip jugs.

7. Sleepy Hollow Font 6c ***
A classic! Climb the left prow of cave from a sit start on plinth. Match sloping hold, hook and slap up to shelf, then move left to a layaway and a technical sequence back right to a spike on the slab. Jump off.

8. Hollow Man Font 6c *
The steep roof is climbed from a sit start on a plinth, hard right toe press allows a crux slap up to jugs and juggy finish up left to jump-off break. The roof sit start aiming right through a small crimp and finishing direct is **The Zealot**, a Font 7b.

9. Jack-in-the-Crack Font 5 *
Further north is the obvious Pyramid boulder above a cracked cave. Sit start under the wee roof and slap right to gain the easier crack follow this to the top.

10. Pyramid Lip Font 6c+ *
Pyramid Boulder. Gain the lip from jugs on the left above a slab, then traverse right and beg over the desperate mantel.

11. In Balance Font 6b *
The Balance Stone lies twenty yards uphill above the Pyramid. Sit start the prow from crimps, gain the lip and traverse right on slopers to mantel out the next problem. Pumpy.

12. Out of Balance Font 6a+ *
On right of north face Balance Stone. From a low shelf, throw for the lip, using a heel-hook by your hands. Bunched.

13. Fulcrum Font 6c **
The south side of the Balance stone. Sit start at quartz crimps, throw up for a lip crimp and swing right to a good flat rail, then finish direct. Powerful and twisty.

14. Tut Tut Font 6b *
Two hundred metres further right again is an obvious cave boulder with a quartzy lip. This is Tut's Cave Boulder. Sit start to left of cave, feet on prop boulder, and gain the quartz lip to a rockover out left.

64

BEN LEDI — NN 566 106

Some fine quality schist boulders set high on the 400m contour on the north flanks of Ben Ledi's 'Stank Glen'. They are perched on a small plateau under the boulder jumble that descends from the Ben Ledi pinnacles. These large imposing boulders that made it onto the plateau provide the best bouldering due to the generally flat heathery landings, though there is certainly scope for more adventure higher up the hill. A good late summer venue when the midges have gone and the heather is in full fire.

Approach Notes

From Stirling follow the A84 and signs for Callander. Continue through the town and up the winding road by the Falls of Leny. When this flattens out, take a sudden left-hand metal bridge to parking. A flat kilometre walk north leads to a steep way-marked path up through the forests into Stank Glen. Follow the corrie path to where the pinnacles come into view up on the left. At a bridge, veer left until you come across a white marker post and low boulder: from here follow a small burn up to a sudden plateau, where the huge boulders come into view. A good warm-up walk with a boulder mat! There are plenty of amenable problems on good rock in the lower grades. The most significant problems are listed and named here. Originally climbed on by the Ochils Mountaineering Club in the 1940's, guided themselves by a climbing cobbler from Falkirk called Ferguson.

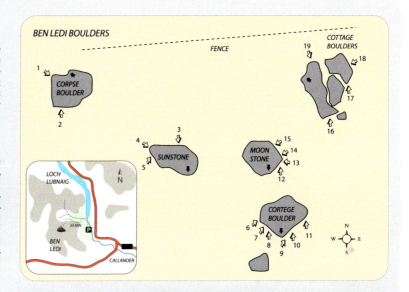

BEN LEDI BOULDERS

65

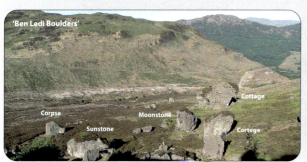

'Ben Ledi Boulders'

Corpse · Cottage · Moonstone · Sunstone · Cortege

Mike Tweedley on 'Trance Mittens'

Ben Ledi Circuit

1. Bernie's Arête Font 4+ ***
The striking north west arête of the Corpse Boulder. Climbed on both sides at various points!

2. Weeping Wall Font 5 *
The central vertical wall of the south face can be climbed through small pockets to a diagonal break and the top.

3. Dawn Wall Font 6b ***
The excellent little groove and Africa-shaped flake on the left side of the Sunstone's north face, finishing up and left.

4. Eclipse Font 6b *
Sunstone. Sit start under the prow, use pockets and butch lunges to an easier top section.

5. Solar Storm Font 6a+ *
The south face of the Sunstone. SS flat holds to quartz pockets, then right to a slot move through the bulge to jugs.

6. The Terrorist Font 6b+ *
The prowed arête on the far left side of the south face of the Cortege boulder.

7. Cortege Crack Font 6a+ **
The thin vertical crack just right of the stream. Descend by the right arete.

8. Pallbearer Font 5+ *
The central wall is a long stretch to good holds. Descend by the right arete.

9. Rude Boy Font 7a+ ***
Hard low traverse across the east face of Cortege boulder to finish up problem 11. SS at the descent arête.

10. Cortege Font 6b *
The hanging crack is hard to get into from a sit start.

11. Cortege Noir Font 7a ***
Sit start at the right arête, gain poor undercuts and holds out left, then up to slopers and crimps to dyno back right to the arête.

66

'The Pallbearer'

'Constellation Arête'

Steve Richardson on the Corpse Boulder

12. *Trooper* Font 6c **
Moonstone. Traverse right along the lip of the cracked roof to finish up the arête.

13. *Ocean of Storms* Font 5 **
Moonstone. Sit start under the overhanging arête and climb it on generally good holds.

14. *Crescent Moon* Font 6a+ ***
The excellent north groove of the Moonstone, using holds on the right wall.

15. *Crises* Font 5+ *
Moonstone. The highball main wall to a high crack. Descend down south face.

16. *The Tombstone* (Crucifix Finish) Font 7b+ ***
The headstone at the south side of the Cottage boulders. Sit start through a hard fingery sequence to a flat hold, break left to gain the arête.. FA Niall McNair 2006.

17. *Constellation Arête* Font 5+ **
Climb the obvious starwards-leaning arête on the east wall of the Cottage boulders.. Excellent.

18. *Past & Present Future* Font 4+ *
The vertical east face is climbed from an undercut to gain the thin pegged crack. First climbed in the 1960's. Highball.

19. *Trance-Mittens* Font 6c+ **
The fun right roof arête of the Cottage boulders, just above the fence. From a sit start, slap and heel hook up to rock over the lip.

20. *Thug Life Arête* Font 6c *
Sit start the prow of the small boulder opposite Cortege boulder. Good wrinkled rock.

'The Moonstone'

Mike Tweedley on *'The Tombstone'*

67

Thug Life Boulder

'The Tombstone'

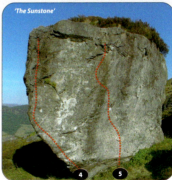
'The Sunstone'

ST. BRIDE'S WALL   NN 586 098

This attractive south-facing schist wall is easily spotted at the start of Loch Lubnaig, just after the bridge to the Ben Ledi car park. There is a convenient layby on the left (if coming from Callander) beside the river, just before the old graveyard of St. Bride's chapel. Park in the layby and skirt the field to the crag in two minutes. Most of the bouldering problems can be finished by traversing or jumping off the sloping ramp which cuts across the crag. The leaning wall is steep and bulging, providing a few classic fingery testpieces over perfect landings. A convenient spot if the Ben Ledi boulders are in cloud. Most of the bouldering problems were developed in the 70's and 80's.

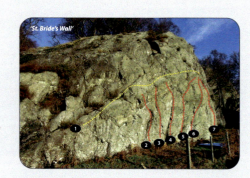

'St. Bride's Wall'

'The Crack'

1. **St. Bride's Traverse** Font 6b *
Left to right traverse along the ramp feature, downclimb the flake crack.

2. **Haemorrhage** Font 6b *
The line of the black stain through two bulges. Sit start.

3. **Brain Teaser** Font 6a+ *
The quartz wall immediately right. Sit start with the left hand on a quartz incut and the right hand on an undercling.

4. **The Crack** Font 6a ***
The excellent thin flake crack from a sitting start. FA I Duckworth 1970's.

5. **Stem Cell Reasoning** Font 6b *
The steep wall via the line of a quartz vein, finishing in a quartz slot.

6. **White Matter** Font 6c+ ***
Sit start the seamed line of diagonal quartz veins to a long reach up and left, which is hard and awkward, or step right and climb through the bulge direct, a superb and better finish.

7. **Grey Matter** Font 6a *
Sit start to right of the last problem and reach up right to a sloping hold, then gain the flake. The bulge direct looks impossible, or is it?

8. **Quartz Flake** Font 4
The main feature of the crag and previously recorded as a VS route.

LOCH KATRINE   NN 483 070

'The Trossachs' are a Victorian wonderland, the original landscape of Walter Scott's romantic idyll of Scottish life, but the Gaelic name refers to a 'rough ground' and a harsher life found in any literature. The landscape is rolling and pined, with many picturesque outcrops and pretty lochs, but the earth is rocky and littered with stones, and only worthy of harvesting for the boulderer. The best of the stones lie on the flanks of Ben Venue, on the south-west banks of Loch Katrine above the dam. The rock is fine-grained compact schist, very quartzy and often reminiscent of gabbro. The boulders lie scattered around the popular rough path to the Bealach nam Bo ('pass of the cattle') and the situation is indeed a scene from a Scots biscuit tin… steamers on the loch, mist in the trees, the rocky summit of Ben A'an with its tiny summiteers. The midges ruin sanity in summer and the bracken hides the boulders, so the best time to visit is a dry spell in spring or autumn. The landings are good on the best boulders, but take a mat to keep your feet dry around the boulders by the burns.

Approach Notes

The boulders lie beyond the path to Ben Venue, a popular Corbett. From the north or east, take the A821 west from Callander to Loch Katrine. From the south, gain Aberfoyle on the A81 and head over the Duke's Pass (A821) to the head of Loch Achray. Take the turn down to Loch Katrine and after 1k park in a layby by the Water Authority road to the dam.

From the layby, walk along the tarmac Water Authority road for a few hundred metres and turn left to a bonny bridge over the Achray Water, following the waymark posts, then turn immediately right along the forested track. Continue along the riverside track, don't head uphill to Ben Venue but continue over stiles until the dam is seen on the right. From here the path gets rougher, but continue along on the left side of the fence to a small burn. After about twenty minutes walk overall, the first boulders come into view and the higher Bealach can be seen. The Fight Club boulder lies in the gravel bed of the stream, beyond this (and over two burn-crossings lie the obvious twin 'Sentinel' boulders (NN 483 070) From here the other boulders can be found in the area. Aside from the classic circuit problems, there are many easier lines and some good harder testpieces in the 7th grades.

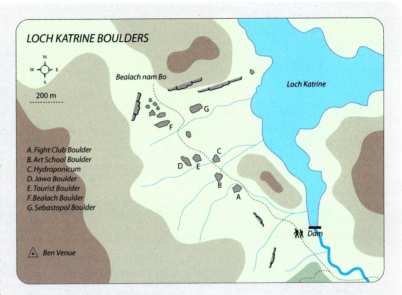

LOCH KATRINE BOULDERS

Bealach nam Bo

Loch Katrine

200 m

A. Fight Club Boulder
B. Art School Boulder
C. Hydroponicum
D. Jawa Boulder
E. Tourist Boulder
F. Bealach Boulder
G. Sebastopol Boulder

⚠ Ben Venue

Dam

69

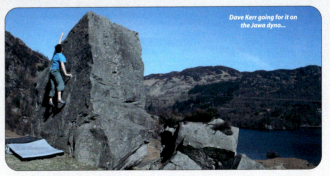

Dave Kerr going for it on the Jawa dyno…

LOCH KATRINE CIRCUIT

1. Fight Club Font 6c+ ***
The Fight Club boulder is the squat boulder in the gravel with a stone patio. This problem climbs the sloping overhang. Sit start at a ledge on a patio of stones, take a good incut, then fight rightwards on slopers to finish up the blunt right nose. Do it when you have good skin! A direct dyno from the jug is Soap 6b.

2. The Art School Font 6b *
The 'Art School Boulder' is well hidden, up over the fence in the burn 50m before the sentinel boulders. This is the committing downstream arête on good rough rock to a high groove. Sometimes a bit green.

3. Watercolour Challenge Font 6a+ ***
Art School boulder. A delightful problem taking the pocketed wall looking up-stream, with a long reach to thankful holds at the top. Finding the best foot sequence is the challenge.

4. Hydroponicum Font 5+ **
Below the Sentinel boulders in a kind of well this boulder leans over a stream just before the sentinel boulders and below the path. Start sitting in the fern-garden and pull up on good holds to finish directly up the groove and over left onto the slab via a good hold. The left eliminate line through pockets is Ikebana Font 7b.

5. Mind Trick Font 6a **
The flat-faced 'Jawa' boulder is the top twin Sentinel boulder. The crimpy south wall to the left on this face has small holds right of a wee hanging groove. Balance on and struggle to lift the right toe higher, then gently does it to the top.

6. Jawa Font 6c ***
A problem that relies on foot technique and flexibility. From the central finger rail, smear high to gain a left hand sloper to press out to the top. Or simply dyno if you get frustrated… it is possible at the same grade.

7. The Nose Font 6b *
A butch problem tackling the snout of the Jawa boulder. Harder from the hand ledge on the left (Font 6c+), easier as a stand-up start. Gain the sharp flange and crank to the top, watch the sloping landing!

8. HB Font 6b+ *
The heathered boulder under the Jawa boulder. Two overhanging arêtes provide the best interest here. The right arête is started from the long hand pocket, which gives a range of choices of holding the slopey arête before a vital two-finger undercling up and right allows a rockover to the top.

9. Tourist Trap Font 6c+ ***
The superb left arête. With subtlety it can be climbed statically through two-finger crimps to the pointy sloper. The best finish is monkeying left to finish in the scooped niche.

70

Anne Falconer on 'Mind Trick'

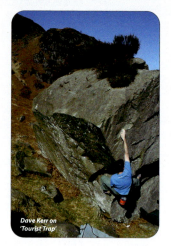
Dave Kerr on 'Tourist Trap'

Dave MacLeod in the Hydroponicum (Ikebana)

Past a boggy boulder with a heather bonnet, climb up to the obvious Bealach boulder field. There are many boulders here, but they suffer from clutter and many are dirty and have poor landings. The 'Bealach Boulder' is the obvious low boulder at the bottom of the cluster.

10. *The Knob* Font 6c *
The central waterworn overhanging wall, from a cross-handed sit-start. Right hand in slot, crank up to gain the lip and use the knob to gain better holds to rock over onto the slab.

In the wee glen below the bealach, follow the stream downhill from the Bealach boulder. There is a large, barrel-shaped boulder below the crags. This is the 'Sebastopol Boulder'. It has a slabby left wall and a roofed right arête with grooves.

11. *Navigator* Font 6b **
Climbs the groove left of the nose from a sit-start at the obvious sidepulls… contort to gain the lip and get established in the left hand groove. Or travel right to the next problem.

12. *Sebastopol* Font 6a *
Climbs the groove right of the nose, using technically demanding slopers and hidden holds in the groove. Finish up the nose on the left.

Testpieces:

Big Up Orra Glasgae Peeps Font 7a+ ***
The Jawa Boulder north face. The right hand wall has an obvious foot ledge. Start at two crimps and if you can mantle on to the ledge and gain the top, you are clever, strong and supple! FA Steve Richardson 2003

Lock, Stock and Barrel Font 7c **
Sebastopol boulder. The sit start to the hanging arête. From under the cave, slap and heel-hook desperately up the blunt arête in the usually vain hope of gaining the good slopers on Sebastopol. FA Dave MacLeod 2003

The Victorian Font 7b **
Sebastopol boulder. From the deep cave start, slap out right and crimp along the lip to the blunt right arête and climb this to the right-hand slab finish. Hard to keep your back off the wee boulder over the crux sequence, but good climbing. FA John Watson 2007

Paralysis By Analysis Font 7b *
On the lower of the sentinel boulders is a short uphill roof over a plinth. Sit start at a right hand pinch and crimpy press, then bicep up to the lip, finishing with a tricky fingerlock mantel onto the slab. One for the weight-lifters. FA Dave MacLeod 2003

John Watson on 'The Victorian'

71

Dave Kerr on 'Big Up...'

Dave MacLeod on 'Lock, Stock...'

STRONACHLACHLAR   NN 392 100

Bloc Notes

This suntrap venue can be great in winter and has a tremendous outlook down Loch Katrine and over Loch Arklet. The rock is mica schist, very slopey in nature and with some fierce crimps - the best quality rock is found on the Long boulder and associated stones clear of the forest. The forest itself is full of hidden boulders, but many are too big and dangerous to climb and the area is a jungle… finding the sports crags and boulders in here is an achievement in itself!

Approach Notes

From Glasgow follow the A81 and A821 to Aberfoyle. Take the B829 north for about 10km to a T-junction at the head of Loch Arklet, parking can be found to the right of the junction. The boulders lie on the hillside above the cottage, the lowest five minutes away, the highest (in the 'An Garadh' woods) about 15 minutes. The circuit follows the best route up to the high boulders, where the hardest problems lie.

72

'An Garadh' Stronachlachlar

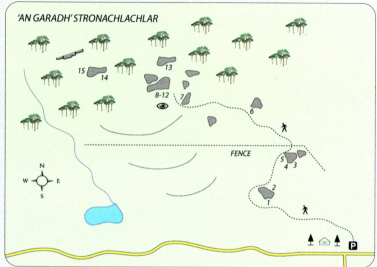

'AN GARADH' STRONACHLACHLAR

1. Mushroom Roof Font 6b *
The Mushroom boulder is the first bloc you come across above the old tractor and overgrown garden above the house. If you squint hard it does indeed look like a sliced mushroom. This problem climbs the roof from a difficult span and reach, exiting left.

2. The Dean Martin Memorial Traverse Font 6c *
Round the back of the Mushroom boulder is a green lip, which brushes up okay after a dry spell. The traverse slaps along from the sapling to round the top edge and mantel. FA Colin Lambton 2000.

3. Sulk Lip Font 6b+ **
Fence boulders. Higher up by the fence lie a few huddled boulders. The south hanging lip can be climbed up and right from a slopey ledge to rock out left as soon as friction gives out.

4. Periscope Arête Font 6b **
A difficult sit start to the arête gains nice technical moves to the apex.

5. Boomer Font 5 ***
The west face of the Fence boulder has a small handrail. Grab it, wind up and boom for the apex jug – a very satisfying dyno hard to pass by.

6. Copernicus Font 5 *
Hop over the fence and head up and left. You pass a nicely featured wee boulder, which can be climbed from the right, slapping left under the nose of the boulder, using heels to make it easier to gain the high jugs.

7. Palaver Font 6b+ *
The low boulder under the Long boulder, pointing down to Loch Arklet. From the lowest slopers, traverse to far left through crux midway slopers and a drop-down.

8. Pimp With a Limp Font 6b+ ***
Long Boulder. The central line climbs out of the right side of the cave to a technical sequence up and left to a high sloping ledge, then a tricky sequence straight up to finish right settles the heart.

9. Toy Soldiers Font 6a+ *
Long Boulder. The right hand line from finger jugs dynamically up to LH crimp, finish right to down climb the groove.

10. Anemone Font 5 *
Long Boulder. The bulge on the far right left of the groove. Butch up slopers, use heel to gain jugs. Short but good fun.

11. Nameless Pimp Toy Font 7a+ ***
The Long Boulder's classic traverse. From the left edge of the cave, boost along the cave lip to a crux arc through *Pimp* to finish up *Toy Soldiers*. Cold conditions needed for crux. FA John Watson 2005.

12. Celandine Prophecy Font 6c **
Behind the Long Boulder on its left is a propped roof. Crouch start from a LH pocket and RH jug, throw up to a palm hold, then take a crux sequence moving left on finger slopers to mantel out on better holds.

13. Virgin Suicides Font 7a+ ***
Another classic traverse. Travels the obvious long lip on the bloc above the Long Boulder. From the far right of the boulder, traverse the lip to finish into the hanging left groove. FA Dave Redpath 2001.

14. Prospero Font 7a+ **
Caliban boulder. Skirt along the bottom of the woods left from the Long Boulder and go up into the woods behind a slabby wall boulder. You'll find a cave with a cairn of stones. From the right-hand cave start, snap back to low holds on the shield, stretch up and right to a sidepull pinch, tiptoe backwards and swing for the lip, then traverse right to a tricky niche mantel. FA John Watson 2005.

15. Ariel's Release Font 6b **
The wee west wall of the Caliban boulder. From a low start behind a tree, climb the short arête to the lip, drop down on slopers to rock out at the far right quartz nose.

Pete Murray on 'Sulk Lip'

73

'Long Boulder'

'Ariel's Release'

LOCH LOMOND EAST   NN 331 100

Though dispersed along a few miles on the West Highland Way, along the pleasant east banks of Loch Lomond National Park, these boulders provide an enjoyable day's adventure and scope for endless bouldering in the densely forested hill-sides where wild goats roam. The shore boulders can be swamped by high water after rain, so a dry spell is essential. The rock is mica schist, but on the best problems presented here, it is of good quality and provides butch pocket-pulling and solid crimping testpieces. There are plenty of easy problems and slabs, especially round the shore boulders and at the Pollochro shielings (ruined houses). There are some great beaches for picnics and swimming, so it's a good place for a family bouldering day out, as well as for the dedicated boulderer. Projects abound, especially on the high alp where the giant Scholar Stone can be found (ten brutal minutes uphill from the Giant Oak), but the vegetation is impenetrable in summer. It's best to stay by the shore, far more pleasant!

Gate Boulders   Pollochro   Rob Roy's Cave

Approach Notes

From Glasgow follow the A81 and A821 to Aberfoyle. Take the B829 for about 10km to a T-junction at the head of Loch Arklet, turn left and follow the road along the loch till it drops down zig-zags to Inversnaid hotel and pier on Loch Lomond. Walk north along the West Highland Way. Rob Roy's Cave is about fifteen minutes walk (turn left at the 'Rob Roy's Cave' sign to access The Bottle problems). There are some pleasant boulders on the loch shore gravel (the best is Holly's Boulder) on the way to the Gate boulders which are a full 45 minutes walk, but probably provide the best bouldering here.

Mike Tweedley on 'Popeye'

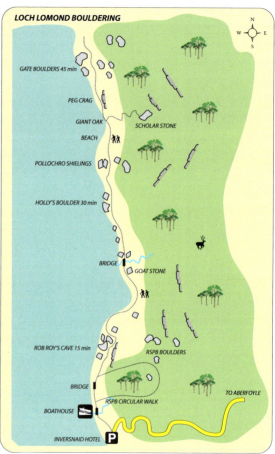

LOCH LOMOND BOULDERING

GATE BOULDERS 45 min

PEG CRAG

GIANT OAK

SCHOLAR STONE

BEACH

POLLOCHRO SHIELINGS

HOLLY'S BOULDER 30 min

BRIDGE   GOAT STONE

ROB ROY'S CAVE 15 min

RSPB BOULDERS

BRIDGE

RSPB CIRCULAR WALK   TO ABERFOYLE

BOATHOUSE

INVERSNAID HOTEL   P

74

Rob Roy's Cave

1. The Bottler Font 6c ***
The tapering bottle-shaped leaning wall which escapes dutifully left to a step-off after things get a bit high. A superb problem from a sit start through quartz slopers and schist sidepull crimps.

2. Out of the Dark Font 7a+ *
The eliminate Pit face left of the Bottle, started from low down in the cave, with a desperate left-hand crimp-press gaining better holds in the light. FA Chris Graham 2005.

3. Is That All There Is? Font 7a+ *
Traverse the lip of the large boulder to the right of the path is it branches left to Rob Roy's cave. From a central quartz jug a series of slopers travels right until you reach another flat quartz jug, move right and rock over onto the slab. FA Tim Palmer 2006.

Holly's Boulder

On the gravel shore a good 15 minutes north of Rob Roy's cave. Has a holly tree on top of it.

4. Holly's Traverse Font 5 ***
From the good sit-start ledge, a fine sequence left and up gains slopers on the lip, gain a high hold from here and rock up onto the vague arête.

5. Holly's Traverse extension Font 6c ***
The extended version from the far right is tricky to get into the original.   Low contortions and excellent slopers.

6. Let' Split Font 7a+ *
Sit start at a central pocket/crimp, left foot on top of ramp, crank up to crimp below Left Lip which is frustratingly just out of reach, then a crux lunge right to quartz nubbin sloper gains Holly's finish. FA John Watson 2007.

7. Left Lip Font 4+ *
Monkey along the left lip and gain the hanging arête to rock left onto slab.

Pollochro

A little further on, there are boulders at the more open ground of the Pollochro shielings, offering some good problems.

8. Talon Font 6c+ **
Climbs the scooped wall on the boulder just east of the path. Crimp from a sit-start on the left to a fierce finish up the groove, or take the wall direct at Font 7a.

9. Pollochro Wall Font 5 **
The excellent wall facing the loch under the trees. Despite a mossy appearance the climbing is good. Step technically up the slabby wall left of the easy groove and gain jugs at the top.

10. Gaelic Bullworker Font 6a *
Climbs the two-edged block behind Pollochro Wall from a sit-start.

Gate Boulders

After the good beach, the path narrows to a tricky fifteen minutes walk to excellent boulders by a gate on the path, opposite the loch narrows and *Island-I-Vow*. The main 'Spinach' boulder has a tremendous south roof and a steep north wall with a short overhang. Sometimes submerged.

11. Out of the Blue Font 7c ***
The challenge of the roof! From the far left flake ledge, heel hook out and right through impossible slopers and crimps to a desperate lunge up and left to jugs. FA Chris Graham 2005.

12. Popeye Font 7a ***
Superb pocket pulling. From a sit-start in the V-groove roof on the north wall, gain the left-hand pocket, then pull hard to Kung-Fu the small mono pocket up right, gain another pocket and boost right to jugs on the arête. Rock out right.

13. Ug Ug Font 6b *
The north wall arête, climbed to the wee tree, is technical and finishes at hidden holds under the vegetation. Best to jump off onto a mat!

'Holly's Boulder'

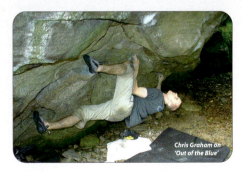
Chris Graham on 'Out of the Blue'

75

Richard McGhee on 'Consolidated', Dumbarton Roc

CLYDE

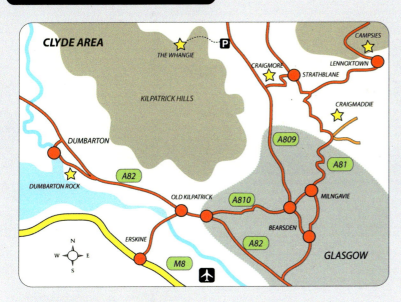

Volcanic Diversions

'Scotland once sat sweating on the equator, its lush tropical vegetation laying down carboniferous coals and limestones. This was when the earth was violent with earthquakes and exploding volcanoes and leaking faults. Magma was everywhere and through the geological eras from the Permian to the Tertiary, lavas bled out as we drifted north and the Atlantic began to flood into the valleys of the Clyde and Forth. It must have been like a scene out of Mordor, with steam spumes and fire and lightening in the clouds. This was the childhood of our 'central belt', our bouldering grounds for the cities of Glasgow and Edinburgh. It is almost a nod to this vibrant geology that our heavy industries fired metal and quarried rock and built great ships in these cities - it is a burly land of steel and strength, of industrial focus, dense and hard and everywhere cradled by this basic philosophy of stone.'

Dumbarton - Scotland's premiere bouldering venue, worth a visit from any part of the world. Despite its industrial outlook, it is an absorbing place to boulder, historical and home to most of Scotland's hardest problems up to Font 8b.

Clochodrick Stone - a little further south in Renfrewshire, but within easy driving reach of Glasgow, this erratic stone provides perfect landings and about a dozen short problems and traverses. Grades from Font 3 to 7a.

Court Knowe - inner city bouldering in a small quarry in the south side's Linn Park, this has about a dozen problems up to Font 7a+. A good option if you are stuck in the city and don't want to go indoors!

Craigmaddie - sandstone crags with a stunning outlook over the city, providing steep problems on walls and roofs. Good in dry weather, with superb 'grit' problems up to Font 7b. The rock can be fragile in places.

Craigmore - a wooded basalt crag with associated bouldering. Needs a dry spell, but idyllic when in condition. Mainly eliminate problems and short solos from Font 3 to 7b. Some classic technical testpieces.

Campsies - small but numerous basalt boulders on grassy slopes above Lennoxtown. Limited but some good hidden classics and a fine sunny aspect. Mainly a low grade venue, with grades from Font 3 to 7a.

The Whangie - overlooking the Southern Highlands, this pleasant basalt crag has some good bouldering from Font 3 to 7a. Good for traversing and working some stamina, or just a lazy Sunday boulder!

77

DUMBARTON   NS 399 744

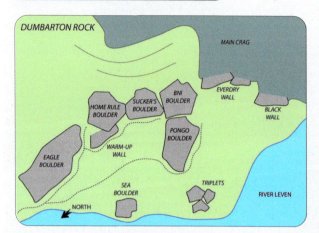

DUMBARTON ROCK
MAIN CRAG
EVERDRY WALL
BNI BOULDER
BLACK WALL
HOME RULE BOULDER
SUCKER'S BOULDER
PONGO BOULDER
WARM-UP WALL
EAGLE BOULDER
TRIPLETS
SEA BOULDER
RIVER LEVEN
NORTH

78

HOME RULE   SUCKER'S
BNI BOULDER
PONGO BOULDER
EAGLE ROCK   SEA BOULDER

Bloc Notes

The castle at Dumbarton Rock on Scotland's Clyde estuary overlooks five monstrous basalt boulders. It was formed from the Clyde Plateau lavas 340 million years ago, through a throat in the earth's crust. This is where Scottish bouldering was conceived, as early climbers 'practised' on the angular structures of the boulders with one eye on the main face lines, getting used to the slope and treachery of high holds, learning what could be stood on and what couldn't, training the head to stay composed and focused. All the oft-quoted names of Scottish climbing have cut their teeth, amongst other things, on these boulders: Bryan Shields, 'Cubby' Cuthbertson, Andy Gallagher, Malcolm Smith, Dave MacLeod... behind these names are legions of talented climbers and visitors who have climbed at this 'Black Fontainebleau,' who have either run away in fearful confusion, or come back for the blood count of bagging the big or the hard. Problems like *Gorilla, Toto, Mugsy* and *Pongo* do not relent easily, and the modern test-pieces like T*he Shield, Pongo Sit Start, Silverback, Sabotage, Pressure* and *Sanction* require the dedication of the hardened alpinist. Like a Black Hole, Dumby will suck in the light from all other bouldering in Scotland; it is the indisputable heart of Scotland's hardcore climbing.

Approach Notes

Leave Glasgow westwards and follow the A82 to Dumbarton, on the banks of the Clyde estuary, just west of the Erskine road bridge (or follow the M8 west to the Erskine bridge, cross this and turn left). Once in the town, follow the brown tourist signs for Dumbarton Castle and park underneath this. Walk between the 'Rock' and the football stadium to find the boulders under the main crag by the River Leven's estuary, underneath the square-cut corner of the north face. 2 minutes approach from the parking. Public transport is also good… take the train from Glasgow to Dumbarton (Balloch line), it takes about half an hour. Get off at Dumbarton East and again follow signs for the Castle.

Ben Litster on 'Silverback'

Dumby Yellow Circuit – good composure needed, a traditional Font-style alpine cicuit!

1. **Cheddar Direct** Font 4 *
Climb on to the orange slab via a blunt arête with a steep pull to start. Climb up right to the ledges under the next problem.

2. **Imposter Arête** Font 4 ***
The highball hanging slabby arête of the BNI boulder, climbed on its left side to the top. Descend far left of the slab and down the hole, or jump across to ledges under the crag.

3. **Skint Knuckles** Font 4+ *
Through the BNI cave, this takes the left arête of the steep Pongo crack face. Use layaways to pull up and round onto the BNI ledges under the slab, descend the hole.

4. **Volpone** Font 3 *
The 'hidden' slab crack can be found between the two bouldersd, accessed from the back of the boulders. Fingerlocks and smears to top.

5. **The Beast** Font 3+
The juggy arête facing the castle has a couple of tricky moves, reversing it to descend the boulder is even trickier!

6. **Friday's Fill** Font 3+ **
The crack on the warm-up wall is a nice little problem, tricky to start and with a puzzling finish, especially if some holds are wet!

7. **PTO** Font 4
The short bulging wall just left of the descent route, using an undercut and a stretchy move to the top.

8. **Central Slab** Font 4 *
The central slab can be climbed on various lines, but going up the left ramp then breaking right on good holds is a thriller.

9. **Pullover** Font 4+
As the slab starts to overhang, there is a jug on the lip. Pull over here and slap high left to a distant hold to pull over.

10. **Steptoe** Font 4 ***
The Sea boulder's stadium-side arête, don't use the lead hold… juggy at the top, with blind holds and technical footwork.

11. **Chowbok** Font 4 *
Sea Boulder. The central seaward crack, gained via layaways to the top niche.

12. **Sorcerer's Slab** Font 4 *
Climb the left side of the Pongo boulder slab from a tricky pull-on at the bottom. Descend the hole and if you found this a breeze, try the blue circuit!

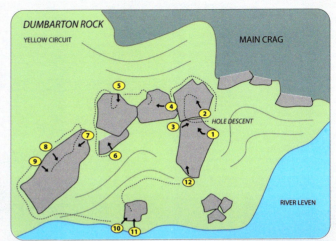

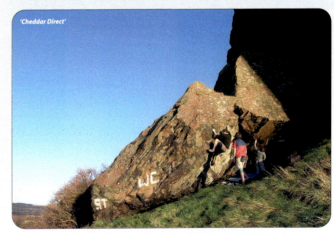

'Cheddar Direct'

Blue Circuit - a little more technical and fingery, but good fun.

1. **Black Wall Crack** Font 5 **
The low wall where the grass ends has an excellent right to left rising traverse. Start at the groove layaways, travel left through a crux reach through the bulging niche, move left on jugs.

2. **The Long Reach** Font 5 *
The triplet boulders. The seaward face of the lowest boulder has a scooped niche. Climb it with difficult smearing to a long reach up and left to a good hold.

3. **Nemesis** Font 5+ *
The hanging groove of the Pongo boulder. A small triangular hold allows a snap for jugs above the left nose. Awkward, good footwork helps get the height.

4. **Lunik** Font 5 **
Climbs the fractured shallow groove just left of the Cheddar arête. Step on to the sloping ramps and gain the high hanging arête.

5. **Deo Gratis** Font 5 **
Climb the central hanging slab side left of the arête above the descent hole. A crucial toe placement allows a snap for the 'thank God' hold above half height. Gulp and climb to the top.

6. **Chahala** Font 5+ *
The hanging face squeezed between two boulders above the cave has obvious hand ledges. Jump to them and campus through the good holds to rock out right onto the ledges.

7. **Friar's Mantle** Font 5 *
The central stepped groove of the warm-up wall, with a crux sloper move in the middle.

8. **Presence** Font 5+ *
Climb the right arête of the Home Rule face, which drops off the warm-up wall shelf. A slopey move gains the good handrail and it's easier to the top.

9. **Central Slab Direct** Font 5 **
Climb the centre of the Eagle slab as direct as possible to a blank section, which relents with small holds and precise footwork.

10. **Zig Zag** Font 5 ***
A classic meandering problem. From jugs at the overhang, pull over onto the hanging slab, then a puzzling section travels left through overlaps to zig zag up the high slab.

11. **Gardner's Girdle** Font 5+ **
Traverse the sea boulder from the stadium face, rounding the second arête (Erewhon) is the crux. More exciting when the tide is in!

12. **Erewhon** Font 5 *
The very polished seaward arête is technical to start but easy to finish. Faith in your feet is crucial.

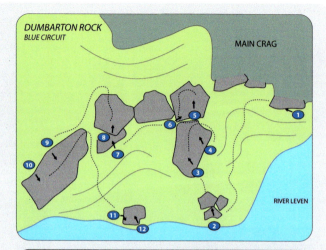

DUMBARTON ROCK
BLUE CIRCUIT
MAIN CRAG
RIVER LEVEN

'Erewhon'

Dumby Red Circuit – some classic hard problems makes this difficult and committing.

1. *Hard Cheddar* Font 6a ***
The hanging rib on the right of *Cheddar Direct*. Climb the lipped edge, using undercut flanges, to a hard sequence to get established on the slab. Little for the feet.

2. *B.N.I.* Font 5+ ***
Start as for *Imposter Arête* but move right onto the hanging orange slab to a good foothold. Continue trickily right through a small flake to finish up the right edge of the slab (*Pendulum*).

3. *Good Nicks* Font 6b+ ***
The cracked face of the BNI boulder facing the crag. Good technique up the crack gains the sharp ledge jugs, then a long stretch left to a crimp on the arête allows a crux cross over onto the slab.

4. *The Railings* Font 6a+ **
A popular modern classic. The lip of the ramp is gained by a long throw from pockets to match a sloper. If you can stick the footholds, traverse the lip left to rock over above the Shield feature.

5. *Toto* Font 6b ***
A technical delight. The vanishing scoop crack is hard to get into and a crux sequence aiming up right to a pinch, then left to jugs has been known to spit out 8a climbers! Jump off .

6. *Mestizo* Font 6a+ **
The hanging left arête of the graffiti'd Home Rule boulder. From a jump start, gain an undercut and snap up to the good hold high on the arête, step left and finish up the wee groove.

7. *Home Rule* Font 6a ***
Not hard but a classic polished Dumbarton testpiece! From the graffiti-covered hand rail, rock up to a press, then gain the higher handrail and finish up right through the jammed block.

8. *Blue Meanie* Font 5+ ***
The shattered orange wall above the slabby rock on the path. Gain the obvious high triangular layaway and lean left insecurely to hidden jugs over the brow of the boulder, romp over the top.

9. *2HB* Font 6a**
The overhanging groove left of the chopped tree. Up through undercuts to a crux 2-finger undercut, then up to good jugs on the ledges.

10. *Supinator* Font 6b **
The obvious crack left of the tree. Get established in the crack and climb it on mainly hidden holds to an insecure rockover onto the slab. Highball, you can easily end up in the brambles.

11. *Gorilla* Font 6c ***
The classic prow. Gain the obvious layaway via a jump or static from the crimps, then stretch up and left to jugs on the lip, rock over onto the slab. Primitive fun.

12. *Pongo* Font 6c+ ***
The wickedly overhanging crack on this boulder can be gained by a jump from the handrail. Custom sequences allow a slot hold to be gained, then lunge for better finishing holds.

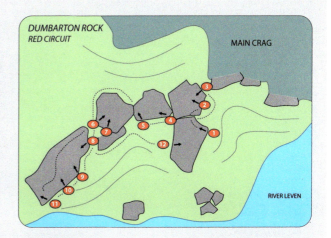

DUMBARTON ROCK
RED CIRCUIT

MAIN CRAG

RIVER LEVEN

'Home Rule'

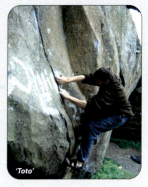

'Toto'

EAGLE BOULDER Testpieces

Zig-Zag Wall

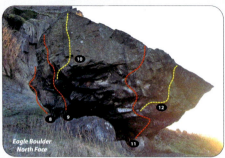

Eagle Boulder
North Face

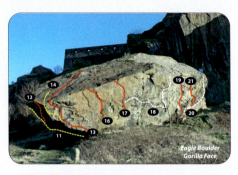

Eagle Boulder
Gorilla Face

82

1. Kev's Problem Font 7a *
From the low undercut hold, gain small two-finger triangles then slap through slopers up through *Pullover*.

2. Ramp Traverse Font 6c *
From the far left sloping ramp holds, traverse the lip rightwards to finish up *Zig-Zag*. Cool conditions needed.

3. Bust My Chops Font 7a **
From the hip-height break, gain crimps above and slap up and left for a right-facing sloper in the corner, finish left or direct.

4. Bust My Chops Right Hand Font 7b *
Start as for the original problem but gain very poor holds on the lip and finish through a flat hold above the lip.

5. Jeremy's Problem Font 6c+ **
An excellent eliminate. Sit start *Zig-Zag*, gain slopers on the lip, then lunge up and left for a sloping pinch, then lunge for a high right sloping ledge, finish direct. No jugs!

6. Zig Zag Sit Start Font 6c *
Sit start at a low undercut and go straight up to match the lip slopers, then into the original problem.

7. Bampot Traverse Font 7a **
Up Bampot arête then traverse the lip left to a crux redpoint sequence through Jeremy's Problem.

8. Bampot Arête Font 6b+ **
Sit start the blunt arête, gain lip and travel rightwards to make a rock over onto *Zig Zag*. Without flat jug it's 7b.

9. Shadow Font 7a+ **
The terrifying black groove on the left. A hard sequence gains a good hold, finish up the wee slab. FA Andy Gallagher 1992.

10. Trick of the Vale Font 7b **
As for *Shadow*, but move right to a ledge then climb the wall direct to the apex. FA Andy Gallagher 1992.

11. Pressure Font 8b ***
Simple: from a wee pillar and flanges at the back of the cave, climb back to the flat jug, finish up the hanging ramp out right (*Smokescreen* Font 7b+). FA Dave MacLeod 2005.

12. Firestarter Font 8a ***
From the juggy ledge on the cave lip crossover right to gain the hanging groove and top. FA Dave MacLeod 2004.

13. Gorilla Sit Start Font 7b ***
The classic flying prow from a sit start at a low front face crimp and a cave sidepull. Two hard moves to get going.

14. Silverback Font 7c ***
From the crimps of *Gorilla*, move left to match poor sloping crimps and gain the incut hold on the arête, then boost for the jug on the nose. FA Dave MacLeod 2001.

15. King Kong Font 8a ***
Sit start *Gorilla*, climb through *Silverback* and finish left round the corner to a tricky mantel. Dave MacLeod 2002.

16. Hoop Font 7c ***
The face right of *Gorilla*. From a finger jug make a long rock over to a crimp on top of the 'ear', then up left to the lip.

17. Bingham's Wall Font 7b+ **
From the juggy rail in the centre of the face, gain a small crimp and make a morphological span left to the lip.

18. Dressed For Success Font 7b+ **
Gain the juggy rail and traverse it right to drop down under the *Supinator* crack, continue along slopers to finish up *2HB*.

19. A Ford Flash Font 7b
The orange groove just to the right of the tree with a long stretch left to better hold. Rarely done, a bit of a mystery.

20. Oceans Font 7b+ **
A committing and desperate solution to the orange groove just right again, from the shallow groove start of the *1990 traverse*. FA Dave MacLeod 2001.

21. 1990 Traverse Font 7b *
Start in the groove right of the tree, layback up a vague crack then traverse hard right to finish up *Blue Meanie*. FA Andy Gallagher 1990!

HOME RULE BOULDER

This boulder has until recently held the lion's share of test-pieces at Dumby. The fashion is now for new testpieces coming out of the cave, as exemplified by Dave MacLeod's circuitous and desperate 'Sosho' girdle. It is the highest boulder on a platform, with a distinctive through-cave and a graffiti-covered front wall.

Testpieces

1. **Mestizo Sit Start** Font 7a+ ***
The overhanging sit start to the sharp arête is climbed from a slopey layaway to slap up left for ledges, then flexible trickery allows a slap to the good crimps on the arête, finish up the original problem. FA Dave MacLeod 2000.

2. **Mugsy** Font 7a **
The centre of the face from the handrail jugs. Jump to the high right sloper, gain a left undercut then throw for distant left jug, finish left on edges. FA Dave Cuthbertson 1980's.

3. **Mugsy Traverse** Font 7b ***
Traverse the line of sloping jugs from the left of the cave into the original problem. The tricky part is doing the crux statically through a sloping left hand crimp. Heel-toe locks possible. FA Andy Gallagher 1993.

4. **Knowledge Is Power** Font 7b+ **
A combination of various problems! From two hanging crimps under the *Mugsy* handrail, boost to the jugs, then traverse right round the *Mestizo* arête to reverse the Home Rule traverse, finish up *Home Rule*.

5. **Hokku** Font 8a *
From the depths of the cave at a spiky jug next to Sucker's boulder, climb backwards out of the cave to gain a shelf which joins the *Mugsy* traverse. Desperate and unlikely starting sequence. *Sosho* is the full girdle from the hanging nose (a long and hard Font 8a+). FA Dave MacLeod 2007.

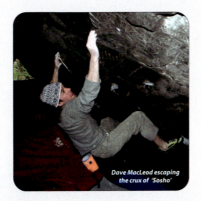
Dave MacLeod escaping the crux of 'Sosho'

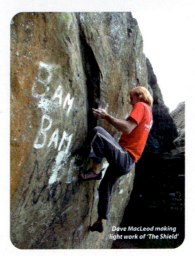
Dave MacLeod making light work of 'The Shield'

SUCKER'S BOULDER

Squeezed out by its bigger brothers and flanked by two caves, this boulder still manages to give us some classic problems: from the polished slab lines to the steeper testpieces of the scooped orange face, where you are likely to find a conspiracy of grounded boulderers contemplating the 'disappearing' crack of Toto.

1. **Toto Sit Start** Font 7a **
From the lowest crimps under the Shield, cross over up and left to join the crack of *Toto*. Correct foot positioning makes the first move possible. FA Cameron Phair 1994.

2. **Totality** Font 7b+ ***
A popular technical modern classic! Climb *Toto sit start* and get established at in the crack, reach right across the wall to a poor crimp, drop down to a sloping left hand hold, then continue with difficulty rightwards to rock over onto *The Shield*. FA M. Casey.

3. **The Shield** Font 7b+ ***
The classic bullworker problem. Clamp the shield anywhere you can (no wee undercut!), pull on and slap for the sloping lip jugs. Sounds easy, doesn't it? FA Malcolm Smith 1994.

4. **The Shield Sit Start** Font 7c **
Gain the pocket then the wee undercut and climb the original. FA Dave Redpath 1997.

Sucker's Boulder

B.N.I. BOULDER

Despite developing equipment and fitness levels in bouldering over the years, there is always the *Bloody Nigh Impossible*! This boulder pays respect to that enduring humility - it is a historic Scottish boulder that has seen epochal ascents. In the late 50's and early 60's, Neil MacNiven and Brian Shields crawled up the 'descent' hole and walked up the exposed arête of *Imposter*, then got the idea of stepping right onto the orange slab, tip-toeing gently further right to the arête of the earlier *Pendulum*, which swings in from the big block on the right, and their classic commitment today gives the boulder its epithet of B.N.I. In the '70's, Willie Todd cranked out the old peg crack of *Good Nicks* which then aims high and left for a stretchy finish round the right arête of BNI. In the '90's, Mal Smith powered straight through the roof onto the slab with *BNI Direct*, and more recently, the awesome dedication of 'Dumby' Dave MacLeod paid off to give *Sabotage, The Perfect Crime* and *Sanction* - a trio of Scotland's most famed and demanding problems.

1. *Chahala Sit Start* Font 8a **
Sit start the arête beside Sucker's boulder (cave) and clamp up this to join the original problem. No bridging on prop boulders. Dynamic and desperate. FA Dave MacLeod 2007.

2. *The Perfect Crime* Font 8b ***
A solution to the cave. From crouching sidepulls at the left edge of the cave, low contortions right lead to a shake-out at the wee hanging ramp where *Sabotage* starts, finish up this! FA Dave MacLeod 2005.

3. *The Serum of Sisyphus* Font 8a+ **
Start matching on the *Railings* pockets, drop down right to join *Perfect Crime* and follow this to the niche, then traverse up and right to *Good Nicks* crack, finish at the halfway jugs here. Contrived but a little easier than finishing up *Sabotage!* FA Malcolm Smith 2006.

Dave Redpath on 'Sabotage'

4. *Sabotage* Font 8a+ ***
Another hard Dumby classic. From a sit start at the hanging ramp, undercut backwards to the lip of the hanging prow under the BHI slab. Gain a poor right sloper and then use the arête to make a rockover onto the slab. Technical and powerful. FA Dave MacLeod 2003.

5. *Sanction* Font 8b ***
The left side of the BNI cave roof. Sit start at good holds and crank left through the flat shattered wall towards the long ramp. Crux move to an inset hold under the lip allows the slab to be gained. Secretive moves and futuristic. FA Dave MacLeod 2006.

6. *B.N.I. Direct* Font 7b+ *
Stand on the stone plinth and start gripping two crimps on the lip of the slab. Pull on and make a long morpho reach to the sharp hold, get established on the slab and finish direct.

7. *Good Nicks Sit Start* Font 6b ***
The excellent groove under the old peg crack, using subtle body positioning and the odd knee-bar to make it easier! Twist into the crack and finish up the original problem stretching out to the arête.

Joe Newman on BNI Direct

8. *You're Nicked* Font 7b **
The excellent direct to the *Good Nicks* crack. From the crack's fingerlock, climb up the wall through crimps to lunge for the wee hold on the arête, finish up the slab. FA Dave MacLeod 2001.

PONGO BOULDER

This - possibly the most worked-on of all the boulders at Dumby - seems unassuming enough until you try the harder problems or the traverses, then it unleashes its brutality and usually leads you scuttling away, badly beaten, to an easier problem. The obvious roof-crack of *Pongo* is a case in point – requiring the utmost of butch approaches and shoulders like tightened Meccano. Originally climbed by Mal Smith, it was a watershed in what was possible in Scotland and is probably the most lusted-after modern problem at Dumby. Traversing came of age on this boulder when the awkward seaward nose of *Nemesis* suggested you could drop down on slopers to continue up and right on the lowest of holds, chalk-bag trailing the ground, to turn the corner and finish by the cave at whatever finish you had the strength left to try. Andy Gallagher started all this off with *Consolidated* in 1994 and now the lowest, thinnest finish goes at Font 7c.

Johnny Morozzo on 'Slap Happy'

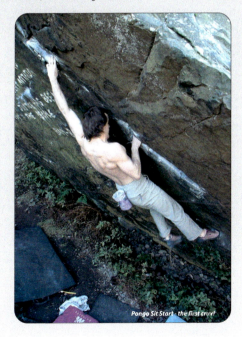

Pongo Sit Start - the first crux!

1. **Slap Happy** Font 7a ***
The leaning wall is climbed through a high sloping crimp, gain the holds just under the lip and dynamically power through to rock over onto the ledges. FA Andy Gallagher 1993.

2. **In Bloom** Font 7c ***
Start on the square hold left of *Slap Happy*, traverse right along the desperate rail and if you can keep your feet on, lunge to the flange on *Pongo* and finish up this. Pure grunt! FA Dave MacLeod 1998.

3. **Pongo** Font 6c+ ***
From the handrail, jump to the flange and continue up the powerful crack with a crux slot move to gain tenuous jugs at the top! Rock-over direct.

4. **Pongo Sit-Start** Font 8a ****
The best problem in Scotland? From permanently chalked sit start holds, climb the leaning crack. Gain the niche and the jammed block, choose how you hold this carefully, then power through two crux moves to finish up the original *Pongo*. FA Malcolm Smith 1998.

5. **Supersize Me** Font 8b ***
An awesome link-up. Sit start right of *Andy's Arête*, climb left to continue into the crux of *Pongo* sit start, then reverse the handrail of *In Bloom* and finish up *Slap Happy*. Easy! FA Malcolm Smith 2005.

6. **Andy's Arête** Font 7b *
Sit start the far right arête and climb it with laybacks on the overhanging side. Use holds on the leaning wall as well. Insecure and feels highball.

7. **Consolidated** Font 7b+ ***
The finest of the traverses at Dumby. From the seaward nose (*Nemesis*), slap up to the lip, drop down right to layaways and traverse low right on slopers to negotiate the blunt arête under *Cheddar*. A crux sequence under the lip gains the big triangular hold, then slap up the hanging arête to finish, or extend it to the cave (Font 7c). FA Andy Gallagher 1994.

CRAIGMADDIE   NS 586 763

The UK's most northerly gritstone venue! Well, it's a form of gritstone, specifically of the 'Namurian Millstone Grit series', which finds its most solid example on the moors above Mugdock, known as Craigmaddie Muir, north of Glasgow. The rock is a sandy gritstone which degenerates in places to a soft conglomerate, but the small crags mentioned here all provide solid bouldering and allow the tired Dumbarton afficionado a chance to toughen up their skin for a visit to the Peak. It has been a quiet bouldering secret for years and 'rediscovered' in the last few years by a few Glasgow boulderers. The outlook of the crag takes in the whole glory of Glasgow and the pleasant twittering of birds is offset only by the flight path to Glasgow airport.

Approach: Go north through the Glasgow suburbs of Bearsden and Milngavie on the A81, until you pass Mugdock and Craigmaddie reservoirs on the left. After a few twists in the road, at a 3-way junction, take a right turn signposted Bardowie (taking the north B-road, not the south). Continue uphill through the forest, past the houses until the road opens out to a view of the city over the fields. Pass the North Blochairn farm with its wall-embedded millstone and continue downhill for a kilometre to a parking layby on the right, with room for three cars. Walk down the road to a gate by an old WW2 bunker on the left and cross the fields towards the obvious crags, but please take care at gates and fences. The Lower Crag is the first encountered, just to the right of the forestry plantation. Best to start at the Upper Crag and work down!

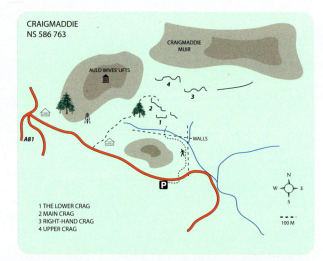

CRAIGMADDIE
NS 586 763

CRAIGMADDIE MUIR

AULD WIVES' LIFTS

A81

WALLS

P

1 THE LOWER CRAG
2 MAIN CRAG
3 RIGHT-HAND CRAG
4 UPPER CRAG

N W E S

100 M

UPPER CRAG

RIGHT HAND WALLS

MAIN CRAG

LOW CRAG

'The Rules'
1. Do not climb here after rain as the rock is brittle… give it a good drying day.
2. No climbing on the main crag March-June as a barn owl is in residence.
3. Respect the farmers' working rights and don't disturb stock.
4. No stripping of vegetation… it just grows back.
5. No climbing on the 'Auld Wives' Lifts' – it has historical carvings.

Marc Sweeney on 'Abracadabra'

'The Mantle' on the High Wall

Right Hand Crag

Lower Walls: composed of two impressive roofs, the left one is best left as a sheep pen, whereas the right provides some of the best roof problems here. The rock is good and the atmosphere very like a classic Peak gritstone venue. The main crag up and left of this is a bit brittle and best left to a nesting Barn Owl.

1. **Filth** Font 5+
The left roof is filthy and friable. Gain a slot in the right hand side of the overhang and dyno for jugs on the lip, work right to top out.

2. **Chockstoner** Font 5+
From the stone-choked chimney at the back of the crag, yard out to the arête using heel locks (or not), cut loose and climb!

3. **Abracadabra** Font 6c+ ***
From a crouching start at the block under the right roof (no block on right), heel hook back to the lip, gain the large pocket and good flat holds, then traverse left along the lip to a tough mantel finish on the nose.

4. **The Plinth** Font 6c *
Sit start on the left side of the plinth at a hidden undercut and RH sidepull, snap up to crimp sidepull and slap again for slopers above the loose block, smear your feet on and lunge for the top.

5 **Farmer's Trust** Font 7a **
Peter Roy's direct line from the far left *Abracadabra* holds finishing right through the annoyingly distant two-finger pocket.

High Wall: continue up past the main crag towards the higher moor onto a plateau. This crag is the highest left wall, with a distinctive vertical face and provides good technical, crimpy climbing. The landings are perfect and many eliminates can be created between the problems.

1. **The Mantle** Font 6b **
Lots of air miles will be gained on this! Climb to the slopey ramp on the left and mantle direct, no holds out right.

2. **Left Crack** Font 4
The obvious crack just right of the high shelf.

3. **Right Crack** Font 5
Pull on at the jugs and gain a RH sidepull on the wall, use this to step up onto the jugs and gain the top.

4. **Flake Wall** Font 6b *
The wall to the right. Use holds in the flake to twist up to a very sharp LH crimp, then dyno for the top.

5. **Undercut Crack** Font 6b ***
Undercut the flared crack on the wall and Egyptian up through crimps, finishing direct to the top.

6. **Right Arete** Font 6a+ *
Using the flared crack, twist up right around the bulging arête and rock up on the nose jugs, finish up the arête.

7. **Lip Traverse** Font 6c *
From the nose jugs, slap right along the lip, gain a sloper under a hanging corner and rock up and left to the crack.

Right Hand Crag: just down and right of the High Wall, this roofed crag sits above a flat boulder. It has some powerful roof problems on sloping holds and a few hard projects. The problems are named after the most distinctive sound here: Glasgow Airport's flight path!

1. **BA** Font 6a+
Left of *Easyjet*. Sit start under the roof and pull through on sloping crimps to rockover left to a big pocket and easy finish along slab.

2. **Easyjet** Font 7a *
From flat holds under far left of roof, gain a LH pinch under the lip, slap right along the lip crimps to join Buzz and rock over.

3. **Buzz** Font 6b *
From the sit start jugs, gain a sharp crimp and lunge left for the jugs on the lip of the roof, pullover onto slab.

4. **Oxygen Mask** Font 6c ***
The superb traverse rightwards out of the cave. Contortions right lead to a hard sequence through the brushed sloper crimps to a lunge for the jugs on the lip.

5. **Cryanair** Font 6b **
From good holds under arête break left through the infamous slopers to lunge for lip.

6. **Emirates Wall** Font 6b
Straight up the scooped wall on the right using crimp presses. Short but tricky.

87

CRAIGMORE
NS 528 798

Approach Notes

From Glasgow the A809 finally gains open country outside of Bearsden. The road winds out to Drymen and Loch Lomond, but before this, just after the biker-haven of the Carbeth Inn, take the first right along the B821 link-road to Strathblane. After the green hut community of the forest, the crag is on the left, hidden in trees by the fields, just before the West Highland Way. Park carefully in a layby or under the trees further east and walk back.

Bloc Notes

North-east facing, it is best in a dry spell in spring or autumn. Avoid the midge season and don't go if it's damp as the mossy old forest retains the moisture. The best of the bouldering can be completed as a Fontainebleau-like circuit, providing a good work-out on varying styles of problem. The Southern section is predominantly bouldering on the main crag buttresses, while the Northern section gives dispersed boulders and walls all the way to the end. The rock is a dimpled basalt which chalks up to good slopers and small crimps. Fingerlocks seem to be the key to many problems, as well as good technique with the feet.

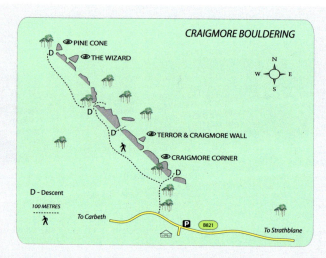

CRAIGMORE BOULDERING

PINE CONE
THE WIZARD
TERROR & CRAIGMORE WALL
CRAIGMORE CORNER

D - Descent

100 METRES

To Carbeth   B821   To Strathblane

Andy Gallagher topping out 'The Wizard'

Pete Murray on 'Wide-Eyed'

Craigmore Corner Area – the walls under the pine tree offer the highest routes here, there are some excellent highball problems and short eliminates as well.

1. **Totem** Font 6a **
Stuck in the corner like a discarded statue is a totemic boulder with an undercut midway crack: pull on to this block in the centre and gain the sloping jugs at the top. Heels ease backstrain!

2. **Wide-Eyed** Font 6c **
A classic! Just right of *Totem* is a crinkle-cut crack in the wall. Lunge to the break in the centre and lock-off up to a foot-popping stretch for reluctant juggy holds, compose and solo or downclimb more easily right.

3. **Harmless** Font 6a **
The crack just to the right. Gain the lock in the crack, where a different sequence is required depending on which hand you use.

4. **Merlin** Font 6b ***
Round the corner is a blunt arête right of a holly corner. Climb the vertical face on the left of this from small foot ledges, slap up and right to poor hold in the corner, then climb the face and snatch to better holds back into the corner. Superb and technical.

5. **Jolly Green Dragon** Font 6b+ **
This excellent eliminate problem sit-starts at a V-hold down and right, reaches up left to the horizontal finger-slopers, then snatches all the way up to a sloping ledge. Finish right.

Terror Head

From a certain angle, this stern-eyed boulder glowers at you as though you're an intruder. The problems on this stone and on Craigmore Wall just to the right are excellent arête puzzlers. The traverse of Craigmore Wall from left to right is a superb technical journey ending wherever you decide to step off.

1. *Terror* Font 5 ***
Puzzles even the most experienced of locals... gain good incut slots on the arête and reach right, step up on smears and gain the good 'eye' hold on the face, then mantle over on the right or left.

2. *Terror Right Hand* Font 6b **
More direct and even better. From the good slot on the right 'chin', climb the mossy face direct with long reaches and a rockover. From the sit start, a link into this this is Font 7a.

3. *Andy's Arête* Font 6c+ *
The arête opposite *Terror* is a real tricky number from the sit start, with poor hidden holds leading to a tenuous move right to the letterbox jump-off jugs. Travelling low right and back left to the letterbox is just as hard.

4. *Samson* Font 6c **
Past Craigmore Wall is a blank wall above an embedded stone. Pull on with poor undercuts and wobble powerfully left to reach and match a V groove.

The Wizard

This conical highball boulder looks like Gandalf's hat. Its main arête can be escaped at half height but purists will want to finish it direct. Spotters and mats are handy as it's a long reach to finish! Paul Savage worked out the sit starts, the most direct of which is the second toughest kid in the infants...

1. *The Wizard* Font 6c ***
Balance, poise, technique and power all combine to produce the classic Craigmore testpiece. Crimp and clamp up the blank arête, with small toe-holds, smears and blind layaways up to a half-height jug. From here step off to chockstone or take your brave-pills and go to the top.

2. *Wizard Sit Start Right Hand* Font 7a *
Sit start in the wee cave and pull up to use the short arête of the cave to lunge up and right for a poor finger sloper, then join the main problem. This will feel a little easier in cool dry weather, the basalt is fussy about conditions...

3. *Wizard Sit Start Direct* Font 7b **
Same as for the above but climb the arête direct without recourse to holds out right. A powerful, barndoory and downright sick eliminate, done for the sake of just being hard. You still have to finish to the top to bag the points!

The Pine Cone

This leaning boulder lies like a dropped cone from the large pine tree at the end of the crag. It catches the evening sun and is a pleasant den in which to spend a while working the problems. Beware though, the rock needs to be cool to make the slopers viable!

1. *Jamie's Overhang* Font 6b ***
The classic original is a good end to the circuit...from the twin crimps in the break snatch to a good left hold on face, then break back right to the far sloper and rockover via central lip layaway and a sharp crimp to break. Good footwork makes this all the more achievable.

2. *Sanjuro* Font 6b+ **
Sit start from Jamie's Overhang, lock toe in far right and cross over to good hold, cut loose and gain the left arête lip jugs, from here it is still hard to suss the crucial toe hold to reach the lip crimp round the corner and a final reach to the good break on slab. Much harder if started on far right.

3. *The Art of War* Font 6c+ **
Same as for Jamie's Overhang but lunge nearly footless direct to the far right sloper, match this then use lip layaway and rockover using the teeth-clencingly sharp crimp.

89

4. *Surprise Attack* Font 7b+ *
From the central crimps somehow dyno to the sloping lip just right of the lip layaway. Hard to reach and just as hard to hold!

CAMPSIE BOULDERS   NS 628 792

'Awa the Crow Road' is an old Scots expression for leaving this mortal world. The eponymous road which winds heavenward out of Lennox-town onto the Campsie moors and summits, passes under the 'Black Craig' and its scree slopes. If you are in no hurry to leave this world, fun diversions can be had on the hidden boulders in these volcanic screes. There are two sets of boulders, one on the west, above a layby after the switchbacks, and another lower down, directly above the communications mast by the golf-course. Though nowhere too big, there are plenty of telescoped problems such as the 'Stink Bug' traverse in the east boulder field and the excellent roof of 'Crow Road' on the first main boulder of the west boulder field. A good circuit can be achieved with a little imagination and the outlook over Glasgow reminds you how easy it is to escape the city and its restless diversions.

Approach

From the north of Glasgow, follow signs for Lennoxtown just under the Campsie fells on the A891. This can also be gained from Strathblane A81 to the east. Follow the 'Crow Road' north out of the town, which winds up past the golf course parking. For the east boulder field, park carefully at a mobile mast on the next corner and walk up in five minutes. For the west boulder field, park a few hundred metres uphill in a layby on the right and stomp up the hill aiming left until the hidden boulders come into view on a grassy alp.

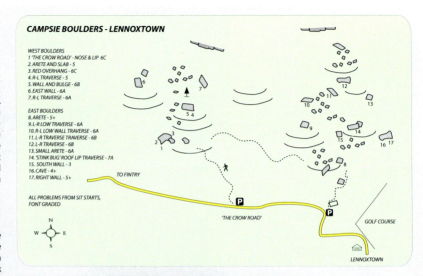

CAMPSIE BOULDERS - LENNOXTOWN

WEST BOULDERS
1 'THE CROW ROAD' - NOSE & LIP 6C
2. ARETE AND SLAB - 5
3. RED OVERHANG - 6C
4. R-L TRAVERSE - 5
5. WALL AND BULGE - 6B
6. EAST WALL - 6A
7. R-L TRAVERSE - 6A

EAST BOULDERS
8. ARETE - 5+
9. L-R LOW TRAVERSE - 6A
10. R-L LOW WALL TRAVERSE - 6A
11. L-R TRAVERSE TRAVERSE - 6B
12. L-R TRAVERSE - 6B
13. SMALL ARETE - 6A
14. 'STINK BUG' ROOF LIP TRAVERSE - 7A
15. SOUTH WALL - 3
16. CAVE - 4+
17. RIGHT WALL - 5+

ALL PROBLEMS FROM SIT STARTS,
FONT GRADED

TO FINTRY

'THE CROW ROAD'

GOLF COURSE

LENNOXTOWN

P

P

N
W   E
S

90

'The Campsies'

'Crow Road'

Classics

1. **The Crow Road** Font 6c ***

The biggest hidden boulder on the west boulder field. Sit start the obvious prow and gain slopers on the lip, then crank right to a sharp hold and continue to a good orange hold on the lip, rock over up the slab to finish.

2. **Stink Bug** Font 7a ***

The obvious low caved slab on the east boulder field, about half way up the hill. Traverse the lip from far left to finish up the hanging arête, rocking left.

CLOCHODRICK STONE   NS 373 612

Resembling a stony brain, this odd erratic boulder lies in the corner of a field on the outskirts of Howwood on the road to Irvine. It is attributed to Roderick Hael, King of Strathclyde, (Clach Roderick in Gaelic) who banished Paganism and Druidism from the area. The Druids were said to use it as a 'rocking' stone to weigh justice and would have found its easy west ramp an accessible climb to decry judgment. It is only 3 metres high but has some good boulder problems and a few traverse problems and is worthy for a summer evening's training. Indeed, Paul Laughlan used it in the eighties and nineties to keep in trim for his raids on Dumbarton and the Tunnel Wall, so any claims of new problems should be taken in context - the holds show a deep polish from decades of bouldering activity, so we must remember we were not here first, indeed, you can imagine Druid kids scrambling up the arêtes in bare feet to show off their climbing prowess. The problems are all on basalt crimps and slopers, best from a sit start. Some polished rock and tricky moves – a little imagination makes combinations of problems good fun and extends the session of circuit problems. Please clear up any litter you find, remember it is an historical site and be friendly to the farmers if they ask what you are doing!

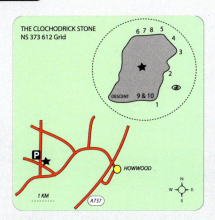

THE CLOCHODRICK STONE
NS 373 612 Grid

HOWWOOD

1 KM

A737

Approach
From the M8 westbound after Glasgow airport, take the A737 signposted to Irvine and after about 6km take a left turn signposted Howwood. The road doubles back and takes a left at the village over the bridge by the station. Continue along the country road for two kilometres to the third (or the fourth also) road on the right, up this for a little until the stone comes into view at a junction. Park carefully in a layby and cross the electric fence at a stone stile to boulder at will.

The Bouldering

1. South Arête Font 6c **
The stand up may be an easy Font 3 warm-up, but this steep arête is hard from a sit start on the east wall at undercuts, pull up left to a pinch hold, then aim for a good incut up and right, gain jugs at top to finish.

2. The Bulge Font 4
The centre of the east wall has a bulge left of a groove. Climb it from a sit start with a tough crimp move to the top.

3. East Arête Font 4+ *
Technique makes this easier than it feels! From low matched jugs gain a pinch hold on the arête with the left hand, then lunge for jugs at top right.

4. The Wall Font 3+
The easy vertical wall through polished holds.

5. North Arête Font 4
From a sit start at good holds, pull steeply up the undercut north arête to jugs at top. No jug on right.

6. North Traverse Font 5 *
Sit start far right and traverse the good handrail on the north wall from right to left to finish up North Arête.

7. West Arête Font 4+
Follow the traverse for two moves but rock up to the west arête using the right-hand crimp. *

8. The Crimps Font 6a **
Follow the traverse a bit further but use the two crimps on the wall to a tough move up and right to the arête.

9. East Wall Traverse Font 6c **
Excellent technical and pumpy work-out. From the jugs on the south wall, traverse low round the south arête (crux 1) to continue under the Bulge (crux 2) to drop down to climb the east arête (crux3). No high jugs allowed!

10. Clochodrick Traverse Font 7a ***
As for above but continue to a tricky technical section along the Wall to drop down and reverse the North traverse.

91

COURT KNOWE   NS 588 600

This pleasant little quarry has a useful bouldering circuit for those stuck in the south side of Glasgow without means of escape. It is at the far east side of Linn Park at the top of a hill which Mary Queen of Scots reputedly used as a viewpoint, or maybe a bouldering venue, who knows?

From Cathcart railway station go left through the pedestrian tunnel, turn left, then right at a roundabout by the River Cathcart to climb Old Castle Road past the Old Smiddy pub. The quarry is behind the railings on the left at the top of the hill, opposite the park. It can be a bit sweaty in summer, damp in winter, and is littered with broken glass and inquisitive youths - aside from that, it's everything a body needs. There is scope for some very hard problems on the leaning wall taken by There Is No Spoon and the project slab on the front face.

'There Is No Spoon'

92

COURT KNOWE - CATHCART - NS 588 600

1. *There Is No Spoon* Font 7a+ ***
Originally chipped and abandoned, this is a solution to the leaning wall on the left side of the quarry. Step off a block by a wide crack and gain two thin crimps in a horizontal break, then pull hard right to the frustratingly out-of-reach finger-ledge. Match this and take the wall direct through another edge and a mono pocket, lunge to jugs at the top. FA John Watson 2000.

2. *Blue Tits Left Hand* Font 5 *
The arête on the far left, taken from the leaning wall side. Gain arête from a sit start on jugs and layback up to a midway ledge, then highstep to flat holds and step out right onto ledge.

3. *Blue Tits Right Hand* Font 5 *
The left arête on the front face. Good but needs a little commitment! Gain a sidepull on arête then bridge up right to snap for a good ledge hold. You can use the crack hold as well, but it's better to have faith and go.

4. *Wullie's Crack* Font 4
Good holds and polished footholds lead to a reach left to a thin crack then reach for the good ledges.

5. *The Press* Font 3+
As for Wullie's Crack but press right at the wee corner and finish on good holds to ledge.

6. *DF 118's* Font 6a+
The wall to the right has a chipped pocket. Gain this and dyno for a high sloper, break left to finish – watch your landing.

7. *Layback Crack* Font 3+
The easy but fun corner can be laybacked on good holds.

8. *Coleptera Traverse* Font 6a *
Start at the arête just right of vegetated crack. Crouch start at flat hold on arête and snatch right to slopers, match these, swap toes and gain the next crack on right, stand up then climb the wall on the right direct. Satisfying eliminate. The other way is *Snowy's Big Traverse* which steps higher on to sloping ledge and reaches left to the big crack.

9. *The Red Pill* Font 7a *
Hard undercutting from the ledge allows the crusty break to be gained, use a hold near the right crack (no crack allowed!) and get stood up on the slabby wall and crank left through insecure smears to reach better holds out left. Eliminate but good.

10. *Thin Fingers Crack* Font 5+
Technical laybacking and smearing up the thin crack, using holds on the left wall as counterbalance.

11. *Mountain Climber* Font 3+
The right wall may be grandly named but it is straightforward. The left side can be eliminate and a little harder.

12. *Ten Year Wall* Font 6a
Up and right is a blank wall, with a good fingery problem.

6 *THE SOUTH WEST*

Pete Murray on 'The Magic Eye', Criffel Boulders

DUMFRIES & GALLOWAY

Quiet backwater or hardcore territory? Both, in fact. Dumfries and Galloway has some fine bouldering stones tucked away in sleepy coves and on the flanks of rounded granite domes. Some of Scotland's most dedicated boulderers have spent days here tending to painfully hard sequences of rock geometry… Paul Savage upped the bar by climbing such lines as *My Evil Twin* at Sandyhills, *Zillion Dollar Sadist* at Clifton, *Chinese Democracy* and *Shrinking Violet* at the Thirlstane, all amongst the first high 7th and 8th grade problems in Scotland. The bouldering is mainly on outcrops and boulders along the tidal fringes of the Solway and the Rinns of Galloway, but on the higher domes of granite, such as Criffel, Clifton Crag, Screel Hill and Clawbelly Hill near Dalbeattie, there are hundreds of granite boulders and walls which provide either blank monstrosities for projects, or generous low-grade bouldering that can fill a whole afternoon with the joy of simple movement on stone. The jewel in the crown is of course the Thirlstane, a sea-drilled cave in an outcrop of slopey sandstone, which has perfect sandy landings and a cool interior which provides hard summer bouldering when the granite is too soapy to grasp. Here are a few of the most recently developed venues and the best of the problems in this undervalued gem of Scotland.

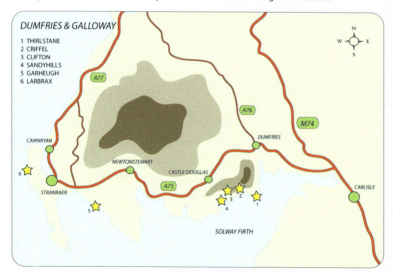

DUMFRIES & GALLOWAY

1 THIRLSTANE
2 CRIFFEL
3 CLIFTON
4 SANDYHILLS
5 GARHEUGH
6 LARBRAX

Larbrax Pinnacle

THE THIRLSTANE   NX 991 567

This wave-worn rock arch lies on a pleasant shelly beach west of Dumfries. It is a hard sandstone outcrop with a tidal borehole right through its core, where some of the best boulder problems in Dumfries & Galloway can be found. There are a few easier walls on the outside of the Thirlstane and a trad wall on the landward side, which provide good warm-up problems. The cave itself is mostly tidal, so check for low tides online before visiting. A 'good drying day' is essential (ie. not humid and damp) to allow footholds to dry out, but when you do get perfect conditions, the harder problems are among the best sandstone problems in the country.

Approach: On the A710 west from Dumfries, the Solway Coast road passes south through New Abbey, under the big mound of Criffel and through the village of Kirkbean, shortly after which is a left turn seawards, colourfully signposted to the resort of Southerness. Take the first left shortly after a farm and carry on for a kilometer to a sharp left bend. Shortly after this, take a right turn at the 'Arbigland' sign down to Powillimont farm, and on to the terribly pot-holed parking by the shore (watch your exhaust). From here it is a short walk eastwards along the shingle beach to the dramatic Thirlstane itself. Bring a dry rag or two, lots of chalk and a good picnic. If the tide is in, you could spend your time soloing the easier routes, or adding more decoration to the shell trees. There is plenty of easy bouldering on surrounding walls, but the cave itself holds the bouldering gems.

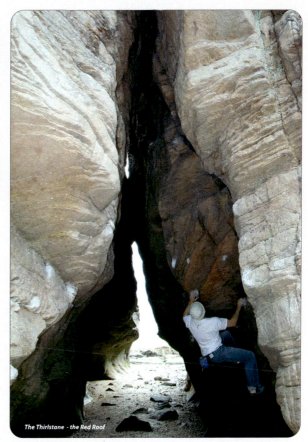

The Thirlstane - the Red Roof

95

THIRLSTANE PROBLEMS

Craig's Wall

Sea Walls

96

EAST WALLS

1. *Grade Obsessed* Font 7a **
Just left of *The Groove* is a leaning wall before the cave opens to the juggy main wall. From a sit start gain a big sidepull and reach up over the lip to match a sloper and crimp, use these to gain holds on the distant break. Traversing into this from Problem 3 is an excellent Font 7b. FA Tim Rankin 2003.

2. *The Groove* (aka Route 1) Font 5 *
Sit start on edges and reach for the flange at the base of the groove, then climb it through improving holds. Joining Problem 3 to an eliminate finish up angled slopers on the right of the groove is *Smack Heid* Font 7b ** by Tim Rankin.

3. *Craig's Wall Left Hand* Font 7b+ ***
Basically a left hand sit start to Craig's Wall. From slopers left of the slots (and just right of the Groove) crank up to match a crimp, get weight on your right toe and a long reach right gains the twin crimps under the gaston of Craig's Wall, finish through the crux of this problem.

4. *Craig's Wall* Font 7b ***
The obvious wall through the vertical slot crack. From the high RH slot and low left undercling, smear on and gain crimps over a bulge, use these or the gaston edge to rock right up to better holds near the corner, gain this and jump off or climb into the light. FA Craig MacAdam 1985.

5. *Shrinking Violet* Font 7c+ ***
The sitter! From a sit start on small slopers gain the low slot, crank up to the higher slot and the crimps. Match the gaston above the high slot and go direct up the wall to a very small two-finger sideway LH crimp then top out with a right hand crimp to better holds (Paul Savage 2003). Standing start is 7b+.

6. *Endrina* Font 7a *
Gain a large undercut under the roof and then a lip sloper and pop for the break, the holds are good and the swing isn't as bad as you would imagine. A toe on the 1st undercut allows the lunge to be controlled.

7. *Insect Kin* Font 7a *
The bulging roof where the walls narrow from the sea. Start as for *Bad Seed*, but continue left to finish up *Lateral Thinking*.

8. *Lateral Thinking* Font 6c *
The roof above the slab. From a pocket and crimp above the slab, blindly reach right to slots on the roof lip, heel-hook to the break.

9. *Eazy Roof* Font 5
The flake crack, on good holds to a break and rock-over.

10. *The Bad Seed* Font 6c+ *
This starts under the most seaward roof, at a curious inverted-heart feature. Take a LH a crimp and RH pocket, boom up and right to unseen pockets, then gain the break. Infuriating to keep the feet on... harder if wet!

11. *Hardcore Superstar* Font 7c **
This traverse is fondly recorded by first ascenscionist Paul Savage as 'awesome'. From pockets by the sea entrance, traverse in over the shingle, drop under the roofs to good edge slots and follow a crux sequence through Insect Kin to gain the finishing holds of Endrina. Complex and mainly footless.

THIRLSTANE PROBLEMS

Sea Wall West

Cave Wall West

SEA WALL (WEST)

12. *Tied Up and Swallowed* Font 7c *
On the west wall of the cave, after a blank section, is a chin-level sloping shelf where several problems start or end their journey: this direct mantel somehow gains the sloping shelf, using a crimp and powerful contortionism to gain a finishing break.

13. *Jihad* Font 7a ***
Monkey left from the sloping shelf through crimps to an obvious pocket, from where good foot positioning and targeting might gain the slopey break. If you latch the throw, traverse happily left to escape. The more direct finish from the crimps is **Nitro** 7a+ ***

14. *Bad Sneakers* Font 6a
Take a pocket with the right hand and slopey pocket with the left, pull up footless and cross to the pocket under the break, top out over the break.

15. *Chinese Democracy* Font 8a ***
When the tide is well out you might want to try your luck with this absorbing and sick-hard sequence from a sit-start at the sea entrance, to finish up *Tied Up and Swallowed* (if you can stomach it after the traverse). This is one of Paul Savage's gnarliest creations. The traverse has few foot-holds and long moves and stays as low as possible. Finishing up *Jihad* is **What's Holy About It** Font 7b.

CAVE WALL (WEST)

16. *The Niche* Font 6a *
A good exercise in footwork and body position. Slightly further in on the right is a darkening pod, which is tricky to get into. A slopey knobbly feature on the right of the niche wall can be matched to allow a squirm up to jugs at the top of the pod.

17. *The Red Roof (Left Variation)* Font 6c *
Between the two niches is a reddish roof. From a two-finger undercut slot, gain the sloping hold above as a RH pinch, reach up left to a good hidden sloper in *The Niche* and travel up and right to jump-off jugs.

18. *The Red Roof (Right Variation)* Font 6b **
From a good crimp grab the big left sloper and go again to a high left pinch, slap your right hand up and gain better holds, finish at a jump-off jug.

19. *The Corner* Font 4
The first groove in the cave on the west wall, forming the right side of the *Red Roof*.

97

Tim Morozzo on 'Jihad', the Thirlstane

CRIFFEL NX 947 590

On the west flanks of Criffel, on the outlying Airdrie Hill, lies a long and impressive granite boulder jumble thinning out as they climb the heathered dome of Criffel itself. Although many of the boulders 'shrink' on approach, it is a great venue in early summer before the bracken obscures the boulders, with its fine outlook over the sun-glittering sands of the Solway estuary. The grades are largely low-grade and the landings grassy. There is scope for endless projects, though the approach can be tiresome. Try not to disturb any adders!

Approach

Continue on the road past west past the Southerness turn-off. Just east of Caulkerbush is a gatehouse to a forested lodge. The boulders are best approached from the forestry tracks higher up. Park near the Gatehouse, or if the gate is open, turn into the forest track (private road to left) and veer right up a track to a locked forestry gate where parking is possible. Take the triple switchback forestry track up right for fifteen minutes until the forestry clears and the granite boulders begin to appear ahead. Veer off on a smaller track across poor cleared ground to the east (right) and cross the old stone dyke and make your way up to the large Viewpoint boulder on a small ridge, which is obvious when you gain a bit of height (25 minutes). From here a veritable smörgasbord of boulders become visible. Projects remain on the cluster at the top of the Track further east. The area was mainly developed by Paul Savage and friends.

CRIFFEL BOULDERS

PROJECTS AREA

WALL

FENCE

TRACK

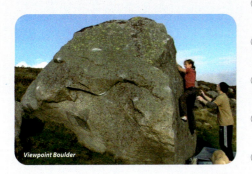

Viewpoint Boulder

1. **Viewpoint Wall** Font 4+ **
Viewpoint boulder (the largest). From a sit-start at the south wall rail, climb to the apex of the boulder (pic).

2. **Magic-Eye** Font 5 **
Climbs the west overlap onto the slab, directly and without using either arête, surprisingly balancy.

3. **Magic Eye Traverse** Font 6a ***
A linking traverse of the last two problems round the blunt arête.

4. **Paul's Arête** Font 7a **
50 m below the Viewpoint boulder is a small boulder with a slopey south arête. Climb this from a sit start.

5. **Concrete Wave** Font 6b ** (bis. Font 7b)
Just up and left of the Viewpoint boulder is a remarkable wave-shaped boulder. Sit start the left arête and traverse up and right, somewhat easier than the low eliminate.

6. **Hobo** Font 6c **
Further left, towards the summit of Airdrie hill, is a bulging cracked boulder. Climb the bulge to a ledge from a sit start and mantel over the top.

7. **No Venom** Font 5+ *
Further east of this small compact area across the jumble lies the obvious Track boulder. Pull on to the crack from a sit-start and span across to the right arête.

8. **Outcrop Arête** Font 5 *
Just below the Track boulder is the outcrop area. This climbs the obvious crack problem on the downhill side.

9. **Bracken Wall** Font 5 **
Above and left of the outcrop are two hidden boulders. This climbs the slabby wall facing the Solway.

10. **The Cannon** Font 6b *
Above Bracken Wall is a difficult nose problem. Surmount this from a standing start.

CLIFTON NX 909 571

A jumble of granite boulders underneath the southwest-facing crag provides some hard test-pieces from Paul Savage and friends. Clifton crag can be approached via the A710, taking the second turning right after Caulkerbush, signposted Southwick Cemetery, up 2k to Clifton farm. Park carefully at the cemetery or past the farm and take stiles and a rough path over the walls north of the farm. The boulder jumble is obvious under the main crag. Three larger boulders lie under the crag and provide some very hard problems. The landings are often bad and require good spotters and a mat or two to protect the ankles. Easier problems can be found in the area, but it is best as a winter hardcore venue.

Clifton Crag Boulder Jumble

1. **Knife Party** Font 7c **
Gate Boulder. Despite the name, this is a very safe problem! Traverse the slopey lip of the gate boulder from the far right to the top left – best done in cold conditions! Starting halfway along the lip is *Half-Knife* Font 7b *.

2. **Study Break** Font 6b *
On the small boulder just opposite the Gate boulder. Climb the small overhang direct.

3. **Trauma** Font 7b+ *
This lies on the perched boulder up and right in the jumble. The central face has a bottomless arête and is climbed from beneath to give a hard and worrying testpiece.

4. **Wall Problem** Font 7b
The difficult and puzzling short wall on the mezzanine up and behind the Trauma boulder.

5. **Paul's Dyno** Font 6b+ ***
On the big boulder at the bottom of the scree. Climb the overhanging wall via a dyno from flat edges to a jug on the lip, traverse left and mantle.

6. **Zillion Dollar Sadist** Font 8a+ **
The desperate blank lower lip of the flat-faced boulder in the scree above the Dyno boulder. FA Paul Savage 2003.

Craig Henderson on 'Half-Knife'

SANDYHILLS NX 891 547

The lovely beach at Sandyhills bay is full of another sort of tourism in the summer, but if you walk west round the headland, over a footbridge and through the nets (make sure it's low tide, or you will get trapped!) and round a couple of sandy coves, you come to a large sandy bay and cave, where you can perform your own rock tourism – the bays have all sorts of eliminate problems and short walls, the highlight being the cave's fin of rock, climbed direct from the back without recourse to larger holds nearby and sneaky heel jams…this gives My Evil Twin Font 8a. There has been a recent resurgence of interest in these bouldery bays and Craig Henderson in particular has been exploring the boulders and walls further along the shore.

Sandyhills Main Bay

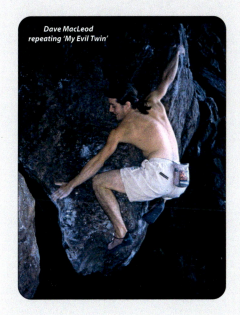

Dave MacLeod repeating 'My Evil Twin'

1. **Mary's Massive Mango's** Font 7a **
Sit start on an undercut and follow crimps and rib to the top pocket.

2. **My Evil Twin** Font 7a to 8a ***
From under the arête follow the roof and up the arête, eliminating all bridging holds and jugs gives Paul Savage's original 8a.

3. **Ejector Seat** Font 6b *
Sit start and blast up the bulge just right of My Evil Twin.

4. **Wall** Font 6b *
Climb the overhanging wall on flat holds.

5. **Twin Flake** Font 5 *
Start on undercut and climb to the shelf using the twin flakes.

6. **The Crack** Font 6b+ **
Climb the overhanging crack.

7. **Flizz Off** Font 6c **
Climb the excellent little slab without using the arête.

8. **SDS Flizz Off** Font 7a **
Sit start the crack to the right and traverse into Flizz Off and up.

9. **Frauch** Font 3 *
Climb the small seaward slab on edges and undercuts.

10. **Toothie Ruthie** Font 4+ *
Climb the bayed overhanging wall without the arête.

11. **Flizz** Font 6a *
Front right of bay. Sit start on flat holds and up on pockets.

12. **G** Font 6b ***
Described by Craig Henderson as the best problem at Sandyhills, back of a small cove to the right of the main bay. Climb the arched wall through the over lap.

'G'

GARHEUGH · NX 267 501

Further west along the Solway, the geology changes from the tan sandstones to a hardened greeny black sandstone called Greywacke, formed by underwater slippages of muddy sandstone from ancient Silurian earthquakes and metamorphosed into a fine-grained rock. At Garheugh, just northwest of Portwilliam, some of this rock has calved into wave worn boulders and this was explored by Dave Redpath, in weekend raids during the summer of 2001. 'Life is Beautiful' is the perfect bouldering conundrum.

Dave MacLeod on
'Curmudgeon'.
Pic MacLeod coll.

Approach Notes: 'Garheugh Port' is a pleasant beach and craggy outcrop on the A747 south of Glenluce between Stranraer and Newton Stewart. From the A75, follow signs for Port William and after a few kilometres, the road starts to skirt the shore. As it rises above a rocky point and drops down, there is parking at a junction with the B7005 Wigtown road. Walk onto the shore and along to the obvious bouldering. It faces south and catches all the sun going, perfect for some photogenic poses! Some of the bouldering is tidal and mats are useful to cover the uneven pebble landings on some problems.

GARHEUGH BOULDERING

'Garheugh Boulders'

1. **Mr. Prickles** Font 6a ***
Slab Boulder. The first slab encountered has a super left arête from a sitting start.

2. **Sense of Danger** Font 5 **
Slab Boulder. The curving ramp on the right of the slab.

3. **Afterlife** Font 6c+ ***
The blank line just left of Sense of Danger, right of the ivy. Bold and technical and highball.

4. **Suck My Woolie** Font 6c **
The excellent hanging arête by the old sheep-pen from a sit start at a jug, undercut and hook up to the nose, cut loose, then mantle onto slab.

5. **Snowhite** Font 6c ***
Sheep Pen 3. From the boss under the arête, slap up right for the lip sloper and pull over onto slab.

6. **Stretch Armstrong** Font 7a+ **
Same start but move left to an undercut and onto the arête and gain the slab.

7. **Nuclear Puppy** Font 6a **
Long Slab. The short crack to right of and gaining the midway ramp, via a crimp move.

8. **Dumby Boys** Font 5 **
Long Slab. Just right of the left arête. From jugs, head right before breaking back left to finish high.

9. **Life Is Beautiful** Font 6b ***
States Boulder east face. The beautiful water-scooped crack-line from a sit start, gaining the right hand ledge and slab to top.

10. **Bowfinger** Font 6c ***
The centre of the east wall via a seam to gain the diagonal crack.

11. **Curmudgeon** Font 7c *
Innocuous looking blunt arête to the right of LIB. From a juggy slot, climb thin crack to gain the ledge.

12. **Mike's Traverse** Font 6b+ ***
The west wall high ramp on the States boulder, finishing by a right groove.

13. **Altered States** Font 7b ***
The undercut flake of the west wall of the States boulder from a sit start finishing up and right.

14. **Changing States** Font 6c+ **
Climb the slabby groove to the right along its edge. SS at crimp behind flake.

15. **Scream Slab** Font 4 **
The slab behind the Long Slab. Start just right of the first apex, using small crimps to climb to the top apex.

16. **The Oyster** Font 6b **
The Main Crag west wall scooped arête, difficult to open! Start left of the crack, gain slot then crank up right through sloper to ledge. No crack and spike.

17. **Barndoor Crack** Font 6a ***
The cracked groove on the east side of the most tidal boulder.

18. **Shadow Dancer** Font 6c *
Tidal boulder. Sit start the slopey ledge on west face and climb the arête, no jugs or flake.

19. **Puma** Font 4+ *
Tidal Boulder. Gain the horizontal break at the left side and mantel to top.

'Life Is Beautiful'

Mike Tweedley on 'Bowfinger'

LARBRAX

NW 967 608

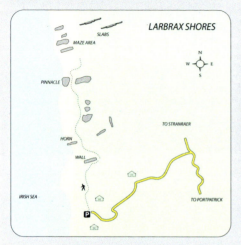

LARBRAX SHORES

SLABS
MAZE AREA
PINNACLE
HORN
WALL
IRISH SEA
TO STRANRAER
TO PORTPATRICK
P

Bloc Notes

Galloway's newest venue has seen plenty of traditional action, but the bouldering potential has only recently been developed. It is a terrific summer venue as the beaches are ideal for the family if you want to mix bouldering and a day out for the kids. It is worth checking the Portpatrick tide tables online and timing your visit if you plan to boulder – the best problems have tidal starts. These thrilling pinnacles and rocky mazes lie on the west coast of the Rinns between Portpatrick and Portobello and the rock is a similar wave worn greywacke to Garheugh.

Approach Notes

To get there, skirt the shore road through Stranraer and head north along the A718 to the village of Leswalt. Take the first left turn in the village (Glen Road) and follow the B7043 for a few miles, past a loch on the left. Shortly after this, take a left, signposted Portpatrick, and after 2 kilometres of wooded driving watch out for an easily missed right turn along a farm track, signposted Meikle Larbrax. This track winds down through a farm and gates to the main beach and parking… watch your exhaust on the track! If the tide is well out, you can walk easily and pleasantly north along the shore to a beautiful hidden beach near Cranberry Point where the pinnacle resides! This bold pinnacle has two excellent highballers on the 'dark side'. The majority of the best bouldering lies on walls and boulders north of this pinnacle, though there are a couple of worthy problems before it.

Pinnacle Traverse

'Paint It Black' dyno

'Craig Henderson on Waning Crescent'

1. **The Horn** Font 6a *
After the North Wall crag is a little sandy cove with a horned overhang. From a sit start climb up and into the Horn feature and surmount it.

2. **Reach or Beach** Font 6b ***
The Pinnacle. Take a deep breath and climb up through obvious holds on the right side of the left arête. FA Julian Lines 2000.

3. **Summit or Plummet** Font 6b ***
This takes the right wall of the pinnacle, aiming for a flake and earlier exit on the right arête. FA Stuart Lampard 2001.

4. **On the Waterfront** Font 6c **
As both Pinnacle problems are bold affairs, a safer combination is to link them via a traverse along the horizontal break. Finish at the right arête.

5. **The Corridor** Font 5+ *
In a short corridor of black rock further north, this problem takes the steep east wall on good holds.

6. **Paint It Black** Font 7a **
Just after is a maze of coves. This dyno takes the tidal black north wall of the main cove. From a crimp left of the arête, dyno over the smooth top to a hidden hold. Barnacled but good.

7. **Black Affronted** Font 6b *
Sit start the slab cut corner arete just to the right and climb it to top using heels. Affected by the tide like most other good problems!

8. **Waning Crescent** Font 6b ***
The small scooped boulder down a narrow cove in the 'maze'. From a sit start on the right, slap left round the blunt arête and gain the lip. Just enough holds.

Little Khumbu NX 865 594

An area of granite slabs and boulders near Dalbeattie under Clawbelly Hill on a smaller hill called Goat Hill. The area was monikered Little Khumbu by local climbers and was developed in the 70's though little modern bouldering has been recorded, Paul Savage did a nice three star wall at Font 5+ he called *Oceans Eleven* (while waiting for tides to go out on his problem *My Evil Twin* at Sandyhills). Approach along the B793 between Dalbeattie and Sandyhills, park near the forestry plantation at the junction with the B road to Sandyhills and walk up hill to the walls above Little Cloak farm.

Craignaw NX 459 833

Famous for the Dow Spout ice route, Craignaw hill also features numerous crags and there is bouldering potential on these 5 metre high granite walls. A long walk in to the Dungeon hills of the Galloway hills, but you can stay in the excellent bothy at Back Hill o' Bush.

Screel Hill NX 784 551

Find the forestry car park for Screel Hill on the A711 south of Dalbeattie. Walk uphill on the forestry paths to small granite walls on the south and north east sides of the hilltop. There is not much but the granite is pleasant to climb on. Craig Henderson climbed a fine wall called 'Happy Days' at Font 6a+ (see pic). Home to a pumpy project known as the *Mega Man Traverse*.

Port O' Warren NX 880 533

1833 Traverse Font 6a ***

Follow the A710 past Sandyhills until there is a sign posted road marked Portling, take this single track road towards the sea and park at the fork in the road (parking for 5 or 6 cars probably) then walk the final ½ mile South towards the Port O Warren Bay – follow signs for the beach. The *1833 Traverse* is obvious - a good outing on jugs getting ever steeper and higher, follow the lip of the wave to its conclusion.

106

'Happy Days' on Screel Hill
Pic: Craig Henderson

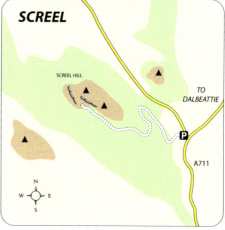

SCREEL

SCREEL HILL

TO DALBEATTIE

A711

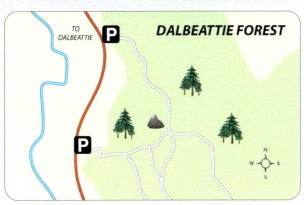

'Craig Henderson on the Hard Rock Roof'

DALBEATTIE FOREST

TO DALBEATTIE

Dalbeattie Forest - *The Hard Rock Roof* NX 841 593

A clean granite boulder located deep in the woods. Parking can be found at the 'Seven Stanes' forestry car park just south of Dalbeattie and the boulder is a further 10 minute walk uphill from here. From the car park follow the fire road east until you see the bike route 'north shore' section, which will be on your left hand side. You can either follow the north shore or a little further along the fire road there will be a dirt track to your left which will also take you to the boulder (5 or 10 minute walk). Please cede passage to any bikers! Start sitting on an undercut and crimp, span out (a long way) to the lip and a good sloper, top out directly from here – it's the obvious line on the boulder.

Lendalfoot NX 132 902

On the A77 between Girvan and Stranraer, this beachside venue is pleasant but tidal. A number of large boulders can be seen on the shore at Lendalfoot. Paul Savage mentioned a hard '8a' project, so far unidentified, and there are certainly some steep problems, developed mainly by Dave Redpath, though they suffer from the tidal damp and need a good drying day. Pleasant summer venue for picnics. Park by the memorial layby and climb at will.

Lendalfoot

7 ARROCHAR

ARROCHAR

Mica-Schist is the rock that dominates the glens under the devil's horns of the Cobbler. It is a densely scalloped rock, squashed by ancient seas, veined with quartz, sometimes flaky as pie-crust, sometimes granitic and rough as high-grade emery paper. For some it is an acquired taste; providing either finger-splitting crimps or endless slopers, (or both!) but it is a technical rock despite its generic form.

Bouldering at Loch Sloy

109

Glen Croe - hundreds of boulders in this dark glen dry out in summer, with some dramatic schist prows such as the classic 'Precious' and 'Turbinal Nose'. Needs dry and cool conditions to hold its notorious slopers.

The Brack - the 'Kennedy' boulder under the shadow of the Brack is the highlight of Glen Croe, a giant stone with good landings and hard testpieces, the Scottish 'Bowderstone'.

Butterbridge - accessible bouldering on a giant stone at Butterbridge, or on nearby boulders at Loch Restil, near the wonderfully named bealach of 'Rest and Be Thankful'.

Coilessan - also known as 'Blaeberry World', this cluster of giant boulders and rocky mazes is still to be fully explored. Excellent bouldering if a little esoteric and remote!

Narnain Boulders - two giant stones on the walk-in to the Cobbler. Historical significance to Scottish bouldering and tremendous rock. A superb small venue in high summer as it is cooler and catches the breeze. Long walk-in but worth it.

Loch Sloy - a variety of projects remain on the distributed boulders on the path up to Loch Sloy dam. Excellent rock and some great lower grade problems with a remote feel.

GLEN CROE   NN 257 041

Bloc Notes

This dramatic glen is a cragger's delight, and recently it has become a decent bouldering venue. There are hundreds of boulders and walls, but only a few with high quality lines, as the ground can be terribly boggy or tree-hidden. That said, there are many easy lines for the explorative, but it is probably best for choosing a project, as these are fantastic natural lines and they have very distinctive and powerful 'schist moves'. The best time to boulder is spring and early summer in a dry spell, as the steep-sided glen gets little sunlight in the winter. The problems described here are the best in the area and most have good dry landings, except the leaking Beer Can!

Approach Notes

The Glen is easily gained from Glasgow by bus (Campbeltown service), or by car along the A83, a few miles west of Arrochar. The boulders are in a bit of a diaspora, so there are a few parking spots.

For the *Precious* boulder and *Supercrack* area, park at the large Honeymoon Bridge boulder spot by the stand of trees. Climb up through the trees on the left for five minutes to the giant boulder. 15 more minutes above this is the *Supercrack* wall.

For the other boulders, climb the hill over the bridge through the gorge to a parking spot by another bridge (Beer Can boulder/Cutting Room), or continue on a hundred yards to a layby on the right to the Roadside boulders (also the Woodwell boulder forestry track for *Turbinal Nose*).

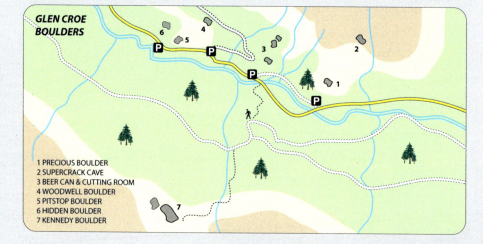

GLEN CROE BOULDERS

1 PRECIOUS BOULDER
2 SUPERCRACK CAVE
3 BEER CAN & CUTTING ROOM
4 WOODWELL BOULDER
5 PITSTOP BOULDER
6 HIDDEN BOULDER
7 KENNEDY BOULDER

GLEN CROE CLASSICS

'Turbinal Nose'

1. **Precious** Font 7c ***
Precious or 'Hideaway' Boulder. A classic and hard 'ship's prow' arête! Sit start at a pinch and climb up to a quartz pocket, where a crux sequence allows better holds to be gained on the leaning wall by a handrail, finish up the airy arête. FA Mike Tweedley 2003.

2. **Supercrack** Font 7b ***
Right of the main crags is a hidden wall left of a wee waterfall. A bit of a trek, but worth it for this one problem! Climb the obvious curving lateral crack on the leaning wall, using an entertaining sequence of slopers and jams to finish up the juggier left crack to a jammed block. FA Dave MacLeod 2002.

3. **Vulcan Wall** Font 6c+ **
100 metres right of Supercrack is a fingery rounded wall. Start just right of the scoop and up right to the 'vulcan' split-finger pockets, reach up to finishing break. FA Niall McNair 2003.

4. **Lopez** Font 7a **
Fernandez Boulder (first wall above the old road and plunge pool). Traverse the vertical wall left to right through a pocket to jugs and finish up the groove on the right wall.

5. **Ace Of Spades** Font 7a+ ***
Beer Can boulder. This is a roofed boulder over a stream and bog, so mats are needed. This takes the obvious hanging right crack. Sit start at a pocket and edge on the arête, climb into the crack to an 'interesting' finish. FA Dave Redpath 2001.

6. **The Cutting Room** Font 7b+ ***
Above the Beer Can cluster is a boggy alp with a few boulders. This climbs the leaning crimpy northwest wall of the drier boulder (left of the Nose). Sit start at a sidepull, wince through small edges and slap for the sloping shelf.

7. **The Nose** Font 6a+ ***
The bulging nose of the Cutting Room boulder. From sidepulls, slap to the lip slopers, then follow these left to a quartz hold and rock to the top.

8. **Rake Humour** Font 6b+ **
The 'pitstop' boulder is the large roadside boulder just past the top layby under a tree. This climbs the right arête and hanging wall from a sit start. Sit start and cross through to the wall jugs, then gain the big pocket and throw for the flat ledge, finish up and right.

9. **Flash Bastard** Font 7b **
Hard to find, this wall lies 50m into the woods north of the Pitstop boulder. If you find it, climb the obvious central wall on crimps. FA Dave MacLeod 2003.

10. **Turbinal Nose** Font 7c ***
Another superb arête! The Woodwell boulder is under the forestry track 400m uphill. From a sit start make a series of dynamic moves up the arête to hook right to a block on the lip, move right and pull back left into the groove to finish (hidden pocket).

Niall McNair on 'Red October', Coilessan

'Rake Humour'

'Here is a field of free action in which nothing is organized, or made safe or easy or uniform by regulation; a kingdom where no laws run and no useful ends fetter the heart.'

W.H. Murray - 'The Undisvovered Country'

'Precious' Boulder

Alan Cassidy working 'Precious'

KENNEDY BOULDER   NN 249 036

Like a schist Bowderstone, but the parking is free and you'll get it to yourself! Once you wind past the Ardgarten tourist centre into Glen Croe, continue up past the Honeymoon parking to various laybys at the second bridge over the River Croe by the waterfalls. Here you can see the giant Kennedy boulder and its heather hat just underneath the dark craggy mass that is 'The Brack'. It's not as far a walk as it looks!

Approach Notes

- From the downhill side of the bridge, follow a fenced enclosure left and uphill over rough ground to a forestry road (5 mins).

- Continue right and uphill round the bends turning right at a junction, then shortly you'll see the sign uphill for 'The Brack 787m'.

- Follow this steeply through the forest for ten minutes and once clear of the forest, continue on the path uphill to where it crosses a wee waterfall. From here, contour across the open hillside towards the Kennedy boulder. A steep 40 minutes at most.

The 'front' face of the boulder is a leaning wall and slab over a perfect grassy knoll, hence the themed names of the problems. The rock is a sharp and quartzy schist giving dynamic power problems. This really is the engine room of Glen Croe bouldering and the sheer concentrated butchness is what this boulder is all about, but there are plenty of other boulders in the area giving good amenable bouldering for all. There is a luxurious howff in the two large boulders just downhill of the Kennedy boulder, if you feel like staying the night. There is a hard problem on the back arete of this Howff boulder called *'Thermostatic'* Font 7c (Dave MacLeod 2003). It climbs the slanting arete facing the Kennedy boulder from a sit start on low holds., through pinches and slopers.

114

Keenedy Boulder in winter

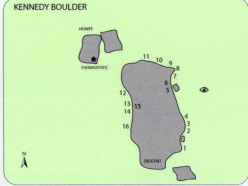

Cavlacade

KENNEDY BOULDER
The front (glen) face has a superb grass landing and a very steep short wall along its length. Crimpy and powerful.

1. Crossfire Font 6a
The left hand side of the main face has a slight bulge where a line of jugs trends up and right from undercuts through a low quartzy boss. A good warm up.

2. Assassin Font 6b *
Excellent steep climbing from a sit start just right of a small plinth. Take the line of good holds trending up and right to a tough rockover.

3. The Hotline Font 7c+ ***
From a low quartz sloper just right of *Assassin*, gain a sloping crimp above and unleash the power to throw for the diagonal jugs up and left. Match these and throw again for the high jugs above. A good Font 6c+ from standing if the sitter is too much. FA Dave Macleod 2002.

4. The Nuclear Button Font 7c+ *
Same start as above at the low quartz slopers, but grunt up and right to the quartzy block, match the holds here and dyno for the lip, which is a frustratingly good Font 7a in itself. FA Dave MacLeod 2002.

5. Trigger Happy Font 7b **
The excellent flakes and pockets problem just right of the embedded boulder. From a low flake get the left hand press and continue up and right through pockets to the lip slopers and rock out. FA Michael Tweedley 2002.

6. Cavalcade Font 7a+ **
As for Trigger Happy but break left to good holds and dyno for the lip. Harder since holds snapped.

7. So Jackie O Font 7b **
From sharp undercuts right of the above problems, stretch desperately up and right to a sloper, match this and continue right through a loose jug to rock over.

8. Conspiracy Font 6c+
The bulge where the main face turns the corner to a shorter steeper wall. From a low crimpy start, slap for the good bulge sloping crimps, then aim up and right to quartz jugs and mantle out.

9. Brinkmanship Font 7b
The low steep wall in the centre, climbed from press crimps to a good lip sloper, then snatch for a jug up and right on slab, and reach high for an inverted jug to finish left.

10. Bullit Font 7a *
A lip traverse of the low roof from the groove jugs all the way left to the groove above Conspiracy. FA Steve Richardson 2002.

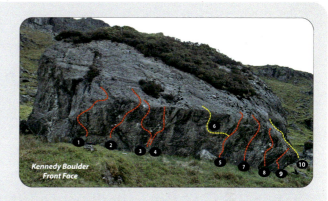

Kennedy Boulder
Front Face

The back wall has a usually wet roof with some good problems if dry:

11. Brains, Shoulders, Knees & Toes Font 6a *
The excellent slab facing the glen, climbing the cleanest rock. Bold and good, but take care. Descent on the other side over the heather is easy.

12. The Grassy Knoll Font 6a
The left hand crackline out of the cave to an awkward rockover on the lip.

13. Vietnam Font 6c *
The back wall of the boulder has a low cave roof. This problem takes the central hanging rail left to a rock out to the obvious cleaned flake. Often wet.

14. Brain Drain Font 7b *
This is a more direct version of Vietnam from the low quartz pinch, direct through the handrail to mantel out using a small sidepull on the slab. Usually a little drier. FA Michael Tweedley 2002.

15. Bullet in Your Head Font 7b+ *
The obvious curving line in the centre of the back roof on the Kennedy Boulder. Sit start at a two finger pocket, lock up to the slot in the crack and finish through lip slopers.

16. Lone Gunman Font 6c
The right hand line in the back cave. From a low layaway feature, reach up to a flat quartzy pocket and break onto the slab via slopers and bigger holds.

115

NARNAIN NN 272 056

Niall McNair on 'Left Wall'.

Bloc Notes

The Narnain boulders have been climbed on for decades by climbers on their way to the peaks of the Cobbler. Once popular as a doss, the Creag Dhu climbed some of the problems and this included an early ascent of *Crucifix*, which was a technical climbing highlight of the late forties and early fifties.

They are situated on the main path about an hour's walk with a mat from the car-park at Succoth. Take a good picnic with you!

116

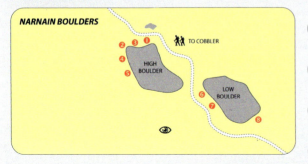

NARNAIN BOULDERS

TO COBBLER

HIGH BOULDER

LOW BOULDER

1. **Cobbler Wall** Font 6b **
High Boulder. To the far left of *Crucifix*, this is a clever solution to a puzzling blankness. From a quartz pinch and low right undercut, position yourself carefully to reach a high left two-finger crimp, then find another undercut to gain the slotted pockets and the top.

2. **The Crucifix** Font 6b ***
This is the striking arête line facing the Cobbler on the higher boulder. Climb it direct with long reaches between holds, requiring balance and technique. First climbed by John Cunningham and the Creag Dhu members just after the Second World War. Try it on rations…

3. **The Tesseract** Font 7a ***
This is the vague scooped wall just to the left of *Crucifix*. Sit start in the groove and climb up and left through crimps to reach the better pockets of *Cobbler Wall*. FA Niall McNair 2004.

4. **Occam's Razor** Font 6c+ *
Round the corner to the right is an impressive rippled west wall. Climb the black weep to the right of the *Crucifix* arête, needing steel in the fingers and grit in the soul.

5. **Two Hot Honies** Font 6b *
This climbs up to a good rail in the centre of the wall, where worrying reaches gain the top.

6. **Left Wall** Font 7a+ **
The lower boulder has good problems over the path. Sit start at a low pocket and press desperately to a three finger crescent hold, from where you gain the big hole on the left, then make like an Egyptian to gain higher holds and leap for the ledge! A standing start it is a good Font 6a.

7. **The Quartz Wall** Font 5 *
The obvious quartz weakness through the centre. Pull directly through the quartz to the top. The caved prow to the right is unclimbed…

8. **The Prow Pockets** Font 6a
Climb the far right-hand section of the roof through pockets to mantle out. Often attempted by fools with tools…

Narnain North Wall

Narnain - Niall McNair on 'The Tesseract'

COILESSAN NN 243 002

Marked as 'Garbh' on the OS 1:25000 map, the nickname 'Blaeberry World' becomes apparent when you walk up here in late summer – a vast collection of boulders and crags below the 500m contour rest on spongey moss and blueberry bushes, with a pleasant southerly aspect overlooking Loch Long and Arrochar. Some of the boulders are huge, the giant red/purple boulder being the centrepoint – 'the Blaeberry'. The bouldering is extensive, but a lot of the schist rock is poor and landings bad, though development is possible on the many boulders surrounding the Blaeberry. The venue may be rambling, but it is worth the walk-in and provides a wealth of eating in the autumn!

APPROACH NOTES

• After picking up provisions in Arrochar, head round the loch-head A83 and swing round the corner past Ardgarten campsite into Glen Croe. Turn off almost immediately at the Ardgarten visitor centre, cross the bridge, turn left and follow the B road for a few kilometres, curiously signposted 'Coilessan Events'. There is a dead-end car-park at the top of a steep hill where the forestry tracks begin.

• Walk along the forestry track 100m, turning right into Coilessan Glen (follow the 'blue bicycle' signs). After 500m at a junction (large boulder), turn left and continue up and left along the forest track for another 800m or so until a white post appears on the right beside a small stream. The crags and boulders are here visible high on the hill.

• Follow the stream religiously uphill for about 15 minutes until well clear of the forest, then head left along the rising plateau towards the boulders, aiming for 'the blaeberry'. Cross a fence and stomp up to the boulders. Allow 45 minutes and bring a change of top. Don't be tempted to descend through the forest by another route – this is the least painful!

18

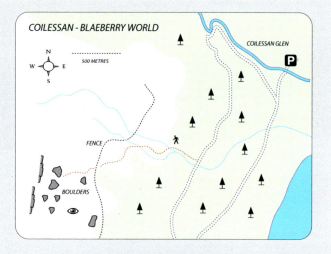

COILESSAN - BLAEBERRY WORLD

500 METRES

COILESSAN GLEN

FENCE

BOULDERS

Coilessan and Loch Long

BLOC NOTES

Red October Font 7b ***
The overhanging grey prow on the front face of the giant 'Blaeberry' boulder, finishing at jump-off jugs. From a low start sitting on the 'plinth', pull on and slap up to undercuts. Gain blind holds round left, tiptoe strenuously on the arête and power up to the slopey ledge jugs.

Blaeberry Crush Font 7a **
Just round the corner to the left of *Red October* on a low boulder, this is the obvious hanging arête in a grassy pit. From the lowest sit start, gain a crushing pinch and power up the arête to rockover onto the slab.

Niall's Problem Font 7a *
The excellent Skyline boulder is the lowest stone overlooking Loch Long just above the forest. It may be small, but it is perfectly perched and has good rock. Climb the blank groove on the right from a sit start. FA Niall McNair 2007.

Colin Lambton giving out free advertising on 'Blaeberry Crush'

Niall McNair on his problem on the Skyline Boulder

LOCH SLOY   NN 299 095

The Loch Sloy hydro station at Inveruglas on Loch Lomond is a remarkable and obvious feature on the A82 north of Tarbet. The walk to the dam is popular and the dramatic glen is littered with giant schist boulders, the best of which are described here. Most of the problems were developed by Dave Redpath, Dave MacLeod and John Watson amongst others. Despite some trekking to get to some of the boulders, there are some quality lines and vast potential for projects.

Bloc Notes

Park or get off the Glen Coe bus at the Inveruglas Tourist Centre (good for a coffee), walk back south past the Power Station and take the tarmac road up under the railway viaduct. This eventually leads to the Loch Sloy dam in about 40 minutes brisk walk, all boulders can be accessed from the road fairly quickly. The Roadside boulder is on a knoll beside the road at the half-way bridge, whereas the other boulders lie on the flanks of Ben Vorlich at various altitudes. The Dam cluster has some very big stones but boggy landings. Take a mat or two for the Roadside boulder. There are lots of warm-up and easy problems over good landings on smaller stones, so there is something for everyone.

120

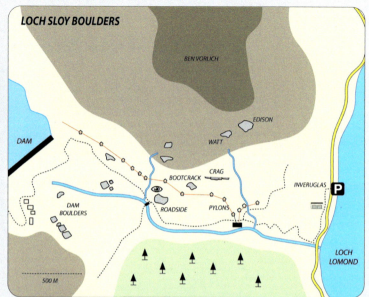

LOCH SLOY BOULDERS

BEN VORLICH

EDISON

WATT

DAM

BOOTCRACK   CRAG

INVERUGLAS

P

DAM
BOULDERS

ROADSIDE   PYLONS

500 M

LOCH
LOMOND

Dave MacLeod on
'Free Energy'

Dam Boulders

Watt Wall and Edison Boulder

These two boulders offer excellent rock and problems up to Font 6c. Edison Wall is high above the switchback road and can be spied under a tree. Just down left of it is the slabby Watt Wall. Hike up the steep slopes just by the burn that comes down the hill before the relay station. 15 minutes.

1. **Edison Arête** Font 6a ***
The Edison Boulder. The steep front wall is thankfully endowed with good holds. SS at a flake, crank up on good holds and pockets, using a pinch on the arête to escape right at the ramp. The middle line is *Edison Wall* 6a+ to the ramp, traverse right to escape.

2. **Watt Wall** Font 5 ***
This is the lovely slabby apexed wall down left from the Edison boulder. This teeters up the central seam, breaking left at the top. Best slab in the area.

Boot Crack Boulder

1. **Boot Crack Roof** Font 7a **
The 'boot-crack' boulder is the obvious large roofed boulder 200 metres uphill after the Relay station. This good roof left of the crack can be climbed from lip crimps through high slopers.

2. **Scissorhands** Font 7a *
Right of the giant 'boot-sized' crack and highball slab is a sharp arête above a flat platform. Sit start powerfully to gain and climb the arête on the right. FA Dave MacLeod 2002.

'Edison Wall'

Roadside Boulder

This boulder lies about half way to the dam beside a junction in the road, opposite the bridge which leads to Ben Ime. The steep north side of this boulder has excellent rock - best stone in the area.

1. **Zero Kelvin** Font 7b+ *
Start up *Enthalpy*, but from the mono go directly to a crimp and rockover into a sloping pocket above, finish direct. No crack out left! FA Dave MacLeod 2003

2. **Enthalpy** Font 7a+ ***
Crouch start at edges on the north overhang, gain a good crimp on the left, then use a mono pocket to slap up to the diagonal crack. A good Font 6a from the stand-up, this is a quality power problem. FA Dave MacLeod 2002.

3. **Free Energy** Font 7b+ ***
The sit start to the north overhang. Sit start at the obvious pocket, lunge up right to the next pocket then go direct through a sloper to the diagonal crack on the wall. Also a left-hand version at 7c. FA Dave MacLeod 2002

4. **Powerhouse** Font 7a *
Sit start and climb the blunt nose with hard moves on slopers to the lip. Follow the edge leftwards into The Economist.

5. **The Economist** Font 6c+ *
Sit start just left of the north overhang below a niche, crank up to a break and crimps lead to a rightwards sloping finish.

6. **Splurge** Font 7a+ *
Sit start in the centre of the back wall at a pinch undercut. Climb up and right and move back left through an undercut break and slap for the top, but watch your landing!

7. **Triple X** Font 5 **
The crack near the left end of the face is climbed from a sit start. Good problem.

8. **Energize** Font 7b **
The traverse of the back wall is technical and excellent. Start as for *The Economist* and travel low left to finish up *Triple X*.

Roadside Boulder

121

BUTTERBRIDGE & REST AND BE THANKFUL

There are two areas worth bouldering at – the boulder cluster at the north-west end of Loch Restil and the giant Butterbridge boulder on the west side of the layby at Butterbridge itself. Both are easily accessed just over the bealach pass of Rest and Be Thankful.

Loch Restil

The set of boulders at the north end of Loch Restil catches the afternoon sun and is a pleasant wee venue, good in winter when the glens are cold and dank. Park at the waterfall car-park for the ridge up Beinn an Lochainn (as the road descends), cross stream and up left over a blind summit to the boulders overlooking the Loch. Lots of easy problems and a few projects.

Restil Boulders

Butterbridge

The Butterbridge boulder cluster is comprised of one giant boulder leaning against another. The south wall has some good straight-ups whereas the road face is steep and has some hard lines. Take a tarpaulin and as a many mats as possible as the grassy ground can be damp under the boulders. The approach is quick but boggy, through the gates by the bridge and up left.

Meccano Boulder

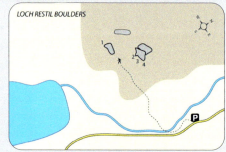

LOCH RESTIL BOULDERS

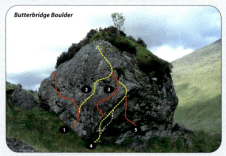

Butterbridge Boulder

Loch Restil

1. The Persuader Font 6a ***
The excellent overhanging groove on the leaning boulder - from a sit start at the arête, climb the steep groove to the top.

2. Meccano Font 7a **
Sit start under nose at crimp, slap for a nose pinch, gain the slopey ramp and surmount this direct.

3. Meccano Traverse Font 6c *
The lip traverse from left to right. Crouch start in groove, gain jug then traverse right along poor holds to mantle out right arête.

4. Meccano Arête Font 6b+ **
The right arête from a sit start, using the sloping ledge to throw for the lip and mantle out.

Butterbridge

1. Butterbridge Wall Font 4+ *
Step on to the wall in the centre and traverse left to finish up a wee groove on the left.

2. The Churner Font 5 **
Step on to the wall at centre and traverse right and up to the right arête. Highball.

3. Buttermaker Font 6b+ **
The wall just left of the arête. From good holds by the arête, rock left onto the slab, then rejoin The Churner.

4. Butterboy Font 6c ***
The arête can be climbed from a sit start with big moves to a ledge on the arête, rock on to this. *Var. Font 7a* - eliminate jugs and use a blunt pinch.

5. Butterknife Font 6b **
Sharp holds on the steep wall allow the ledge to be gained. A sit start on the right will be a possible at a big grade!

GLEN MASSAN   NS 117 867

This collection of boulders provides some remote bouldering on the Cowal peninsula, a relatively forgotten area, which if you were to draw a map of Scotland, would undoubtedly be left out by the tyranny of ignorance. This is perhaps its best asset, its secrecy and remoteness, despite being a mere ferry journey from the industry of the Clyde through Dunoon.

Approach Notes

Travel through Arrochar and Glen Croe on the A83, then turn off onto the Cowal peninsula road and follow signs for Dunoon (A815). At Strone, turn right, then right again at the bend and follow the road up Glen Massan, passing Ben More gardens on the right until the boulders appear on the right at the head of the glen. Park just past Stonefield Farm by the river. Some stones lie near the farm garden, so knocking on a door and explaining what bouldering is would be polite.

A short ferry-ride also goes to Dunoon from Gourock on the south side of the Clyde which can shorten the journey from the east. The biggest, and the best stone, is the giant House Boulder in the field under the trees. There is bouldering higher on the flanks of the glen, as well as in the gorge, so it's more adventurous than you might think. The area was for years a hardcore haunt of Mike Tweedley and friends.

'Crocodile'

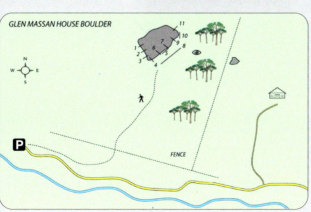

GLEN MASSAN HOUSE BOULDER

FENCE

The House Boulder

1. Pocket Problem Font 7a+ *
North Face. Sit start from the pocket and a hard sequence gains the top.

2. The North Wall 1 Font 6c
Climb the wall direct on small holds.

3. North Wall 2 Font 6a
Further right, climb the wall on crimps and dyno to the top.

4. House Boulder Arête Font 6a *
Climb the wall just right of the arête using pockets to the right.

5. Blade Runner Font 7b+ **
A good but wimp-out problem! Sit start on the middle of the front face and use side pulls and a poor crimp to make a hard move right to finish in a pocket half-way up the overhanging wall.

6. Rapier Font 7c ***
Sit start as for Blade Runner and climb up directly past a sidepull flake and to lock for an edge and sharp mono. Climb the wall trending right on two-finger pockets to a thankful finishing jug. Technical.

7. Broadsword Font 7c ***
The true finish to Blade Runner! Climb Blade Runner to the pocket, continue up to a finger-pocket, keep going on more small pockets, moving left at the top to a flat jug. Highball thriller. FA Dave MacLeod 2002.

8. House Traverse Font 7b ***
Traverse from the left arête to finish up the right arête. Make strenuous moves right to undercuts, then a pocket moves gains a spike on the right arête.

9. Crocodile Font 6b+ ***
Start at the right arête and use the 'crocodile' hold to gain and climb the wall above.

10. Highball Font 6c *
Start on face left of Crocodile at a large flake. A hard move gains the arête, turn this on to the right face, finish carefully up this.

11. Right Wall Groove Font 6a+ *
Climb the groove on the right wall, from a crouching start it is 6c+.

123

8 LOCHABER

GLENCOE

For all its dramatic rock faces and mountainous grandeur, Glencoe has spawned precious few boulders, as though keeping the place jealously dedicated to the traditional climber. However, there is some good bouldering to be found on solid volcanic rocks and there are enough quality testpieces to be worth seeking out. The walk-ins vary from five to fifty minutes, but in general, the remoter the rocks, the better the quality! There are five main areas which provide bouldering, all accessible from the A82 main road, or from the Glen Etive B-road.

The Lost Valley

1. Gleann a Chaolais - numerous but remote granite boulders with top-end potential and in a fine spot for high summer bouldering. Accessed from Ballachulish, these stones have some hard clean lines.

2. Loch Achtriochtan Boulders - a collection of fractured andesite boulders with one particularly prominent stone, seen just east of Loch Achtriochtan farm by the turn-off to the Clachaig Inn.

3. Lost Valley Boulders - some fine remote rhyolite boulders in a tremendous hidden valley, with the highlight being the Alpine-like 'Leaning Bloc'. Plenty of project potential and a great place to go wild-camp bouldering.

4. The Chasm Boulders - two large rhyolite boulders underneath the south face of the Buchaille Etive Mor, with the Chasm boulder providing excellent mid-grade problems with a stunning outlook.

5. The 'White Stones' - a collection of mostly small but clean white granite boulders recently revealed from a cleared and burnt forest area above Loch Ba on the Rannoch Moor. The highlight is the Rannoch boulder which has some fine problems five minutes from the road.

6. Loch Etive Boulders - small boulders underneath the Trilleachan slabs above Loch Etive, the best being two stones right on the shores of Loch Etive. They are easily accessed and provide some quality problems on superb granite.

125

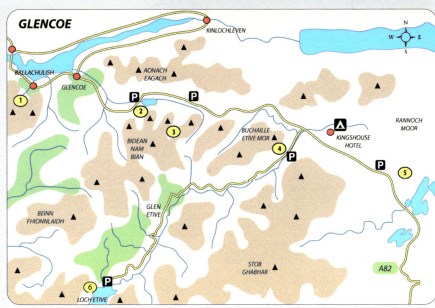

GLENCOE

ACHTRIOCHTAN   NN 141 563

At the bottom of Glencoe there is a pretty loch with a white farmhouse at its west end. On the far shore of the loch are some boulders, obvious to the east of the farmhouse. Park as for the walk-in to Stob Coire nam Beith in a layby by the River Coe, opposite the entrance to the Clachaig road. Follow the field edges to the boulders in about ten minutes. The best boulder is the vague ship-shaped boulder, the *Marie Celeste*.

1 *Pooped* Font 6a *
Marie Celeste boulder. Sit start on the flat hold under the west prow and go over the lip onto the wall via a crimp.

2. *The Black Pearler* Font 7a *
Marie Celeste. Sit start at the obvious hold under the left overhang and an undercling to the left, reach right to small pockets on the lip and crank over using bigger pockets.

3. *Keel-Hauled* Font 6c (var. *Foxy Traverse* 6c+) **
Marie Celeste. The full low-level traverse from *Pooped* left to finish along lip pockets and up *Black Pearler*, or extend it further for more of a stamina test. Can be climbed left to right as well to finish up the arete.

126

Tom Lee on 'Foxy Traverse'
Pic courtesy of www.cubbyimages.com

There is also a good roof boulder higher up the glen on the Aonach Eagach side, under Am Bodach, opposite and above the Stob Coire car-park (5 minutes stomp) with two very hard roof problems, the right of which is the excellent *Bittersweet* (Font 7b+). It is hidden about grid NN 164 571.

GLEN A CHAOLAIS   NN 037 568

'Some nice aretes, hard boulders and small smooth crags to boulder on. All granite... lots of scope, beautiful setting...'

Jo George

The stones in Gleann a Chaolais (Glen A Chulish) provide some remote but excellent bouldering on clean granite, particularly pleasant in summer when the sun gets into the glen. Developed largely by locals Dave Cuthbertson, Jo George and friends.

Bloc Notes

'Glen A Chulish' is the forested glen behind South Ballachulish. Enter the village from the A82 (just west of Glencoe village) and go to the end of the road to the forestry car park. Follow forest track (best on mountain bike) for fa ew miles to grid ref NN 037 568 at a bend in the track.

The first large granite boulder is in the woods (visible from forest track) on the bend just at the start of the path which leads up to the coire. The main boulder field itself is located between Coire Dearg on east and Coire na Capuill on the west. Aim for slabs on the left (south) side of the coire and you'll come across them.

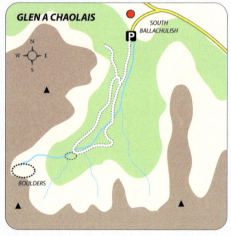
GLEN A CHAOLAIS
SOUTH BALLACHULISH
BOULDERS

The easiest approach is to follow the main track into the coire, climb over the stile and then follow a stream immediately after the stile on the right. A small but good path follows the stream all the way to the top of the hill but it gets a bit vague near the top. There's a good large boulder at the top of the hill next to the fence above the forest. From here, the rest of the boulders are visible, both nearby and further up the coire - they don't get much sun till summer but they are generally clean. There are more clean boulders hidden in the forest!

LOST VALLEY   NN 167 556

Bloc Notes

When you finally step down into the Lost Valley after a hike through the gorge of the Allt Coire Gabhail, you might expect to see Velociraptors running about in packs, such is the hidden mystery of the place. It is a choked hanging valley with smooth turf and gravel beds tumbling into a chaos of boulders and hidden streams. There is a lot of bouldering here though most of it has angular blocky landings. The best bouldering is just as you drop down into the high valley, where a giant slabby pyramidal boulder provides a focal point. There are many steeper project lines roundabout for the ambitious, but probably the best dedicated problems are on the clean rhyolite of the obvious propped boulder that is the Leaning Bloc, fifty metres northeast of the Pyramid. As big a mat as you can carry is useful for the other problems in the area.

Access Notes

The A82 is the main road through Glencoe. Once you swing past the waterfall gorge down into Glencoe proper, the Lost Valley is the first high glen on the left (south). Continue down past the white cottage and park in the first small layby on the right (or the last as you climb up through Glencoe). If this is full, park in one of the main car-parks in the Glen, where the pipers usually play. Take the path downhill off the West Highland Way to a gorge bridge over the River Coe and continue uphill through the steepening gorge on its right. The path eventually gets lost a bit in the gorge, so the best advice is to ford the river below a boulder-choke, then continue up the left bank (south side) of the gorge. The path climbs up and over to the sudden alpine vista of the Lost Valley itself. The boulders are obvious on the grassy flats and alluvial gravel. The forty minutes hike is worth it for the scenery alone.

128

The Leaning Bloc - Lost Valley

1. **The Bulge** Font 6c+ *
The blunt arête of the bloc from a sit start at sidepulls. Gain lift-off and grovel up right through the bulge groove, with a long move to a poor right hand hold allowing better holds to be gained, rock out left onto the arête and slab. No escaping early…

2. **Helipad** Font 7a **
The left hand line on the main face of the bloc. From the right hand crimp, jump left to a sharp incut hold, find your feet then throw for the sloping ramp above… if you hold this without helicoptering off, pull left to the flake and rock over.

3. **Diesel Canary** Font 7a+ ***
The excellent direct crimp line on the bloc. From a left hand sloping crimp and high right-hand crimp/thumb-press, rock left to foothold, creep upwards then throw dynamically to the sloping ledge frustratingly out of static reach. If successful, match and pull left through the finish of *Helipad*. Powerful, but may be easier for the tall.

4. **The Groove** Font 6b *
The far right groove line on the other side of the prop boulder. Climbed by a slap to the lip and an awkward contortion into the hanging groove, finish boldly or escape out right.

'Diesel Canary'

CHASM BOULDERS   NN 229 539

For such a rocky mountain, the Buchaille Etive Mor could have been more generous with its boulders. However, there are a couple of worthy stones underneath the south face of Central Buttress: the roofed boulder hidden in a small gully underneath Central Buttress and the excellent Chasm boulder, on a perfect grassy plinth just to the right of the entrance to the Chasm gorge.

Chasm Boulder - warming up on the slabs on perfect rock

To access them, drive exactly one mile down the Glen Etive road, park carefully by a blue sign. From here you can see the Chasm boulder just to the right of a crag at the entrance to the obvious long gash that is the famous Chasm. Walk up directly over the heather in about 20 minutes. To reach the Central Buttress boulder, contour right from the Chasm boulder for 300 metres till you stumble over it by a small burn beneath a pale scree slope.

The Chasm Boulder

This large boulder lies on the 350 metre contour and has a steep south face which holds the best bouldering. The west slab is good for warm ups and the north face is still a little dirty. The front face lies above a perfect grassy landing and the outlook over the Rannoch moor is stunning. A good spot in summer and not too midgy as it is exposed and gets the wind. The sun finally rises above Sron na Creise to warm the south face in March.

1. *Murray's Traverse* Font 6c *
From a sit start at a flake on the right wall, gain the slopey arête and climb it to good hol;ds at top, then swing left and traverse high along to finish up The Groove.

2. *Soap Glove* Font 6b+ **
Sit start at a good incut, crank up and left to sloping ramps, heel hook and gain the soapy RH hold and jump for jugs. Gain good high holds and finish left along the Traverse. Excellent.

3. *The Groove* Font 5 ***
The excellent juggy central groove can be romped via a technical and difficult press sequence at the start. Finish on jugs out left.

4. *The Bulge* Font 6c *
A hard blunt undercut start in the central wall gains a high left sidepull, twist up right to better holds, slap for jug and climb more easily up through the bulging nose.

5. *The Ramp* Font 7a **
The wee cave is climbed from a sit start at a RH nubbin, aim to LH sidepull, then crux RH undercut sidepulls allows jugs to be gained far left, finish up the hanging ramp.

6. *Screamer* Font 6a
The left arête can be climbed from a sit start, either finishing left or better to break right and finish up the hanging ramp.

Central Buttress Boulder

A well hidden boulder invisible until you almost fall over it! It lies in a little burn gully in the far right scree fan under South Central Buttress. Only go in summer when the burn dries out and the cave is cool and dry, otherwise it's too wet. Hard roof problems offer an alternative to the Chasm boulder's technical wall, but there is a fun traverse along the lip at about Font 6a.

129

RANNOCH MOOR   NN 305 510

Perhaps the greatest curse of the Scottish landscape for the last number of decades has not been the windmill but the spruce tree. This monoculture cash crop has infested the Highlands with great swathes of barren green geometry, leached the soils and turned boulder hunting into a nightmare! Now it seems much of this forestry is being cleared at last, revealing the bounty of rock underneath. In one such case on the Rannoch Moor, a cleared forest was burnt and revealed clean white granite stones a hundred yards from the A82. These are the 'white stones' of Rannoch Moor. Most of the granite boulders on the Rannoch Moor are too small to play on, or too wrapped in a lichenous gortex, but these accessible stones are worth a play if you are passing.

Access

From the south or north the A82 reaches its highest point on the Rannoch Moor before it dips down to Loch Ba. At the highest point of the road as it turns a corner, there is an old blocked forestry layby overlooking the expanse of Rannoch. Park a few hundred yards up towards Glencoe at a layby and walk back. The burnt forestry is hard-going underfoot, but the best boulder is only five minutes downhill.

The Rannoch Boulder

Below the layby are a number of granite stones, some a little too small, but others are worth a few short problems. The best boulder is the Rannoch Stone, sitting on its own by a tree down in the forestry scrub, about five minutes north-east of the corner of the road. It might not look big, but grows in stature as you approach. The other boulders roundabout on the moor might also provide some good testpieces, depending on how far you want to walk!

Colin Lambton cruising 'The Stretch'

The Rannoch Stone

1. The Stretch Font 6a ***
If this was Font it would be a blue circuit slab.... in other words, desperate! Climb the faint grooved slab to the top. A superb balance problem.

2. The Groove Font 3
The good groove, tricky to start but easy to finish, also the descent.

3. The Hook Font 5 *
Climb the arete starting with a heel hook, good tension allows cross-over moves on slopers to a high balancy sequence.

4. Galtee Merci Traverse Font 7a+ **
From a low crouch start at the left arete, slap right along slopers to the good handrail then a long reachy rockover gains the stand-up problem.

5. The Jump Font 6a *
From the good handrail holds, dyno up and left to flat lip holds then climb the balancy high section.

6. Galtee Merci Font 6b *
From the good handrail, pull on and sort feet to gain a diagonal hold over the lip, then a powerful rockover gains the high ripple and an entertaining finish.

ETIVE BOULDERS   NN 106 444

The long winding road down Loch Etive goes through some awesome scenery and finally ends at an old pier at the head of the sea loch, where the famous Trilleachan slabs can be seen on the hillside, usually streaked with black weeps like a barcode. Just south along the west shore lie a few clean granite boulders, which Dave Cuthbertson developed. There are not many lines, but the existent problems are all on perfect granite and provide a few good testpieces worth seeking out.

It's a good spot for a family picnic and the boulders aren't too far a walk, though the path is usually boggy, so access the boulders more easily along the rocky shore. The first two boulders lie on the waterline, the larger providing a good low traverse or two, and an even better boulder lies ten minutes away, hidden on the shore by an alder tree. This provides a few more testing problems.

Dave Cuthbertson on the Etive Boulders
Pic courtesy of www.cubbyimages.com

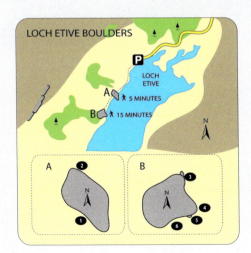

A - The Micron Boulder. Some easier slabby lines and some short roofs. The best of the problems are:

1. *Cubby's Traverse* Font 7b ***
The south face of the overhang is started at a low right jug, then a hard crimpy slappy sequence leads left along the lip and round the corner to rock out onto a small hanging slab. Excellent and technical.

2. *The Roof* Font 6b
The short north roof can be mantled out onto a slab.

B - The Alder Boulder. On the shore under the Trilleachan slabs by an alder tree.

3. *The Ramp* Font 7a **
The obvious shoreside ramp. From poor holds on the ramp, heel hook up the arete to lunge left to a good quartz vein hold, then continue slapping up the arete to mantle out. Superb. No prop boulder for feet!

4. *The Vein* Font 6c *
From a sit start, climb the bulge right of the wee hanging corner, using crimps and poor holds to gain jugs high right above the quartz-vein, travel right and rock back left.

5. *Vein Traverse* Font 6b+
From the same start as the above, travel left along the south lip on better holds to rock out at the inland arete, which is a good 6a in itself.

6. *The Lunge* Font 6c+ *
The south face has a low flake with sharp crimps. Sit start at the flake, use the crimps to lunge up and right to jugs and mantle out direct. Very little for the feet and a big move.

Dave MacLeod on the crux move of
'Deep Breath', Font 8a, Glen Nevis

GLEN NEVIS

One of Scotland's finest glens, this Scots Pine wonderland is covered in crags and boulders, with many projects still out there and some of the best quality schist in Scotland - compact, wavy, rough, crimpy, slopey... perfect for the boulderer. Midges and wet ground can be a problem, but a cool breezy day in summer is a fine time to visit. Best of all is a dry autumn day when the glen glows in full technicolour finery and the stones catch the low light. All areas can provide a good day's entertainment and quality problems can be found at all grades. The highlight for the dedicated boulderer is Sky-Pilot (High Crag), which was developed mostly by Dave Cuthbertson and Dave MacLeod. From Fortwilliam take the sign-posted Glen Nevis road south which follows the river's west bank for about five miles until it winds eastwards into the upper glen, where the crags and boulders come into view.

1. CAMERON STONE   NN 147 685

This steep stone lies just above the road and is the first boulder seen on crossing the bridge to the Poll Dubh area, two hundred metres past the Falls car-park. Park considerately in the gravel laybys and walk up to it in two minutes, maximum. Take a tarpaulin and mats as the ground, though grassy and flat, can be wet.

2. HEATHER HAT   NN 147 685

This superb roof boulder lies about 100 metres east of the Cameron Stone on the same contour. It has a west roof and three vertical walls, oh, and a heather bunnet. Classic roof problems and some crimpy walls to boot.

3. PINNACLE RIDGE BOULDERS   NN 147 685

A selection of distinctive boulders under the wee Pinnacle Ridge crag, another hundred metres along the glen. There is a gravel path up to the crags, the boulders lie to the right of this, including the 'Standing Stone', the 'Heart Stone' and the impressive 'Deep Breath' bloc. Drier than the other areas.

4. 'SKY PILOT' aka HIGH CRAG   NN 147 685

The best rock in the glen with some classic problems and traverses. It is the high skull-shaped crag seen from the road and has a leaning front wall over a perfect grass alp. There are various steep and sweaty approaches but the best follows the rough path up through the crags (veering right) past Cavalry Crack buttress and the Secretaries slabs. About 25 minutes.

5. SCIMITAR AREA   NN 147 685

Follow a small burn and glen up the craggy ridge to the obvious 'scimitar' boulder. Lots of quality low-grade problems and slabs. 10 minutes.

6. RIDGE BOULDERS   NN 147 685

From the 'halfway bridge' parking layby, there are hidden boulders and walls on the forested ridge above the road. 5 minutes.

7. WHALE ROCK   NN 147 685

Cross the footbridge and aim up towards the crag. There are some good smaller boulders below the crag. 10 minutes.

8. PINE ALPS AREA   NN 147 685

Continue up past the obvious Whale Rock crag to two boulders amongst pines on a high alp by a waterfall. 25 minutes. Higher alps await development.

9. CAR PARK AREA   NN 147 685

From the car-park, strike down to the river and ford it if possible to the obvious boulders in the flat area under a small crag (10 minutes). If the river's high, approach from the halfway bridge in twenty minutes.

10. THE GORGE & MEADOWS

Head along the gorge path from the car-park. there is bouldering in the gorge in a dry summer and some bouldering by the Meadows. 30 minutes.

133

'History has it that a short way above the lower falls one of the MacSorlie chiefs was murdered in the early part of the 17 th century... he was out checking his cattle and while drinking from the river he was shot by an arrow , which was rumoured to have pinned his drinking bowl to his own head. The murder was attributed to a malevolent dwarf known as Iain MacAindrea who was hiding behind a boulder... so watch out.'

134

Cameron Stone

Jo George on the Cameron Stone
Pic www.cubbyimages.com

1. **Ye Ken** Font 6a *
Sit start on the left at low block and climb from the ramp direct up the vague arête.

2. **The Shelf** Font 5 *
Just right is a smooth sloping shelf, hang this and go through the big slopers left or right for variable dynamic fun.

3. **A Dram for Donald** Font 6a *
From the start of *The Shelf*, go diagonally out right on crimps to better holds and a mantelshelf finish.

4. **Man of Mystery** Font 7a **
Sit start at crimps right of the shelf, gain good crimp up left (crux), divert to a good far right crimp before lunging back left to the juggy groove of Problem 3. Hard to get going... maybe easier from a crouch start.

5. **The News in Pidgin Gaelic for White Settlers** Font 7c+ ***
Described by Dave MacLeod as 'a stunning and desperate crimping battle!' Start in the depths of the cave on a block undercut and crimp, go through a minute crimp and somehow continue through crimps rightwards to the inset finger jug near the top.

6. **Shifting Sands** Font 7b+ *
Climb the arête using small crimps, slaps and bear-hugs. Full-on desperation and a struggle, success once described 'as dependent on your hairstyle as anything else'.

7. **The Right to Silence** Font 7b ***
Sit start on the rail in the cave and use a heel-toe to gain the lip, move left to crimps on the arête then move back right to finish up the wall of *Inspector Cleuso*. FA Dave MacLeod 2002.

8. **Inspector Clueso** Font 6b *
Climb the wall right of the arete using a variety of small crimpy things through the bulge.

9. **Woolly Jumper** Font 4 *
The obvious crack up the centre of the wall with a tough wee pull-on to start.

10. **The Nose** Font 5 *
Step off from the right and climb the hanging prow, finishing right to mantel out.

Heather Hat Boulder

Just east of the Cameron Stone, this boulder has a distinctive square-cut roof on its west side and some thin vertical faces on the other sides. Linking the problems in various combinations is also possible. It can be easily accessed from the gravel parking space by the river, lying under the obvious crags of Poll Dubh, but please park carefully and don't block the road.

Dave MacLeod on 'The Pagan Direct'

Heather Hat

Midnight in a Perfect World

1. **Maizie Gunn's** Font 6b ***
The classic perma-chalked line on the left of the roof from a sit start. Follow holds left out of the roof to escape up the hanging arête.

2. **Pagan Uilleann** Font 7a+ ***
Sit start right at the back and move out to peg scar holes in the square cut roof corner, reach for lip and mantle out at any point.

3. **The Pagan Direct** Font 7b+ **
The central roof at its longest span. Sit start on crimps in the centre at a good footledge. Slap into the *Pagan Uillean* sloper shelf and do this problem's crux but more direct to the jug rail (without the pin scars). Now make a huge slap to tiny ripples on the lip at the roof's widest point, avoiding the easier options either side (crux).

4. **Under the Hat** Font 7c *
Sit start on tiny crimps near the right side of the roof, reach for the sloper rail and make a careful deadpoint to the inset jug (almost a pocket) just right of the next sloper rail. Holding the swing is desperate. FA Dave MacLeod 2008.

5. **Midnight in a Perfect World** Font 6c+ **
The obvious lip traverse from right to left. Sit start far right, traverse round both arêtes to finish up *Maizie Gunn*.

6. **The Wall** Font 6c **
The superb thin wall on the back, climbed at its highest reach! Bit of a crimpy heart-flutter but very good.

135

Poll Dubh

High Crag

Pinnacle Ridge

Cavalry Crack Buttress

Heather Hat

Cameron Stone

'Sky Pilot'
High Crag

136

1. Beatle Back Font 7c ***
Uber-classic traverse. Start sitting on the pedestal and traverse right along the horizontal break to a hard sequence through two poor pinches, followed by a drop-down to a low shelf and along to a break, take a gasp and keep going to finish up *Auto Roof*. FA Dave Cuthbertson circa 2000.

2. Catch 22 Font 7c **
An infuriatingly good dyno, just right of the pedestal. LH on a crimp sidepull, RH on a low pinch in the horizontal crack of *Beatle Back*, pull on and boom for the obvious sloper… swing, grunt, match and hoot. (A sit start adds a grade and there is an easier method to the left at 6c). FA Dave Cuthbertson 2000.

3. Sky Pilot Font 6c+ *
Sit start below the fault and horizontal break. Climb up and left past good hand jams then travel back right on slopers. Up to niche, then left to jump-off jugs. A Font 7a variation climbs direct from the niche slopers. FA Dave Cuthbertson 1981.

Dave MacLeod on 'Catch 22'
Pic courtesy of www.davemacleaod.com

4. Auto Roof Font 6a ***
The excellent niche groove on the right, finishing at jump-off jugs in the niche. Undercuts and sidepulls combine with good technique to make a class problem. A sit start from the right makes it Font 6c. FA Kenny Spence 1981.

5. Burning the Candle Font 7b+ **
Sit start *Auto Roof* and go up to a protruding block, which allows an undercut slap to a high tan RH sloper. Toe-hook and slap right again for the boss above, match and go left to niche. FA Dave MacLeod 2002.

6. Press Gang Font 7c+ ***
On the far right is a left-facing corner. Sit start just left of this and use press holds to gain an undercut pinch. Slap for the slots and continue through the bulge to a quartz hold. Jump-off. No corner allowed! FA Dave MacLeod 2002.

7. Lip Traverse Font 7a+ *
The very slopey R to L lip traverse just right of the corner, finishing by reaching jugs at top of the corner. Don't roll off too far backwards!

GLEN NEVIS CLASSICS

Mike Tweedley on 'Deep Breath Arête'

Tim Morozzo on 'Tim's Arête', Boothill Boulders

John Watson on 'Sylvestris', Pine Alps

Dave Cuthbertson on Sky Pilot
Pic courtesy www.cubbyimages.com

Pinnacle Ridge Area NN 152 685

Just east again of the two big stones is a roadside collection of boulders under the Pinnacle Ridge crag, just right of the wee path. Some distinctive stones and some very hard problems, but also some good easy problems on the front faces.

1. *Deep Breath* Font 8a ***
This stone is just under the Pinnacle Ridge crag and has a steep west face hiding under the birch trees. Sit start at the bottom right of the leaning face at a pinch-sidepull and low edge, move up to the thumby crimp then climb direct up through slappy holds to aim right to grab the right arête, finish up the arête (a superb 7a sit start in its own right). FA Dave MacLeod 2007.

2. *Shorelines* Font 6a ***
The stone to the right has an obvious groove in the centre, place a mat strategically and keep your technique together up the highball slab above the groove.

3. *Hidden Wall* Font 4+ *
The stone behind the trees. Climb the nice wall leftwards.

4. *Hamish* Font 7a ***
The 'standing stone' is the obvious nosed boulder on the right. Sit start from a crimp, make a Gaston move to gain undercuts and slap up and left to escape this hard wall. Moving right from the undercuts to lunge for flat jugs is *MacTavish* Font 7b.

5. *The Prow* Font 5 **
Climb the challenge of the prow… the sit start is Font 6b or so.

Boothill (Blar Ban) NN 166 688

Boothill - This area is the field of obvious boulders opposite the high Gorge car-park (marked Blar Ban on the 1:25000 map). There are a number of excellent stones in a linear trail under the crags south of the river all the way to Whale Rock. They can be gained at low–water across the gorge by the car-park (there's an old weir), but if the water is high, access from the halfway bridge under Whale Rock, heading east along the riverside. Lots of enjoyable low-grade lines on good rock.

Classics

1. *Finch Attack* Font 6c ***
The first boulder across from the car-park has a big arête and steep north wall. This superb problem climbs from a big central sloper, aims up and left to cross-over layaways then uses opposition to gain the top.

2. *Tim's Arête* Font 6b+ ***
Climbs the main river-facing arête without the wee boulder underneath, useful if you're tall!

3. *Flying Roof* Font 6c ***
Further west under the wee Boothill crag are a number of boulders. The large roof under the big tree has a great dyno problem. From the centre, climb up and left to a committing dyno to a crack jug, finish left.

Other Areas

The Scimitar Font 4+ ***
Scimitar Ridge has some good low-grades walls and arêtes with the highlight being the distinctive Scimitar rock. Start up the front slab direct on smears and climb it to the apex, a little highball but an excellent problem.

Sylvestris Font 7a ***
Pine Alps. High above Whale Rock are two giant boulders on a hidden alp opposite a waterfall, under some mature Scots Pines. The front face traverse of the cave boulder starts in the central tan cave, crank left to a sloping ledge, then continue along the slopey shelf to the flying arête and climb this to jugs on the right, jump off.

Waterfall Arête Font 5+ ***
Pine Alps. The big arête on the first boulder facing the wee waterfall. Gain good holds on the arête and continue directly.

The Wanderer Font 6c ***
Allt Coire Giubhsachan NN 183 695. Walk east out the back of Steall Meadow and hang a left up the valley behind Meall Cumhann. The arête of the large boulder on the left as you walk up the valley. Step up using flakey holds, out right to a pinch on the arête, feet on the perfectly placed footholds, then cross through with left hand to the large hold and pull through to the top. FA Tom Charles Edwrads.

138

Pinnacle Ridge

Boothill Area

Pine Alps

ARDGOUR NM 857 604

These impressive boulders lie in west Glen Tarbert and have been known for years as holding some of the hardest projects in the north west. They are clearly visible from the road on the way to Strontian, and though they seem small from a car window, they swell on approach into blank gneiss monsters!

Approach Notes

Catch the Corran ferry and head west past the Garbh Bheinn car-park on the A861 till it rises up into Glen Tarbert and crosses the pass here. As it drops down by a forest on the right towards Strontian and Loch Sunart the stones can be seen down left across the Carnoch river. Park in a forest layby at the closest loop of the river and follow a small burn down to ford the river (if low!) to the stones. There are futuristic projects on the lower giant boulder but some good easier lines and one or two testpieces on the others. There is scope for more bouldering at all grades along the length of Glen Tarbert and on the steep crags above the boulders. Food and fuel can be found at the nearby town of Strontian.

'Futuristic'

'Them Bones'
Pic www.davemacleod.com

'Cubby was going on about them for years but wouldn't tell me where! *Them Bones* is a classic…especially if you are good on big slopers and body power.'

Dave MacLeod

Small Boulders

'Them Bones'

Tall Boulder

'Futuristic'

139

Them Bones Font 7b+ ***

The smaller high boulder in the loose cluster across the river has a fine slopey weste facing nose. Climbed from a sit start up and right through powerful sloper moves, requiring good body tension. FA Dave MacLeod 2006.

9 *WEST COAST*

ARDNAMURCHAN   NM 473 673

The Ardnamurchan 'Ring Cycle'

Ardnamurchan is one of the most remote peninsulas in Scotland and the furthest west the mainland stretches before dipping into the sea and becoming the Hebrides. The peninsula itself is a volcanic caldera with hundreds of boulders and gabbro crags. The rock is so rough it's almost impossible to slip off the slabs in sticky rubber, so bouldering and even soloing feels very secure. It is a terrific summer venue with fine sandy beaches at Sanna and great for wild camping.

Walking the ridge tops of the volcano is long enough, but add on a few highball problems and easy solos makes for a very interesting and exhausting day's climbing. Start at the central camp-site by the wee river (before Achnaha), go up the back of Creag an Airgid and circumnavigate the boulders and crags anti-clockwise to finish over the craggy back of Sanna and the long ridge home to the campsite. Climb anything that looks good. The best bouldering is around the crags and boulders between Creag an Fhir Eoin and Achnaha Buttress, but doing the whole thing will provide up to 1000m of actual climbing on rock, depends how much you want to do!

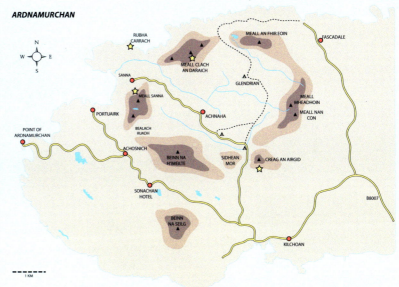

ARDNAMURCHAN

Dave Kerr on the 'Ring Cycle'

Access Notes

To get here, cross Loch Linnhe south of Fortwilliam by the Corran ferry and follow the signs west for Ardnamurchan and Sanna, driving through the villages of Strontian, Salen and Kilchoan. Fill up with fuel at Fortwilliam, as it's a good hour and a half drive on small winding roads. Parking and camping is possible at various laybys within the volcano caldera, but is not permitted at Sanna itself.

141

MORAR   NM 741 920

Loch Morar Boulders

On the main road past Arisaig on the way to Mallaig, take a right turn signposted to Morar, then take the next right by the river before the village, follow this small road which winds along the north shore of Loch Morar. At the dead end a few miles later, at Bracorina, a path leads along the shore for two kilometres to a large schist crag overlooking the loch. This is Creag Mhor Bhrinicoire and underneath it is an alp of fine gneiss boulders, still awaiting full development. A good mat is required, as well as an assortment of wire brushes, but the rock is solid and good on the main problems and many challenging lines remain on these impressive boulders. The two twin boulders on the alp and the boulders up near the crag provide the best problems. Lots of easier lines can be climbed at will.

'Loch Morar Boulders'

Chris Graham on 'The Sword'

1. **The Groove** Font 6b **
From the good holds on the sloping ledge of the first twin boulder, pull left into the wee groove and a tricky slap gains the top, downclimb ledges to left.

2. **Morar Monster** Font 7a ***
The excellent sloping nose on the first twin boulder. Climb the obvious nose from a sit start down left under ledges, gaining the prow through slopers and climbing it to the top, using the right wall as well.

3. **The Bad Twin** Font 6c ***
The second twin has a smooth arête at the left of the 'corridor'. Jump to gain holds on this and climb it to the top.

4. **The Muffin** Font 7a **
The small coloured boulder behind the Twins. Sit start in the wee cave, where butch pulling allows sharp holds to be gained on the lip to a tricky mantel over the nose.

5. **Lip Traverse** Font 6a *
The low boulder higher up has an obvious right to left traverse. It is not high and can be obscured by vegetation in summer.

6. **Tree Wall Arête** Font 6a
The left arête of the obvious Tree Wall higher up. A little highball and needs mats for security.

7. **The Sword** Font 7c+ ***
The superb and outrageously steep sword-edge below the main crag from a sit start right at its base. Dynamic and powerful moves up the blade lead to a difficult slap between two slopers either side of a chockstone (not used!) and then to the top. FA Chris Graham 2005.

'The Morar Monster'

APPLECROSS & TORRIDON

Torridonian sandstone is an ancient rock - compact, baked and red as its desert origins. It is a pebbled rock much like its gritstone cousins, but is wonderfully warped and folded into rounded shapes and lumps. The natural weathering of this rock has made for some attractive bouldering stones and features. It provides hard sloping testpieces as much as generous and juggy easier problems. In terms of future development, it is almost unlimited, with crags and boulders littering the natural rock terraces on the flanks of some of Scotland's finest mountains such as Beinn Eighe and Liathach. Only the most accessible of the bouldering potential has recently been developed, the remote corries are full of king lines and remain largely unexplored.

1. Kishorn Boulders - large, distinctive erratic boulders on the flanks of the famous Bealach na Ba road to Applecross village. Fine features, good landings and immaculate rock make this a popular roadside venue. There are plenty of other boulders along the shores of Loch Kishorn and on the flanks of Meall Gorm and Sgurr a' Chaorachainn.

2. Applecross Area - lots of short crags, boulders and walls provide easily accessible bouldering, the best of which is on the Brae boulders and the remarkable Stone Age cave roof at 'Sand' - a beautiful beach a few miles north of Applecross. Good in the rain!

3. Torridon - superbly accessible rock walls and boulders at Torridon campsite and nearby Annat provides some of the best testpieces and circuit bouldering in the North West. The Ship Boulder is the highlight, despite being a little aquatic!

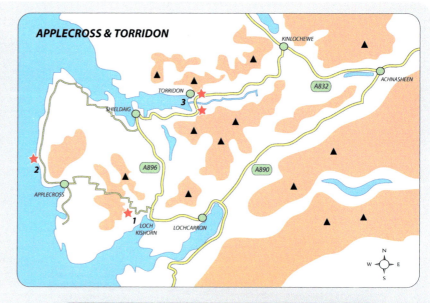

APPLECROSS & TORRIDON

Lee Robinson exploring Kishorn shores

KISHORN BOULDERS NG 813 406

Travelling to the North West of Scotland fills any climber with hyperactivity, much like a child that's eaten too many Smarties - there are just too many boulders to swallow in one go and things get a bit manic. It is best to pick an area, stay there a while and get used to the balanced tension of climbing on Torridonian sandstone, learning the angles of the sloping holds, what pebbles can be stood on, what apparent jugs you gamble on hitting with a dynamic throw. As good an area to learn these tricks of nuance and experience would be the great boulders looking out over Loch Kishorn under the nose of Sgurr a' Chaorachain. Dumped by a long-vanished glacier, these erratic stones were plucked from Coire nan Arr and deposited on a blunt ridge west of the Russell Burn.

Most of the climbing is in the easier grades and the rock is clean and heavily featured, the landings are good and there are plenty of new projects and open lines still to be climbed on the boulders. The views speak for themselves and the midges aren't too bad as there is often a breeze. Cold conditions are needed for the harder sloping testpieces. Descents are all generally down easy problems, or jump-offs. There is also some good bouldering further west along the shore of Loch Kishorn and on the terraces on the higher plateaus..

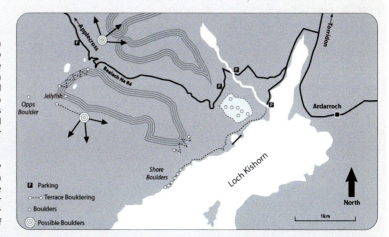

Parking
○┈┈ Terrace Bouldering
○ Boulders
◎ Possible Boulders

145

Approach Notes

From Lochcarron, head west over the hills on the A896 till it drops down to Loch Kishorn. As the road meets the loch it swings north and there is a B-road turnoff over a bridge at Tornapress, signposted to Applecross. If coming from the north, this is at the mouth of the River Kishorn. The B-road climbs and winds up to the alpine Bealach na Ba. The boulders are littered around the Russell Burn after about 3 kilometres. Parking can be found where the burn crosses the road, or further up a few hundred metres past the sharp bend, where space for one car can be found. The boulders are obvious downhill. The largest is the obvious Kishorn boulder, which distracts the eye as you climb the road. The Russell boulder is hidden in a hollow nearer the road.

Kishorn Classics

1. North Wall Font 6b *
Russell Boulder. Just down from the road, this large boulder is quite well-hidden below a rise. North wall: crimp and sidepull to break, easier to top.

2. Changed Days Font 7b ***
This climbs the north-east arête from a sit-start, slapping desperately on poor depressions and slopers to finish up and right. FA Dave MacLeod 2004.

3. Mike's Problem Font 7c+ **
Sit start at undercuts on the steep wall of the Russell boulder, gain a sidepull then cut back right to edges and an easier finish. FA Mike Adams 2006.

4. Undercut Wall Font 5 **
The central front face of the Kishorn stone, gain the undercut flake and climb through this to the top.

5. Pressing Matters Font 6a+ *
Eliminate but good line to the right on the blank section left of the triangular ledge, direct to top, no holds out left. FA Stewart Brown 2007.

6. East Crack Font 4 *
Kishorn Boulder. The left hand of the two cracks on the east face is good fun. The right crack is good as well.

7. Kishorn Dyno Font 6a **
Kishorn Boulder. The blunt south arête facing the loch. Jump for the sloping top from good finger rail holds on the south wall.

8. Deno's Dyno Font 6b **
Climb the obvious south ramp then jump up and right to better holds. Wet in winter. FA Lee Robinson 2005.

9. IQ Traverse Font 4 **
Brains boulder. The crack on the west wall, traverse up and left to finish up the north wall.

10. Synapse Groove Font 6a ***
Brains Boulder. The obvious groove can be finished right or left. Tricky to finish either waybut excellent rock.

11. Good Ass Font 6b+ **
Takes a more direct line up the Brains Boulder just left of the groove. FA Lee Robinson 2005

12. West Crack Left Font 4 *
Swamp boulder - the drier boulder surrounded by small boulders further downhill. Good holds all the way on the left-hand crack on the west face.

13. West Crack Right Font 4 **
The right crack - maybe a little harder and a bit highball, but terrific nonetheless.

14. South West Arête Font 5 ***
Swamp Boulder. Swing out to the arête from the south wall and finish direct. Superb.

15. South Wall Font 6c+ **
The south wall of the Swamp boulder. Start near the left edge of the wall, at a jug, gain a lateral V-hold and crank up and right to a crinkly flake edge.

16. Donkey Kong Font 6b **
Sit start at a jug and ape your way up juggy slopers to the right above the cave and through the bulges.

17. The Cave Font 6b *
The east cave of the swamp boulder. From a deep triangular hold, jam feet in break and reach back and right to good lip holds, finish up the juggy arête.

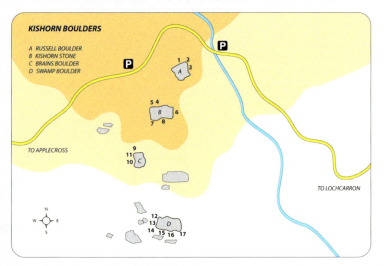

KISHORN BOULDERS

A RUSSELL BOULDER
B KISHORN STONE
C BRAINS BOULDER
D SWAMP BOULDER

TO APPLECROSS

TO LOCHCARRON

146

Russell Boulder from north

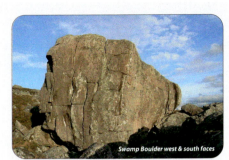

Swamp Boulder west & south faces

'Kishorn Shores'

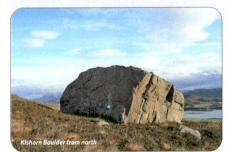

Kishorn Boulder from north

'Good Ass'

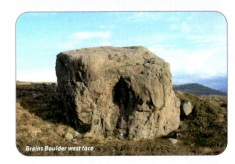

Brains Boulder west face

Swamp Boulder west crack 1

"Deno's Dyno"

SAND BAY — NG 683 493

A few miles north of Applecross village, the road drops down to a lovely beach aptly named 'Sand'. At the parking spot by the road down to the MOD station, there is a remarkable roof feature. Though a plinth of rock underneath it makes it scary for bouldering through the roof itself, there are some good perma-dry traverses on the back wall and a few good straight up problems. Nearby, on the boulders above the road on the 'brae' (south of Sand), there is some bouldering developed by Nic Ward.

SAND BAY

MOD ROOF

MOD

SAND BAY

BRAE BOULDERS

500 METRES

TO APPLECROSS

Orange Wall

Orange Wall

On the left of the roof is an orange wall which has some good vertical warm-up problems though the rock is a little sandy.

1. Orange Wall Direct Font 6a
Without recourse to large holds in the left or right cracks.

2. The Seam Font 4+
The seam on the right of the orange wall left of the crack.

3. The Crack Font 3+
The rising rightwards crack is straightforward.

4. Neolithic Orangeman Font 6b **
Sit start at layaways under the roof and climb it through good holds over the lip, aiming right to a ramp then back left to join the Crack at the top.

5. Flake Wall Font 5
Climb the flaked wall on the right, some sandy holds lead to jugs at the top.

The Roof

6. MOD Traverse Font 6c **
From the centre of the main roof, climb leftwards along low juggy holds to a crux sequence dropping under the flying ramp nose feature to finish left round the corner.

7. The Right Roof Font 5+ *
The right hand side of the roof has a line of jugs leading left to lip jugs, jump off here.

8. Ministry Of Offence Font 7a **
2m right of the central pillar of the cave is a large ledge at the back. Reach from this to a smaller flat slot with your right. Cross with your left to a crimp sidepull and make a large reach up and right for an incut hold. From here pull through to the jugs on the lip. FA Nic Ward 2008.

9. Hanging Wall Font 6b *
The right side of the right hand roof has a flat hanging wall. Climb along this from the back, matching a crimp to lunge for lip jugs.

MOD Roof

Sand Bay Brae Boulders

The boulders are situated half a kilometre south of Sand Bay car park, in a stunning setting looking across to Raasay and Rona. GF 686 487. Heading north towards Sand Bay from Applecross Village, the road drops to a car park firstly, then a hideously steep brae ensues. 50m before the top of the brae, park on the left and ensure your car is not encroaching on the road too much. There are currently 2 boulders on which there are documented climbs. They consist of Torridonian Sandstone. The upper of the pair is a huge roof which is comprised of disappointing rock on the underside, but above the lip is good. The lower boulder is an obvious block 20m south which consists of perfect rock and climbing to match. On the up-hill side is a slab, and facing the road is a 10° overhanging wall littered with small sloping breaks. Nothing is highball in nature but a pad is essential as the ground is somewhat broken and spotters are few and far between!

Brae Boulders

Upper Boulder

1. **Braelle Trail** Font 6c *
Start at the obvious low jug 3m from the right hand end of the roof. Traverse leftwards along the lip toward the arête and top out staying just to the right.

2. **Braece Yourself** Font 5+ *
Near the right hand end where the space under the roof begins to increase again, there is a jug at the back. Start here, pull to the jug on the lip, and turn the roof to top out.

Lower Boulder

3. **Braerut** Font 6b *
Start toward the left hand end of the slab. Start lying-down. Pull on using small crimps and cunning heel work to finish slightly right via a large obvious hold at the top.

4. **No Braener** Font 6b *
Sit start with hands and feet on the obvious large jug right of the arête. Climb the arête on its right and top out.

5. **Braeby Back Ribs** Font 6c ***
Brilliant. Sit start with hands on the same large hold as the previous problem, and right foot further back on this feature in a heel-toe cam. Pull over and climb the wall on a series of sloping breaks, avoiding the arêtes, finishing on the jug on the lip.

6. **Holy Braeil** Font 6c+ **
A great problem if slightly contrived. Start on the same hold as above but climb more direct to finish on the same jug.

The view from Applecross

The Ship Boulder, Torridon, Lee Robinson on 'Dandy Dons'

TORRIDON NG 907 557

'Hardly anyone ever comes here…'
Queen Victoria

Approach

From Garve, between Inverness and Ullapool, take the good new road west to Achnasheen, head on to Kinlochewe, stock up on goodies from the shop or petrol station and turn off down the picturesque single-track A896 road into Torridon, watching out on the bends for oncoming traffic.

The road sweeps past Beinn Eighe on the right, its grey ramparts usually in mist, until the boulders come into view at a stand of trees by the loch-head. The area can also be approached from the south via Applecross.

From the Tourist Information centre car-park, walk back up the A896 a hundred yards, then cross the bog between the two plantations in a north-east direction by the forest edge on the left. The first boulder you arrive at lies under a leaning crag and if you look round its back side, you will find the delightfully petroglyphed slab of the 'Celtic Boulder'. 3 minutes.

Bloc Notes

The rock is a superb grit-like red Torridonian sandstone. It takes a while to get used to what you can and cannot step on, which pebbles are good and which are 'poppers', and never dyno in hope…it's usually a poor sloper and you'll not hang it! The features are generous and there is scope for endless adventure on the terraces and hidden boulders. A popular bouldering circuit over the years, first ascents are given only for the more recent testpieces. Best in dry sunny spells in winter, spring and autumn out of the midge season - in summer pray for a breeze!

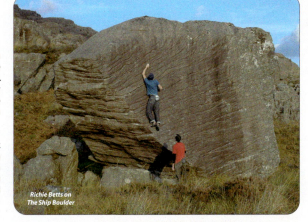
Richie Betts on The Ship Boulder

Lee Robinson on 'Squelch'

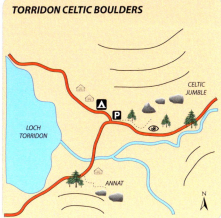

THE CELTIC CIRCUIT - TORRIDON

Celtic Boulder   Spaceship Area   The Ship   Dinosaur Area

TORRIDON CELTIC BOULDERS

CELTIC JUMBLE

LOCH TORRIDON

ANNAT

N

'The Celtic Circle'

1. The Ramp Font 4 *
The Celtic Boulder lies underneath a leaning crag with soaring arêtes. Climb left to right over the symbol.

2. Scott's Wall Font 5+ *
Celtic Boulder. The wall direct on the right is a little trickier.

3. The Crack Font 6a ***
The excellent hanging crack on the main wall opposite the symbol has good holds to a top-out on the slab. Gain the slot, then a good ledge, cross over to a high hold by the heather and finish up the high slab.

4. Blankety Blank Font 7a **
Sit start on *Frantic* undercuts to the right of *The Crack*, straight up to good hold through crimps. FA Ian Taylor 2007.

5. Slot Wall 1 Font 6a+ *
The wall to the right of the last problems. Gain the left hand slot from a sitting start and crank out to easier ground.

6. Slot Wall 2 Font 6c+ *
A harder proposition, with the sit start crux to the right-hand slot leading to a crimp and slopers to pull over the lip.

7. The Traverse Font 5 *
The boulders beneath the walls here have good easy warm up problems on all walls. There is a good traverse on the back of the square boulder at the front of the area.

8. Hanging Arête Font 6b **
Just to the right of the warm-up boulders is a pyramidal arête. From good holds at the lip, heel-hook and press up to better holds and an easier top-out.

9. Spaceship Wall Lefthand Font 6a ***
The 'Spaceship' is a large squat boulder with slabby sides, looking a bit like a crashed UFO. The steeper east wall has a wee roof. Step onto the lip and pull left on crimps and sidepulls to gain height on foot slopers. Finish left. Careful!

10. Spaceship Wall Righthand Font 6a+ ***
Step on at the same place but swap hands on crimps and aim up and right through poor slopers to a wobbly exit.

11. Celtic Knot Font 6a ***
The 'Conundrum' Boulder' lies down and right of the Spaceship, over the edge of the bog. This classic stopper mantles the central ledge and presses out the groove without recourse to the right arête. Puzzling.

12. Conundrum Font 4+ *
The right arête of the wall can be made easy with an unlikely heel-toe lock. Finish up and left at the last problem.

13. Muir's Wall Font 6b+ *
Above these boulders and to the right is an excellent vertical wall above a good landing. This is the direct line between the easy left arête and the right-hand crack.

14. Groovy Font 6a+ *
The 'cave boulder', to left and behind The Ship, has a good east face groove just left of the cave above a black pool. Climb it direct from crimps.

15. Sostenuto Font 6c+ **
The slopey west face of the caved boulder has a right to left lip traverse over the plinth.

16. Bench Press Font 6a+ *
Above the Ship on a mezzanine is a hanging prow boulder. Take the midway shelf from a prop-boulder jams, heel-hook rightwards then mantle out back left onto slab.

17. Angel Wall Font 5+ *
Further right still lies a series of overhanging walls. Straight up through the cave via a sloping ledge.

18. Richie's Wall Font 6a+ **
On the steep wall to the left of Dinosaur. From a low juggy shelf, take a line of crimps up the left hand side to a slopey finish with fat pebbles… pad the landing.

19. Dinosaur Arête Font 6a *
The 'Dinosaur' is far right and looks like the hoof of some extinct beast. Its front arête is tricky, the mantle out even harder.

20. Slipstones Thing Font 6b **
Round the corner from Dinosaur is a steep slab with an obvious flat ledge about head height, then a pebble about 5 foot higher. Looks straight-forward to mantle the ledge but its not!

21. Finish the circuit with a choice testpiece on the Ship boulder!

Bench Press

Celtic Knot

Spaceship RH

Torridon Testpieces

Celtic Boulder Area

Frantic Font 7c *** ☐

The hardest problem in Torridon to date. On the right of the cracked main wall opposaite the carved slab is a hanging slab lip. Sit start just left of the right-hand arête on undercuts, pull up and gain the ramp lip slopers, follow these left to the crack to pull over. FA Dave MacLeod 2004.

Lawrence Hughes repeating 'Frantic' Pic: Ian Taylor

'It looks like it should be fairly easy as it contains the only real features on the face, and these look massive compared to the blank wall to the left which is just covered in shallow ripples and pebbles. However, it ended up being much harder than it looks: reachy, crimpy and tenuous...'

Richie Betts : 'The Mission'

'The Mission'

'Malcolm's Arête'

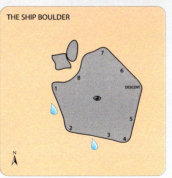

THE SHIP BOULDER

N

The Ship Boulder

Though it suffers from squeezing up bilge-water with its own weight, if you have a mat and can place flat stones strategically, the problems are superb. A tarpaulin is handy. One of the best boulders in the North-West.

1. **Squelch** Font 6c ***
The obvious challenge of the left-hand west-facing arête, butching up footless to a difficult top-out on slopers, hence the name!

2. **Malcolm's Arête** Font 7a+ ***
The awesome arête to the right is a super-classic. Can be climbed from a sitter, but the stand-up is hard enough! Crank up good holds to lunge for a left sloper, bring your toes up and dyno for the top, either right or direct, mantle out and celebrate. FA Malcolm Smith.

3. **The Mission** Font 7b ***
The vertical wall to the right has been climbed! On the right is a faint groove. Climb it direct on small and balancy holds to a hard deadpoint dyno to a good hold just below the top. Can be gained from the right arête at a grade lower. FA Richie Betts 2007.

4. **Dandy Don's** Font 6b **
The arête on the right of the vertical wall, aiming right at the top. Good and technical and not as hard as the last!

5. **Bogmen** Font 6a+
The wall right of Dandy Don's.

6. **North Face Direct** Font 5+ ***
The north wall is a superb outing, steady but technical to rock over onto the slabby top.

7. **Swamp Monster** Font 6c **
The blunt arête from a sit start just by the corner. Undercut up right to slopers, then a crux lunge gains the arête slopers, continue up wall to a technical rock out left from quite high. Don't go too far right over the bad landing!

8. **Indentation** Font 5
The groove just left of *Squelch* and right of *Swamp Monster*, finishing left of the prow. Not a great landing!

153

TORRIDON OTHER AREAS

Annat

A series of walls and boulders above the cemetery at the hamlet of Annat provides lots of low grade bouldering. To access them, park at the new house layby just before the cemetery and aim up to the obvious terrace walls and boulders above the road.

There are two particularly hard problems to date:

1. **Three Streaks (and you're out)** Font 7a+ ***
The higher level, left of a cube boulder. This wall has a distinctive triplet of black streaks and a shallow central groove. A tough sit start from an undercut and crimp allows a right hand sloper to be gained, stand on the foot-ledge to the left and reach to a blind crimp high on the left (if you're short you'll just have to be strong). Shift left to further crimps with blind foot moves gaining the faint groove above to finish more easily. Steely technique required. FA Michael Tweedley & Dave MacLeod 2004.

2. **Total Bullworker** Font 7c *
About 5 metres right of *3 Streaks* is a prow on the left edge of a chimney. Sit start and pull on using a sidepull on the left, crank desperately up the smooth arête to find a jug and finish more easily. FA Dave MacLeod 2004.

'Three Streaks'

The Balgy Boulder

This is a prominent sandstone erratic on the south side of Upper Loch Torridon. It is 7km (4.5miles) west of Annat heading towards Shieldaig on the A896. The boulder can be clearly seen on the east side of the road. The boulder was developed by Nick Carter and Donald King. Further details can be found at *www.alphamountaineering.co.uk*

Approach

Park at a lay-by on the right side (at 837542). Opposite the lay-by head up a vague stream line for 30sec, turn left onto a path and after 2mins you will find the boulder. As the boulder is quite short most problems have sitting starts. The prow is a must do if you are operating at the grade.

1. **The Balgy Prow** Font 7a ***
Clamp your way up the obvious blunt arete from a sit start.

2. **The Mantelshelf** Font 5+ *
Starting on the obvious break to the right of the Prow, step up and make a mantel to ascend the block. (pic)

Nick Carter on the Mantelshelf

10 NORTH WEST

Achnahaird Wall, Reiff

THE NORTH WEST

The accesible bouldering from the North West capital that is Ullapool is the gateway to some of the best landscapes in Scotland, where bouldering can easily dissolve into thousand yard stares. If you do manage to focus on the bouldering, the problems all require finger strength, technique and friction on some of the roughest and cleanest rock in Scotland.

1. Inchbae - hundreds of small granite blocks with some hidden gems, though new problems require a lot of brushing and cleaning. On the way from Inverness to Ullapool and worth exploring.

2. Mellon Udrigle - beautiful vistas and clean Torridonian sandstone makes this coastal venue fun to explore with plenty of development potential around the headlands.

3. Rhue Blocks - very similar to gritstone, these rough sandstone blocks and walls provide skin-shredding classics in a stunning location overlooking the Summer Isles. Accessible and great for circuit climbing.

4. Ardmair - a butch roof on a beautiful pebble beach, Ardmair is a local training ground and very accessible. The problems feel easier once the 'secrets' are pointed out.

5. Reiff in the Woods - fine hidden bouldering on Torridionian blocks under the ramparts of Stac Pollaidh. Some hard testpieces and a great place to watch sunsets.

6. Reiff- sunny walls and crag bouldering at the classic trad venue. Great testpieces and a super place to hang out in the high summer. Best in winter for holding the slopers, but watch the seas!

7. Achmelvich & Clachtoll - beautiful secluded beaches with associated gneiss bouldering. Explore at will this wilderness of small walls and slabs. Excellent mobile bouldering in summer.

ASSYNT & COIGACH

157

INCHBAE   NH 375 701

'...originally a porphyritic granite with abundant orthoclase phenocrysts, but is now a coarse biotite-granite gneiss in which the phenocrysts are largely deformed to augen wrapped round by a streaked-out matrix of quartz, biotite, potash feldspar and plagioclase...'

A geologist's explanation of the Inchbae Intrusion.

Approach

The A835 links Inverness with Ullapool. Shortly after the Garve turn-off to Kinlochewe, the road continues past the looming hulk of Ben Wyvis on the right, then begins to climb up to a rocky plateau by Altguish Inn. Before this the road swings along briefly beside the Black Water river, from where numerous small erratic boulders can be seen south and north of the road.

Bloc Notes

The Inchbae erratics are hundreds of granite boulders scattered like litter by a glacier. The biggest boulders lie hidden in hollows south of the river, so it's best to park at the big layby by the Black Bridge and cross the bridge to strike over the low hills south of the river. Aim for the highest hummock (Carn an t' Sneachda) and you will see the main boulders spread out across the bog and heathery moor. The best boulders are the biggest and the cleanest, whereas the smaller boulders seem to be covered in resilient black lichen.

'The Inchbae Erratics'

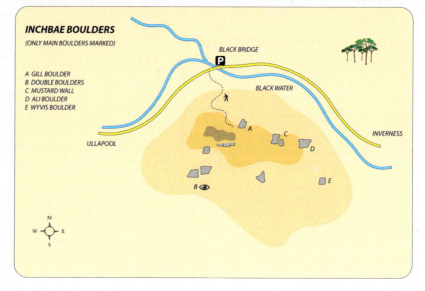

INCHBAE BOULDERS
(ONLY MAIN BOULDERS MARKED)

A GILL BOULDER
B DOUBLE BOULDERS
C MUSTARD WALL
D ALI BOULDER
E WYVIS BOULDER

BLACK BRIDGE

BLACK WATER

INVERNESS

ULLAPOOL

1. **Half Way Landing** Font 5 *
Double Boulder – the highest and best boulders with grassy landings, over the back of the craggy hummock. The left arête of the face.

2. **Phenocrysts** Font 6a ***
Double Boulder - the slab direct to the apex, no wimping out leftwards. Start sitting at the flake, go left, then back right to a highball finish through the slab.

3. **A Long Winning Streak** Font 6c ***
Doubler Boulder - the direct line up the white streak wall of the left boulder. The arête to the right is Font 5.

4. **Xenolith** Font 5 *
The balancy left arête of the right-hand boulder of the Double boulders.

5. **The Scoop** Font 6a **
Double Boulder - the excellent central scoop hard from the ledges. The right arête is easier.

6. **Gill Shadow** Font 6b **
Gill Boulder – the central split boulder in the middle of the cluster. From the cave right of the arête, sit start and climb out powerfully on good holds and surmount the nose to a high 'shield' on the wall, mantel up and step right to the mossy slab to downclimb.

7. **Jam Crack** Font 5 *
Mustard Wall– a yellow-coloured granite face with a split jam crack through it. No using the arête! Jam the crack to the top.

8. **Colonel Mustard** Font 6b **
Sit start the front arête over the plinth and climb into the mustard-coloured technical wall and gain a saddle hold at the top to rockover.

9. **Rope-a-Dope** Font 6b+ ***
Ali Boulder – shaped like a giant fist, this horizontally cracked roof boulder is closer to the river. The east face roof on the right is climbed from good slots up to the hanging blunt flake crack and rock over. Technical. Traversing all the way along the crack from the west to finish up this makes it Font 6c+.

10. **Champion** Font 6a *
Ali Boulder - same start as above but travel left along the crack to rock out the jugs far left, with some very enjoyable moves.

11. **Wyvis** Font 6c **
Wyvis Boulder – a small roofed boulder further east from the Ali boulder. A good problem on the left side of the face that looks towards Ben Wyvis.

'Double Boulders'

9 var. start
'Ali Boulder'

159

'Champion'

'Colonel Mustard'

RHUE BLOCKS NH 098 974

Cleric's Wall

The excellent cluster of south-facing walls and blocks on the west flanks of Meall Garbh, behind the houses looking out over Rhue lighthouse. From Ullapool, drive north over the Morefield hill and drop down to a bridge, turn left at the Rhue sign and follow the road to a car-park at its end. Continue on foot below the houses to cross a gate and meander up the edges of a bog to the walls and blocks in about 5 minutes. Please don't cut through the houses. There are three main boulders at the right end with a line of small crags extending left behind them. The furthest left crag on a high escarpment is the excellent juggy 'Cleric's Wall' with easy but highball problems beside a large detached block.

'Rhue Blocks'

1. The Deceiver Font 6c **
50m left of the walled cave is a steep nose forming the left wall of a corner. Sit start and make a long move up and right to a good hold above the nose and belly flop over the top.

2. Disney Tour Traverse Font 6a *
From jams at the back of the cave span backwards to good holds out left then traverse left with heels to finish up and left.

3. The Scoop Font 6a *
Further right is small boulder with a scooped face. Climb the right edge of the scoop from a sit start. Technical.

4. The Concave Wall Font 6a *
Next right is a concave wall. Can be climbed using the left arete, the direct is a hard technical challenge, crimpy and dynamic.

5. The Forge Font 6b+ ***
The Forge boulder. This is the massive boulder with a cave on its right side. Climb the front face of the boulder from a good left pocket and dynamic slap up right to a sloper, undercut the break and rock up the slab on pebbles. Superb.

6. Right Forge Font 7a ***
Climb into the original problem from a crouching start on the right along a slopey break. No foot block.

7. Slab Layback Font 6a *
Start just left of the cave and use the flake on the slab to pullover.

8. Skinshredder Font 6c ***
Sit start and hook toes at back of cave then climb right along crux slopers on the smaller boulder, with a bridging move allowed. Finish right with a mantel. Font 7a+ with no bridging.

9. The Bear Hug Font 6a *
A few metres right of Cave Boulder is a small rounded boulder. Sit start, clamp both arêtes and gain the top.

The Forge Sit Start
Pic: Tess Fryer

Ian Taylor on 'Skinshredder'

160

Ian Taylor on the Forge, Rhue Blocks

ARDMAIR BEACH   NH 107 978

Ullapool's premiere training ground, this excellent sandstone roof provides powerful and technical wall and roof-problems. It's just a short cycle or drive over the hill north of Ullapool, at the south end of the pebbly Ardmair beach. Park at the campsite layby and walk back along the beach.

The beach roof itself can weep heavily after rain and needs one or two mats to pad out the rocky landing at the main left roof, as well as covering the seaweed!

Richie Betts on 'Cup Run'
Pic: Ian Taylor

Ardmair Ruins

The 'Ardmair Ruins' problems lie across the road by the old croft ruins. There are a number of good problems hidden here, the best of which are on the propped cave boulder 80 metres along the crags past the roadside ruin. Cross the road, hop the gate and turn left along the craggy edge of the field.

1. **Hanging Corner** Font 6a **
The hanging corner from a sitting start. A bit of a stretch to better holds!

2. **Cressbrook** Font 6b+ *
Start left of the corner, hanging off a good finger hold on the lip. Gain two crimps on the wall above, then the top. No right arête.

3. **Corkscrew** Font 6c ***
Start under the block at a good hold and crimp on the left wall. Crank to the break (no lower wall) then climb right along the lip to finish up the hanging corner.

4. **Sidey** Font 6b+ *
Sit start under the roof on undercuts, feet on the prop boulder, span right to the good hold under the corner and finish up this.

5. **Crucifix** Font 7b **
Start with hands and feet on the cave boulder and crank out using flat undercut sidepulls to the good hold under below the corner, no supporting boulder allowed, just good body tension! Contrived, but the hardest problem in the Ullapool area? FA Mike Tweedley 2005.

Angus Murray on 'Watch Your Back'

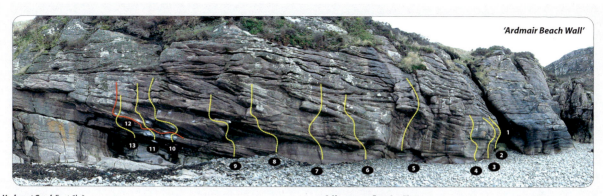

'Ardmair Beach Wall'

1. **Undercut Crack** Font 6b *
SS undercuts on the left wall of the cave, pull up via a rectangular niche in the crack and go straight over.

2. **Stones and Seaweed** Font 6a ***
Just to the left, undercut the crack, then reach up left to a shallow pocket then slap for jugs!

3. **The Pockets** Font 6b **
Sit start with left hand on a three-finger pocket at the top of a vertical seam. Up rightwards to a shallow pocket, gain better holds above and pull over.

4. **The Ledge** Font 4
Start sitting just left of the undercut nose and finish standing on the ledge.

5. **The Pebbledash** Roof Font 5 **
From a sit start at a slot under the rectangular roof, climb over the roof.

6. **A Right Bulger** Font 5+ *
Start on undercuts at the right end of the main roof. Make a blind move to a good hold then pull over.

7. **Smiley Problem** Font 6a+ **
Sit start at a pocket on the lip and gain the smiley hold and the crimp to its right, then slap up to a better hold and pull over on jugs.

8. **Jumping Bristletails** Font 6b
From a small corner, twist out backwards to a hold below a blocky jug then finish through the jugs.

9. **Youzyernee** Font 6a+ **
From a cramped start at the square roof corner, use crimps to span backwards to the half-moon jug on the lip, cut loose and climb up on jugs

10. **Watch Your Back** Font 6b+ **
Start 2m left of *Youzyernee* at the back of the cave, gain a flake in the middle of the roof, aim for the slopey pinch with the left hand, then struggle to better holds on the lip.

11. **Changing the Locks** Font 6c+ ***
Sit start at the back sloping rail, gain the two crimps in the roof then lock up to the break. Heel and toe hooks are the key.

12. **Cup Run** Font 7a **
Traverse the cave slopey rail, lock back to the crimp in the tan roof, slap backwards again to the next crimp then make a crux lunge to a tan sloper under the roof, continue left.

13. **Boulder Ding** Font 6c **
The furthest left problem. Starting from a good undercut, make some fun manoeuvres to gain good holds over the lip. No shelf on the left!

The Grand Traverse Font 6b **
Start with hands on *The Ledge*. Follow breaks left until past *The Pebbledash Roof*, drop down until feet are on the lip, then continue left along the lowest good holds to the yellow ledge.

The Lower Traverse Font 6c **
Start at *A Right Bulger*. Go left, undercutting and using small holds on the lip of the roof, to the half-moon jug. Continue crimping left along the lip of the main roof to the yellow ledge.

Tricky Lippy Font 7b+ **
From the *Smiley* pocket, traverse the main roofs left along poor lip crimps without the back wall!

163

REIFF IN THE WOODS   NC 092 094

Bloc Notes

North of Ullapool, the landscape ages dramatically: cores of Precambrian Torridonian sandstone have been gnawed down by the invisible teeth of time to produce the great peaks and buttresses of Coigach. The pebbled red sandstone is hard and baked, rasps against the fingers and has remarkable foot friction. Most problems, due to the generous sculpture of the rock, lie in the lower grades, with some steeper lines providing the impetus for future return.

'The Crack'
Pic: Richie Betts

Being so accessible, yet so hidden, and in such a wild landscape, this arcadia of bouldering exhibits the generosity of superb climbing and constant movement for which Coigach is rightly renowned.

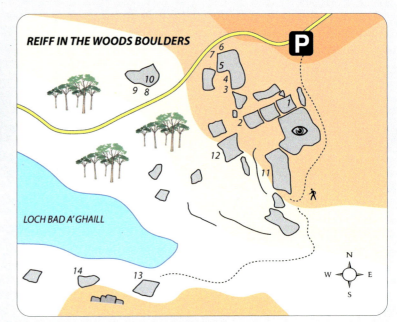

REIFF IN THE WOODS BOULDERS

LOCH BAD A' GHAILL

'TP & QC' Pic: Ian Taylor

164

Approach Notes

North of Ullapool, turn west off the A835 signed Achiltibuie, the single-track road winds along Loch Lurgainn under Cul Beag to the unmistakeable towers of Stac Pollaidh. Two kilometres after the car-park to this remarkable peak, just before the road drops down to Loch Bad a' Ghaill, the forested hill overlooking a craggy peninsula hides some of the best of the extensive bouldering in Coigach. A small parking layby lies at the top of the hill and the boulders and walls can be explored at will over generally mossy landings.

Torridonian Landscape - Stac Pollaidh

'West Wall Traverse'

REIFF IN THE WOODS CLASSIC PROBLEMS

1. *Haven* Font 6c+ ***
The first cube roadside has a recess. Pull on small fingery holds on left of vertical wall, using arête at about half height, gain better holds at top: fingery and technical.

2. *Cube Arête* Font 4 *
On the third cube, climb the blunt arête through a bulge on its right side with long reaches.

3. *Avoiding the Main Issue* Font 6c *
On the right of the wildly leaning wall, start with right hand on a spike pinch, traverse up left on slopers and pull over onto ramp and direct finish.

4. *The Main Issue* Font 7b ***
An astonishing dyno from the central handrail on the steep wall up to the obvious lip, which is not as good as it looks - cold conditions needed and a positive commitment is vital for success…needs mats and cat-like reflexes. FA Richie Betts Nov 2006.

5. *The Pokey Hat* Font 6b **
The left arête of the bay finishing with a long move for the pokey hat at the top - stretchy and technical.

6. *Pebble Beach* Font 6b *
Step on to the slabby roadside arête 5m left of *The Pokey Hat*, climb to a steeper precarious finish.

7. *Clach-mheallain* Font 7a ***
Sit start under the right side of *Pebble Beach* arête. Gain the better holds on the overhanging arête with heel-hook to a tough last move. Mats needed to pad landing. The name is Gaelic for 'little stones', more commonly known as 'hail'. FA Ian Taylor 2006.

8. *The Crack* Font 7a+ ***
The roadside boulder (across the road downhill). The left-slanting crack on the right side has few footholds!. From a sitting start traverse into the crack, then gain a groove to better holds. FA Mike Tweedley 2004.

9. *Pebble Mill* Font 7a ***
To the left of the crack are two obvious sloping jugs, gain these from a sit start, then use a poor break and broken pebble to struggle over the top.

10. *A Man in Ascent* Font 6c **
Sitting start as for *The Crack*. Up to large layaways, then gain large flat hold, then escape right. FA Ian Taylor 2006.

11. *The West Wall Traverse* Font 6b ***
The clean and striking west wall is a delightful example of the best rock here. Traverse from far right arête, with the crux move gaining the spike hold in the middle. Finish up left arête.

Var. ***The Final Countdown*** Font 7a+ ** (FA Dave MacLeod 2005) - when passing the spike, drop down using poor holds then follow a low break to finish up the left arête.

12. *TP & QC* Font 7a ***
Howff boulder. Technical, Powerfull & Quite Committing! Crouching start on crimps and avoid the block on the right. Somehow gain holds above the lip, go right and finish up the right arête. FA Lawrence Hughes 2007.

13. *Teewhuppo* Font 6c ***
On the other side of the wee bay is a craggy peninsula with a towered crag. The 'Patio' Boulder is the large heather-capped block lying just below this. Climb the west arête wall – highball. The escape rail leading right is the excellent *Breathalyser* (Font 4).

14. *Bullworker* Font 6c+ ***
Climbs the blunt right arête of the next good bloc along from the Patio Boulder. A modern classic and worth seeking out.

165

Ian Taylor on 'Clach Mheallain'

Lawrence Hughes on 'TP & QC' Pic: Ian Taylor

REIFF   NN 566 106

Bloc Notes

All the rage for trad climbers in the 80's and 90's, Reiff is as much a paradise for boulderers. Skirting the western edge of the remote peninsula of Rubha Mor, and copping any good weather available, it is Scotland's version of climbing in the Med. The bouldering is now as popular as the routes due to the attractive solidity of the sea-sculpted sandstone. In fact, many of the routes are short enough to solo out with mats, though one would advise caution… as with all crag bouldering, it's up to you how high you climb! Described here are the best of the problems in the main areas of the 'Pinnacle' and the 'Bouldering Cliff', which is actually a cliff so jump-offs or downclimbs are advisable. There are plenty of other sea-platforms with flat landings for the adventurous, just go exploring in calm weather and take a mat to protect your ankles. Watch out for swelling seas and do not attempt to cross tidal platforms awash with rogue waves.

'Wave Traverse'

166

REIFF

TO ACHILTIBUIE

500 m

Approach Notes

For the Pinnacle and the Bouldering Cliff, the approach is the same. From the limited parking at the Reiff crofts - mostly kit-bungalows - cross the concrete bridge and jump the gate onto the machair. Skirt the edge of the lagoon until you cross a smelly sea-gully, then drift uphill towards the cliffs which come into view. Locate a square stone ruin on the cliff-tops – this is a good marker and meeting point.

1. The Pinnacle Area - just down and west of the ruin on an easy stepped gully onto sea-platforms. The *Detached Block* and *Earthshaker* walls are obvious, with the Pinnacle itself just around the corner.

2. The Bouldering Cliff - lies northwest of the ruin - descend a slimy gully by a green pool. The square-cut walls are obvious and most problems are located around the three main arêtes.

'Leaning Meanie'

1. Pinnacle Area

1. Tiny Creatures Font 6a+ *
The Detached Block has a few good warm-up problems, but the best is this fingery test up the wall just right of the central crack, no escaping out right!

2. The Salt Pans Font 6c+ **
Climb directly up the left edge of the wall from the pocket and crimp, using whatever you can…thin and fierce. Finish on the ledge and jump off.

3. Earth Shaker Font 6b ***
The excellent central line on the attractive leaning wall - an old-timer's classic and named before mats existed. From the good holds under the block, layaway up and right dynamically, then continue to the jugs on the ledge and jump off, or continue at E2 solo. FA Brian Lawrie 1970's.

4. Earth Shaker Right Hand Font 6b+ **
A little harder - come in from a sit-down start on the flake on the right, with tough presses gaining the halfway holds on the original problem.

5. Reiff Case Font 6c+ *
Climb the wall to the right of Earth Shaker via a triangular layaway to good holds and downclimb right.

6. The Wave Traverse Font 7a ***
Traverse from the right edge to the left up and down Earthshaker to a tough fingery crux through a small pocket and crimps to gain good holds on the far left and a finish past Salt Pans. Going direct under Earth-Shaker via an undercut and slap down to a sloper to finish up SP ups the grade significantly.

7. The Green and White Men Font 6c **
The obvious prow of the pinnacle over the drop-off! Place mats and spotters strategically, then sit under the prow on the left at a big RH undercut and LH crimp, power on and slap up left for poor holds, gain juggy pockets on the right then aim up and left for layaway pockets and the top mantle. Linking it to the Blue Men is Bluegreen 6c+.

8. The Blue Men Font 6c ***
The excellent prowed-roof direct from jugs in the depths out through shapely jugs to a finger-slot move through the lip to ledges. Use mats but keep your body tension tight to avoid bum-brushing, or even springing your spotter into the sea!

Reiff Earthshaker Wall

Reiff Pinnacle Roof — Link

Angus Murray cranking out 'The Green and White Men'

167

Reiff Bouldering Cliff

Reiff Bouldering

The Bouldering Cliff

1. *White Horses* Font 6b **
Sit start and slap up the short first arête to a match, gain a left hand ramp and continue up to a sloping ledge, traverse this right to the wee corner and downclimb.

2. *Golden Eyes* Font 6a **
The obvious cracked corner gives a struggle to ledges. Climb down, jump off on mats or traverse right and down.

3. *Razorback* Font 7a ***
The big scooped arête, nothing like a razor. From obvious jugs at head height, use a crimp round to the left to pull on, get your feet high and launch to the big jug which is light-years away up and left then power on up to the big break, traverse left to escape.

4. *Romancing the Stone* Font 7a ***
The thin crack to the left of the scooped arête is technical and desperate. Find a way through layaways, crimps and crap pockets to the break, traverse boldly off left down the ramp. The most failed on problem at Reiff!

5. *Undertow* Font 7b *
The raspberry ripple wall has high undercut holds just left of centre. Crank into these somehow and continue to the ledge, then jump off. For every inch you lose under 6 feet, add a grade.

6. *Leaning Meanie* Font 6c *
The cave under the left arête has good holds leaning out to a poor hold at the bottom of the crack. Find a way to gain the distant jugs up and right, jump off and blow your cheeks.

White Horses

Razorback

THE FAR NORTH WEST

Once you cross the Kylesku bridge into the 'far northwest', you understand how radically Scotland can change its landscape. From the younger Torridonian sandstones, quartzites and limestones further south, you are now aware of being on the rocky base of the world… gneiss. The landscape is rolling and craggy with ancient swirled rock everywhere. Swollen boulders and striped crags catch the eye and it is a dream for the explorative climber. It is such a remote area, and feels so 'away from it all' that bouldering has traditionally been 'visitational' and problems rarely recorded… it seems to provoke wanderlust rather than the desire to colonise. However, there are some accessible venues and big stones that are worth a mention. Development of them has been sporadic, but if you are in the area, these are probably the best areas to visit. The area around Rhiconich and west to the Sheigra seacliffs offers the best bouldering on some very old rock!

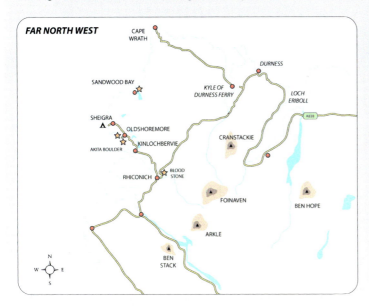

Bouldering at Oldshoremore Beach

169

Akita Boulder NC 203 577

Bloc Notes

This giant gneiss boulder sits below a small outcrop on the headland south of Oldshoremore. Steep on three sides with excellent quality, clean rock, crimpy and powerful climbing. The landing is assorted rocks and pits, so big mats and spotters are essential. If you don't like the commitment involved, there are lots of smaller boulders roundabout with easier lines. Boulder at will. Turn off for Oldshoremore and take the left hand fork immediately after. Follow this to the end of the tarmac and park in a small layby. Ascend the slope above the road and walk due south, crossing a couple of faint ridges crowned by curious small erratics. The boulderfield is obvious down in a small valley not far above the shore. 15 mins. Developed by Dave MacLeod.

1. **90's Rock** Font 6b+ ***
The leaning crack and right arête, starting from the obvious jug. Committing.

2. **Something Worth Crimping For** Font 7a **
Sit start as for Problem 4 and travel left to fight up the crimpy wall.

3. **Kobi** Font 6b+ *
Sit start and climb the obvious arête utilizing a good undercut to jugs and a thinner top-out.

4. **Akita** Font 6b+ *
Sit start as for Kobi just right of the arête, gain a small pocket and finish direct.

5. **Growlers** Font 6c
Start again at Kobi, climb Akita but take the pocket with your left hand and finish right.

6. **Rubbish Guard Dog** Font 6b+ *
From low-down crimps, crank up to an incut and finish direct.

The Rhiconich Bloodstone NC 266 529

Bloc Notes

The Rhiconich hotel on the A838 lies north of Scourie and is the junction for the road down to Sheigra and Oldshoremore. Just north of it, up the hill 1km beside the river and the road, is the giant red 'Bloodstone'.

This is the centrepiece of a good explorative area, with lots of gneiss walls and erratic boulders. It has a number of good problems and projects and has a distinctively red overhanging north face.

1. **Odysseus Crack** Font 6c **
The left-hand crack on the north face is hard to get into and a little tricky to finish onto the slab.

2. **Blood Music**
The central red bulge was a good problem until a hold snapped, now it's a real challenge! Climb out of pockets right of Odysseus to an impossible-looking sequence through the central wall aiming right to better holds.

3. **Penelope** Font 6b ***
The right hand cave wall over the bog by the pocket. Crimp and layaway to flat hold, gain pinch and reach for lip. The crux is getting onto the slab.

4. **Rhiconich Arête** Font 6a ***
The best arête of its grade in the country? The south wall arête can be gained by a crimpy step off to lunge for the arête and a ledge. A committing sequence gains good blind holds round the arête to finish thrillingly up the easy top ledges (cover shot).

170

Oldshoremore

Oldshoremore NC 192 586

Take the winding B801 west for a dozen kilometres through Kinlochbervie to a signpost to the beautiful beach of Oldshoremore. Turn left then immediately right downhill to a parking area by the old graveyard. Hop over the hill to be presented with a superb beach. There is good bouldering on walls and boulders at the west end of the beach and along the headland past the island. Superb clean rock.

Droman Pier

Backstage Boulder NC 257 537

The 'Backstage Boulder' is a good looking piece of rock near the crag of the same name, providing a number of easy problems and a few sit starts. It is superbly clean and is visible from the road just west of Rhiconich on the B-road to Kinlochbervie.

Gneiss!

Sheigra NC 182 601

Sheigra is a great spot to base yourself here for climbing and bouldering in the summer months. There is a beautiful camping spot at the 'end of the road' at Sheigra itself, and nearby some good tidal bouldering blocs at Droman Pier NC 185 592 (the first road down left before Sheigra, or walk south round the headland from Sheigra beach). The rock is superb but hard on the fingers!

Sandwood Bay
Pic by Dave Wheeler

171

Sandwood Bay NC 225 654

Perhaps the jewel in the crown of remote Scottish beaches, Sandwood Bay can only be gained by a 5km hike along a path by the lochs north of Blairmore (just before Sheigra). The bouldering is located on cliffs and outcrops at the east end of the beach. The rock is truly exceptional and a feature in itself. There are some good hard lines and projects developed by Dave Wheeler and friends, should you wish to stay here for a few days camping and going wild, though it's a place where even the most dedicated boulderer might be distracted by grander things!

Backstage Boulder

11 THE ISLANDS

Claire Youdale on the
Sannox Boulders, Arran

OUTER ISLANDS

SHETLAND

Shetland is our most remote climbing outlier and home to some ancient stones, though it really is a different country, more of a republic! If you are travelling here, or working here for a bit, there is bouldering on the seacliffs and various erratic boulders, but the best bouldering is on the cleaned gneiss bloc-giants called the 'Stanes of Stofast', which have recently been developed by Paul and Al Whitworth and friends, who run the excellent *www.climbshetland.co.uk* website, where news of bouldering can be sourced.

Stanes of Stofast HU 505 720
For the 'Stanes', take the A968 north out of Lerwick and continue to Voe where you turn right onto the B9071. Continue north through Vidlin and on to Lunna and parking on the Lunna Ness peninsula at the road-end at Outrabister. Walk southeast across the moor to the large boulders.

Eshaness HU 205 784
Crag bouldering and shore bouldering under the spectacular seacliffs round Eshaness lighthouse. Head north on the A970 to take the B9078 west to Eshaness lighthouse.

Su Stanes HU 418 638
About 30 or so problems on the stones above the village of Hillside, east of the A970. They can be gained from the B9071 above the Loch of Voe.

RUM - HALLIVAL NM 404 959

A lost island which often lies like some Jurassic Park set on the misty horizon west of Mallaig. Take a Calmac ferry to Kinloch and stay at the campsite or the Castle (it's not that expensive for self-catering) - it's best to go outside the midge season (Easter or September are good times) You can do the round of the Rum Cuillin, but if you're prepared to take a small boulder mat, check out the corries under the ridge. Possibly the most unique are the incredibly clean and rough 'allivalite' boulders perched on heather under the east flank of Hallival in Coire nan Gruund. They can be approached by climbing Hallival and dropping down, or by the pleasant path from Kinloch to veer off up the Allt na h'Uamh burn up into the corrie. There are excellent problems at all grades on the incredibly rough rock.

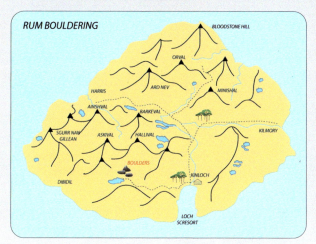

RUM BOULDERING

BLOODSTONE HILL

ORVAL

ARD NEV

MINISHAL

HARRIS

AINSHVAL

BARKEVAL

SGURR NAN GILLEAN

ASKIVAL

HALLIVAL

KILMORY

BOULDERS

DIBIDIL

KINLOCH

LOCH SCRESORT

Eshaness
Pic www.climbshetland.co.uk

LEWIS & HARRIS

The Outer Hebrides are a must-see if you enjoy travelling: wild landscapes, surfing waves, white beaches, huge skies and yes, good bouldering! Though it is maybe not a place to seek out solely for bouldering, there are now a number of areas where you can combine traditional climbing and a little summer bouldering. Dave MacLeod, James Sutton and Niall McNair and others have all raided some areas and created some reliable problems described here. The rock is a superb and multi-coloured Lewisian Gneiss...the very best and oldest rock you can get!

Niall McNair on 'Traighd Route' at Traigh na Berigh
Pic by Emma Stevens

Lewis & Harris

Butt of Lewis — ⚓ Port Nis
A857
Barabhas
Isle of Lewis
Carloway — A858
Traigh na Berigh
Miavaig — Callanish Stones
Stornoway ⚓
A859
Huisinis — Clisham
Harris
⚓ Tarbert
Ferry from Ullapool
Ferry from Uig, Skye

Port Nis NB 538 633

The Butt of Lewis is the very north tip of the island and Port Nis is a small harbour hiding from the brunt of weather fronts. Drive north out of Stornoway on the A857 and follow signs for the Butt of Lewis and Port Nis. Park at the harbour and walk south along the beach to the obvious crags and the obvious lone boulder known as the 'sea peanut'. The rock is a tidal gneiss, sometimes a little wet, but good quality.

1. **Sunday Surgery** Font 6b **
The Sea Peanut. On the overhanging south face of the Peanut, sit start right hand in crack, reach for the lip and use the arête to mantle over.

2. **Hiding From God** Font 6b **
On Sea Peanut again, same start as above but climb out right to mantle.

3. **Fear of Drowning** Font 6b+ **
Right of *Hiding from God*, sit start the sloper lip gain the higher lip and traverse left to *Sunday Surgery*.

4. **Lip Service** Font 7b+ **
Further south along the cliffs is an overhang with a wave-worn shelf. A great lip traverse can be done along the roof. Sit start on the ledge sloper, slap up to the lip and follow it all the way round on slopers to pull over at the right hand end on edges. FA Dave MacLeod 2005.

Traigh na Berigh NB 108 354

On the far west of the island are terrific beaches east of Uig sands (where they found the Lewis Chessmen). Traigh na Berigh is the beach south of Bhaltos. Follow the A858 southwest from Stornoway to a left turn before the Callanish stones onto the B8011 which eventually leads to Miabhaig. Turn right off here onto a loop road, the left turn takes you to Cnip and the campsite further on by the beach of Traigh na Berigh. The excellent crag at the east also has associated bouldering on and roundabout it. The rock is a superb gneiss.

1. **Raspberigh** Font 6b+ **
The original problem on the long roof below the main crag, following the thin crack near the left end. Sit start.

2. **Wannae Cnip Ma Pal?** Font 7b ***
The roof and headwall direct, just right of *Raspberigh*. Sit start and pull through an undercut, then use a thin break to a slopey top-out direct. FA Dave MacLeod 2003.

3. **Cnipped in the Bud** Font 7a+ **
The roof and square recess right of *Cnip Ma Pal*. Sit start the good break, use a right press in the recess, turn the roof through crimps to an easier finish.

4. **The Cnipper** Font 7a ***
The classic fingery traverse on the main face. Start at a good hold in a crack above a pedestal, traverse left across the fingery wall to finishing jugs. Technical. FA Niall McNair 2001.

5. **Traighd Route** Font 7c ***
Immaculate traverse of the main crag. Start high near the right end of the face, standing on twin blocks. Climb left down to a thin break, continue past an easier section to a thin crux (above an embedded block) to sustained climbing at low level to a break (shake-out) over the pedestal. Finish along 'The Cnipper'. FA Dave MacLeod 2003.

6. **Traigh of Torture Instruments** Font 6c+ **
Under the main face is a right-facing overhanging nose. Clamp up this to a left hand break then climb across the nose on slopers. Direct is *No Traighdbacks* Font 7a.

Miabhaig NB 081 346

On the road to Mangersta, just after the Bhaltos loop road turn off at Miabhaig, you enter a mini canyon. Underneath the overhanging prow on the left there are a couple of boulders over the stream. The Gravestone boulder has a steep triangular face and the neighbouring boulder is a rectangle with a hanging nose. The best problem is:

Crofter's Concern Font 6c ***

The hanging nose of the boulder facing the 'Gravestone'. Sit start the slopey left arête, heelhook right and pull through to the flat ledge. FA James Sutton 2005.

Clisham Pass NB 191 097

The pass over Clisham to Tarbert is the entry to Harris. The north side of the pass has some terrific boulder clusters overlooking Loch Seaforth. They are good in summer when the bogs dry out, are exposed and catch the wind and there is plenty to do if you are in the area! They are best reached from the Tarbert ferry port on the A859, though if you are travelling south from Stornoway, they are worth stopping at. There are plenty of easy circuit problems and no shortage of projects. The best testpiece is this one:

Hard Lines Font 7a+ ***

10m east of the large 'heather-hat' boulder, below the road (40m from layby). The downhill steep face with an undercut rail sit start. From this, gain a crimp and snatch for the double sloper above the lip, then again to the jug. FA Dave MacLeod 2005.

Clisham Boulders

MULL - LOCH BUIE   NM 621 244

Mull is a magical island for climbing and bouldering, with varied rock and terrific isolation. Apart from the granite at Fionnphort, the best bouldering lies in the sleepy bay of Lochbuie on the south coast, hidden away from everything.

Approach Notes

From Oban, regular ferries sail to Craignure, from where the A849 can be taken south for 10k, to a left turn onto a B-road at Strathcoil. This is taken for about 12 kilometres to the shores of the picturesque Loch Buie. From here, a walk eastwards past the gatehouse and along the shore past Moy Castle leads to the crags and boulders by the land-rover track which runs to Laggan Sands. If you're on a bike, cut down the track following signs to Laggan Sands B&B, it's a bit quicker.

The 'Popcorn Wall' is the first textured wall of the embedded buttress behind the tree. The other walls and boulders lie by the track. The best boulder is at the end, the 'Mushroom', which grows in a field in front of a cave. The rock is a very rough dimpled gabbro. It was developed mainly by Daniel Brooks, Mark Somerville, Mike Tweedley and Dave MacLeod.

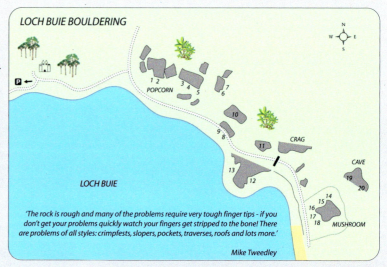

LOCH BUIE BOULDERING

POPCORN

CRAG

CAVE

LOCH BUIE

MUSHROOM

'The rock is rough and many of the problems require very tough finger tips - if you don't get your problems quickly watch your fingers get stripped to the bone! There are problems of all styles: crimpfests, slopers, pockets, traverses, roofs and lots more.'

Mike Tweedley

176

Kirsty MacBirnie on 'Danny's Wall'

Graham MacBirnie on 'Gunge Pool'

Kirsty MacBirnie on 'Flesh'

Dave MacLeod on the Mushroom Boulder's 'Nipple Attack' Pic: MacLeod Coll.

1. **Hook and Go** Font 7a ***
Popcorn Wall. Climbs the superb steep arête right of the overhang, using heels and dynamism, Font 7b from a sit start.

2. **Tried and Tested** Font 7a+ **
Popcorn Wall. Takes the right wall direct on small crimps and pockets.

3. **Higher than the Sun** Font 6b+ **
Pink Monsters Wall. The central left line is steady but highball.

4. **High as a Kite** Font 6b+ **
Pink Monsters Wall. The line just right again.

5. **Pink Monsters** Font 7a ***
Takes the technical hanging arête which is very hard to get established on and crimpy to the top. FA Mark Somerville.

6. **Perfect Day** Font 5 *
The boulder with the square-cut corner on the right, viewed from the track. Takes the arête just to the right of the corner.

7. **Flesh** Font 7a **
Just right of the corner. Takes the central wall on painful crimps and involves long immersion in confusion and pain before success.

8. **Beefcake** Font 7a+ **
The 'Beefcake Boulder' overhangs the track. The obvious crack from a difficult sit-down start.

9. **Jimmy da Cricket** Font 6a *
Just left of the above problem, dyno from crimps to the top.

10. **Danny's Wall** Font 5 ***
The pockmarked wall, with a wee cave embedded in it. This takes the obvious overhanging flakes on the left of the wee cave, with a puzzling top-out, excellent rock and great climbing!

11. **Zippy Lippy** Font 7b ***
The next big boulder you can walk underneath! The only line so far, this traverses the slopey lip rightwards to exit above the walk-through. FA Mike Tweedley.

12. **The Gunge Pool** Font 6a ***
Sea Promontory. On the east walls, this travels right from a thigh-height ledge by the obvious nose of rock, where the tallest part of the wall is climbed. The nose direct left is Font 6b.

13. **The Black Seam** Font 4 **
West wall of sea promontory. Climb the left edge of the black seam, delicately at first on sea-worn footholds.

14. **The Mushroom Traverse** Font 7b ***
Mushroom Boulder. This works left to right around the boulder from the back to finish standing on the slopey ledge at the front.

15. **Freebase** Font 6c ***
Mushroom. Climbs the vague crack line left of the nose, from a sitting start at frustrating slopers. If you can do this move, the rest follows easily up the nose.

16. **Nipple Attack** Font 7a+ ***
Mushroom. Sit-start under the nose at a crimp-rail, out left to a left-hand crimp and a slopey boss, where a horizontal twist and slap gains the finishing holds.

17. **Naked** Font 6c ***
Mushroom. This climbs straight through the crimped front roof from a sitting start.

18. **Streaker** Font 6b+ **
The short clean cut corner at the front from a sit start. Named after an occasional visitor on the beach.

19. **Cut Loose** Font 6b **
Cave. Climbs from the back of the shelf to a good hold on the arête, cuts loose and climbs to the top.

20. **Sonic Mook** Font 7a+ ***
Cave. The left arête of the right wall, climbed from a low start and long reach with the left hand, then heel hooks allow technical progress to be made all the way up.

Gunge Pool Wall & Nose

'Nipple Attack'

177

Sunset at Loch Buie

SKYE - COIRE LAGAN

Gabbro is a super rock to climb on, raspingly rough, allowing some element of security on the more highball problems, but be warned, a day's hard session will strip the skin and chew up finger-tape. Vaseline, cocoa-butter, or maybe an old-wife's remedy is required if you want to pull on again the next day! The best arrangements seem to echo the thoughts of Douglas Milner on the efforts required to climb in Skye: '…one day sitting and thinking, one day on the ridge, and one day just sitting.'

Approach: Having crossed the Skye Bridge, the A87 winds through Broadford, on round Loch Ainort past the hump of Glamaig, then diminishes westwards at the Sligachan hotel onto the A863. After a few miles there is a left turn signed to Carbost, from where a minor road drops down through Glen Brittle. It is hard to keep your eyes on the road as the mighty mother-lode of the Cuillin looms. This is where signals on mobiles simply vanish and compasses begin to spin. Accommodation can be found in bunkhouses or at the campsite (01478 640404).

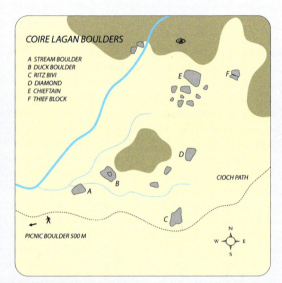

COIRE LAGAN BOULDERS

A STREAM BOULDER
B DUCK BOULDER
C RITZ BIVI
D DIAMOND
E CHIEFTAIN
F THIEF BLOCK

CIOCH PATH

PICNIC BOULDER 500 M

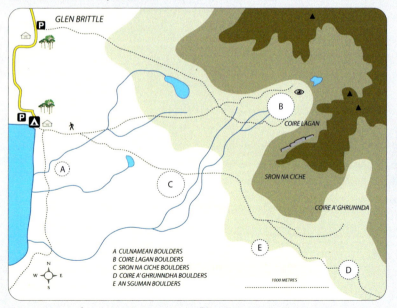

GLEN BRITTLE

B

COIRE LAGAN

A

C

SRON NA CICHE

COIRE A'GHRUNNDA

E

D

A CULNAMEAN BOULDERS
B COIRE LAGAN BOULDERS
C SRON NA CICHE BOULDERS
D COIRE A'GHRUNNDHA BOULDERS
E AN SGUMAN BOULDERS

1000 METRES

"The magic and magnetism (real and sentimental) of the great bare ridges of The Coolin grape blue in the morning sun…"

C. Douglas Milner
Rock for Climbing - 1950

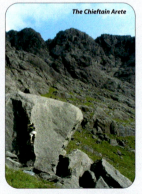

The Chieftain Arete

1. *Jawbreaker* Font 6b+ **
Picnic Boulder. Situated by the path east of the loch on the walk-in. Climb the crack on the west face, gained by smearing feet and twisting side-pulls - an excellent introduction to gabbro.

2. *Criss Cross* Font 6c ***
Picnic Boulder. Climbs the overhanging arête over the bog (do your duty and bring a stone from the path to help fill it in), clamping the seamed arête with toes and hands to stop swinging off into the pool.

3. *Jump for Joy* Font 6b **
Picnic Boulder. Just right of the north-east arête, start on the angled slab, through an edge and sloper to a better edge and the top.

4. *North East Arête* Font 7a *
Picnic Boulder. Niall McNair's technical addition to this boulder, sit start the east slab using an undercut and continue pretty much relying on smears all the way.

5. *East Face Crack* Font 6a *
Picnic Boulder. Climbs the vanishing crack to finish on slopers.

6. *Lucky Break* Font 6c+ ***
Stream boulder. On the large steep face, sit start at slopers and gain head-height edges, then a power lunge to a break allows an easier finish to the top.

7. *Surf's Up* Font 6a **
Duck Boulder. The large boulder with smaller ones on top. This climbs the far left sloping bulges through the small roof.

8. *Naismith's Route* Font 3 **
Duck Boulder. Climbs the easiest rock on the left above the gravel apron on polished holds. Blame Naismith for polishing the rock with hobnails!

9. *Collie's Route* Font 4 *
Duck Boulder. Climb the left hand slabby groove from good holds. FA Norman Collie early 1900's.

10. *The Groper* Font 7a **
Duck Boulder. Sit start low left and follow the holds right to jump to the bra-shaped hold, match a sloping hold above, then finish lengthily on better holds. 6c from the bra.

11. *Tiggy's Pinch* Font 7a **
Duck boulder. A couple of metres left of the right arête. Difficult pinching leads to a good left sidepull on the lip, then the right hand snaps to another lip pinch, from here it is a matter of willpower to fight through the small edges onto the slab.

12. *Duck Boulder Arête* Font 6b+ ***
The right arête. A long stretch to get started, but good holds gain height and a slap for the sloping bulge to the right allows the trucking slab to be gained.

13. *The Ramp* Font 4 *
The Ritz Bivi has three cracks above its entrance, all worthy of a tip. The ramp feature on the north-west face looks easy, doesn't it?

14. *The Flunky* Font 6a **
Ritz Bivi. Right of the ramp. Climb the excellent north crack and arête.

15. *The Lift Attendant* Font 6a **
Ritz Bivi. Bridges up over the bivi-wall and into the diagonal crack, finishing right. More like a Masonic handshake than a climb!

16. *Skins* Font 6a+ **
Diamond boulder below The Chieftain. 2m left of arête, crank from crimps rightwards to the diagonal undercling then follow the crack. *Ben's Problem* is a Font 6c variation direct up the wall to jug.

'True Stories'

17. *The Chieftain* Font 6c E4 6a ***
Clach Ceann-Feadhna (The Chieftain). More of a solo route and a terrifying act of commitment up the scooped weakness of the west wall. Step right into a dish at half height, then mantle out with brave-pills. Pad the landing.

18. *Chieftain Arête* Font 6c E4 6a ***
Another hard and scary teeter up the right side of the northwest (left) arête, crux at the top. Mats needed. FA James Sutton 2006.

19. *Chieftain Groove* Font 6a **
The left-hand groove left of the arête is still intimidating. Rocks up with increasing commitment to easier ground at the top. Descend left.

20. *True Stories* Font 6a ***
The 'thief' block above the scree. From the mezzanine, step left out onto the bold arête and wobble up it with a heart flutter or two!

21. *Revenge* Font 6c **
Thief Block. From the mezzanine, gain the slopey lip and mantle with difficulty.

Sron na Ciche NG 430 199

These boulders provide a less stressful atmosphere, but a rough and rude challenge to the boulderer's strength. The path to these boulders veers off right across the stream from the Coire Lagan path, past a wee loch to the lower reaches of the Coire Lagan burn. Just before the burn, turn right across a small bog and over the first brow appears the fern-barbed peak of the Venom Boulder. 200metres further east is a complex of boulders 50m before the burn on the right. This triplet cluster with the cave has a steep blank face in the middle, around which the best problems lie.

'Snake Attack' on the Venom Boulder

1. **Snake Attack** Font 6c+ ***
Venom boulder. Climbs the steep west face from a sit start along a flake crack to lunge up onto the slab and is one of the best problems in the area.

2. **Bass Line Venom** Font 7a ***
The obvious sloper traverse of the south face from a sit start, slapping from right to left to finish round onto the slabbed corner.

3. **Morning Wings** Font 6c **
Cave arête left. Sit start round the corner at a sloping shelf, follows the slopey traverse right along the lip to finish up the left arête.

4. **Evening Wings** Font 6b+ **
Applies the same philosophy to the right arête from a low start.

5. **Thunderhead** Font 7b/7c ***
A hard slopey traverse on the boulder opposite the arêtes cave. Start below the triangular nose, negotiate this and drop down to the lip and traverse left to hopefully pull through onto the slab. Grade depends on if you use high holds round the nose or not!

6. **Howling Gael** Font 6b ***
A few metres to the right of *Evening Wings* is a wee bulging roof. This excellent problem pulls over into a diagonal seam and smears up right to finish.

180

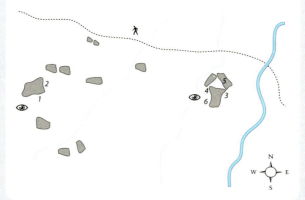

SRON NA CICHE BOULDERS

'Howling Gael'

The Culnamean Boulders NG 417 200

From behind the toilet block at the campsite, turn right along the landrover track. The boulders lie along the south edge of the first stream, about ten minutes walk south. There are a string of boulders offering good problems and traverses for the lazy boulderer. The best boulder here is *Bob the Boulder*, the large overhanging, heather-hatted boulder in the middle of the line.

Bob 1 Font 6b ***
The original. On the west side, take a sit start at a good hold, stretch for a ledge and boom to the top.

Bob 2 Font 6b **
Go left from the same start to gain a slanted hold and a sloper.

Bob 3 Font 6c **
The low traverse along the thin crack from a far left sit start, follow the seamed crack to finish up the block. Continuing to the far right adds a grade.

Coire a Ghrunnda & An Sguman

Further southeast, the path continues to Coire a Ghrunnda in about another half hour, (taking the right fork in the path), where large boulder clusters come into view around the path on the east side. Directly downhill through the marshes from this viewpoint is the 'Phantom' boulder. Heading east along the path leads to the visible cluster with the odd tree leaning over them. Find a cave with a very obvious lateral crack! Some easier slabs lie round about as an alternative.

1. **Pump Up the Jam** Font 7a ***
An Sguman east. A ten metre tape-up! Jam along the perfect crack in the huge roof from the far right, aiming up and left to pull round the crack in the nose. Hard as nails. FA James Sutton 2005.

2. **Phantom Face** Font 7a ***
Phantom boulder, An Sguman west. The black leaning east face, start using a crimpy right sidepull and an undercut, reach up left to a slopey sidepull and aim for the jug up right.

Tape Up!

Mal Meech on 'Phantom Face'

'Pump Up the Jam' Pic James Sutton

CARN LIATH   NG 497 567

Aside from the great (but painful) gabbro boulders of Coire Lagan, there is also a collection of finer-grained basalt boulders at Carn Liath off the A855 to Staffin. Described by developer James Sutton as 'truly mental'.

Approach: they lie about 13km north of Portree, before the hamlet of Rigg and the conifer plantations, two burns tumble down from Carn Liath hill on the west. Approach up the main grassy ridge to the west onto the flat boggy moorland (the main cliff is visible high up ahead). Aim for a mini col at about 300m, right of the cliff. From here you can see a couple of thousand boulders. The main bouldering area is on the flat area at about 250m. It is a complex place to explore but there are some terrific natural problems.

Lee Robinson on Mr Ben Direct

Rob Jones on Giant Haystacks

Lee Robinson on Skyeline Crack

'You'll be utterly gobsmacked, but don't be intimidated by this vast boulder field. To get the best of this dramatic landscape return via the Old Man of Storr.'
Lisa Wastling

1 **Pyramid Area** - Various grades *
Nice clean rock to warm up on. Lichen-free zone.

2. **Swing Arête** Font 6c+ **
Climb across the overhanging arête from left to right using the finger pocket. Try not to swing off onto the block below. Handy heel-hook to top out.

3. **Twin Arêtes** Font 6a *
Sit start the obvious short arête and similar to the right.

4. **Mr Ben** Font 6b ***
An excellent face of rock. Straight up the left hand end using the mono: 6c without the mono.

5. **Divot Do That** Font 6a *
Just right of Mr. Ben. Start with your feet on the big sloping ledge, reach for the spike and continue with an awkward mantle.

6. **Tigers** Font 6b *
Uphill from Mr Ben. Sit start and traverse right to left to the roof centre and over.

7. **Dimple Slab** Font 6a **
Straight up the middle is the most satisfying - the higher you go, the harder it gets. Escape right or left if you get the jitters.

8. **Skyeline** Font 5 **
The diagonal crack on the main face of The Wrestling Block.

9. **Arêtenaphobia** Font 6a ***
Wrestling block. Climb the perfect arête.

10. **Giant Haystacks** Font 6c ***
On the rear of the wrestling block, right to left layback, then campus moves to top.

11. **Sheep Can Levitate** Font 6b **
The Sheep Boulder. About 100m up the hill from Mr. Ben is a large boulder buried in the hill. From a sit start on slopers, gain a jug then a crimp and undercut. Continue over the top slab.

12. **Sheep Dip** Font 6c ***
The Sheep Boulder. From a sit start head straight up to a triangular ledge, then pull over the slopey basalt via a tiny crimp, if you can find it!

13. **Cetorhinus Maximus** Font 6c ***
The obvious and striking shark fin arête. Sublime if a little scary.

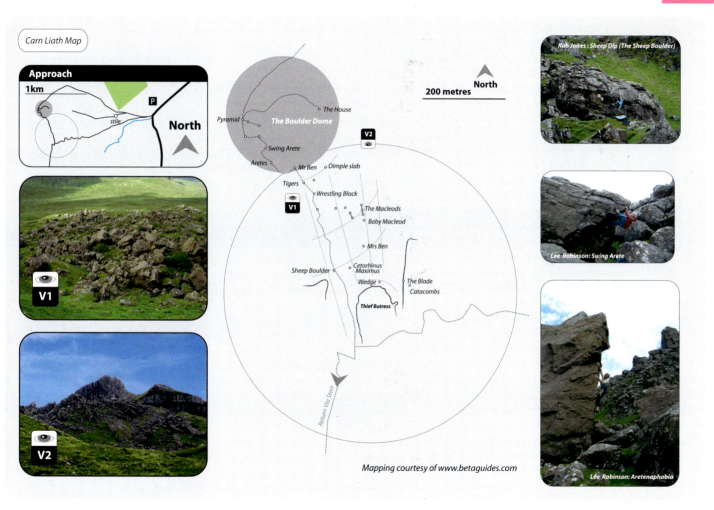

Carn Liath Map

Approach

1km

P

stile

North

The House

Pyramid

The Boulder Dome

V2

Swing Arete

Aretes

Mr Ben Dimple slab

Tigers

V1 Wrestling Block

The Macleods

Baby Macleod

Mrs Ben

Sheep Boulder Cetorhinus
Maximus

Wedge The Blade
Catacombs

Thief Butress

Return Via Storr

200 metres **North**

V1

V2

Rob Jones : Sheep Dip (The Sheep Boulder)

Lee Robinson: Swing Arete

183

Lee Robinson: Aretenaphobia

Mapping courtesy of www.betaguides.com

ARRAN BOULDERING

Arran is a stunning geological jewel stuck in the middle of the seafaring clutter that is the Clyde. Its youngest rocks are the excellent granitre erratics and boulders on the north of the island, but it also has old red sandstone bouldering and some gabbro bouldering on the south coast.

Caledonian MacBrayne operate regular ferries from Ardrossan, winter and summer, so it's easy to take the boulder mat over for a day's bouldering and catch the last ferry home. It takes no more than two hours fast stomp to the highest boulders in Glen Rosa, whereas the coastal bouldering is all extremely accessible from the bus routes that tour the island, some of the drivers even know the names of the stones!

1. The Mushroom *NS 026 387* - an old red sandstone outcrop in the woods of Brodick Castle grounds.

2. Corrie Boulders *NS 024 420 (Clach Mhor GR)* - four excellent granite erratics on the road verges between Corrie and Sannox.

3. Sannox Boulders *NR 996 455* - hidden boulders in a small gully underneath Cnocan Donna, accessible from Glen Sannox.

4. Glen Catacol *NR 918 488* - a pleasant stone on the northwest of the island on the side of Glen Catacol, known as *Clach a' Chait*.

5. Glen Rosa - the whole glen, from the bridge at the Garbh Allt (NR 982 386) to the higher Fionn Choire (NR 972 424) is littered with excellent boulders which improve in quality with altitude.

6. Kildonan *NR 022 208* - a geological hot-point at the south of the island, these gabbro outcrops are obvious on the shore. Climb at will.

184

Tim Morozzo on the fine granite of Glen Rosa

1. THE MUSHROOM

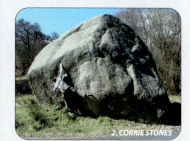

2. CORRIE STONES

3. GLEN SANNOX

LOCHRANZA

CATACOL

④

SANNOX

③

CORRIE

②

⑤

①

ARRAN

BRODICK

LAMLASH

BLACKWATERFOOT

WHITING BAY

1 KM

KILDONAN

⑥

N
W   E
S

4. GLEN CATACOL

5. GLEN ROSA

6. KILDONAN

185

ARRAN - Corrie Boulders

Delightful granite boulder erratics which are extremely accessible to say the least. They provide a satisfying circuit which gradually gets harder. From Brodick pier, catch the North Island bus to Sannox (ask to get off at the Cat Stone) and walk back via the boulders, which are all close to, or actually on, the main road.

The Cat Stone NS 020 444 - lies on the road between Corrie and Sannox. Watch for traffic!

Clach an Fhion NS 023 429 - this boulder stands by a layby in the centre of Corrie, on a grassy verge, south of the bad bend harbour.

Clach Mhor Druim a' Charn NS 024 420 - this giant boulder is on a mezzanine just south of the last village house. Walk up through the field to climb a short steep slope, or cut across from the path to the Roof Boulder.

The Roof Boulder NS 025 418 - just by a small burn south of the field is a layby and path into the woods. The Roof boulder is obvious up and left on the slope.

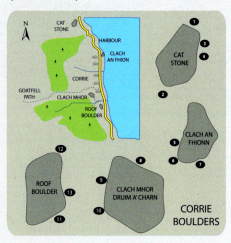

1. Roadside Slab Font 3
Cat Stone. Step onto the slab by the shot-hole and step right to finish up the wide crack.

2. South Arête Font 3+
Climb the blunt south arête via the scoop to finish leftwards at the descent flakes on the back.

3. Shothole Direct Font 4
From the roadside shot-hole, use a polished crimp to gain good holds above and follow the flakes to the top.

4. Shothole Traverse Font 5+ **
From a sit start at the shothole, pull left through polished sidepull slopers to match crimps, then crank up through big edges finishing rightwards.

5. Hero Slab Font 6a
Fhion Boulder. Step on to the slab just left of the easy flake crack, using a poor RH pocket, aiming high and left for another pocket and bigger holds.

6. Roadside Arête Font 5+*
Climb the cracked arête to a wobbly finish.

7 The Fhion Gaston Font 6b **
Sit start at the obvious pockets on the right, walk up the ramp and use the blunt arête to gain a high Gaston through the crack to the top - technical and good.

8. The Slab Font 4 *
Clach Mhor. Highball and excellent. Just right of the cheatstone crack is the steepest part of the slab. Climb it direct from a flake ledge, aiming for the good high pockets.

9. The Snare Font 6c ***
The steep back wall direct through the obvious sidepulls. Gain a high sharp pocket, try not to snare your fingers and crank left to sidepulls and a smeary escape left.

10. The Balance Font 6a+ *
From the ledges left of the saplings, balance upwards using a blunt arête hold and go direct to a hidden ledge above on the lip. Mantle out right to finish.

11. Left Wall Font 6a+
Roof Boulder. Sit start at the horizontally cracked left wall, gain jugs on the lip, then mantle up and left to a big pocket.

12. Right Arête Font 6c *
Sit start at a pocket and use the plinth for feet, gain holds on the arête then a good LH pinch allows a rockover to the blank lip and finish right.

13. The Roof Font 7a **
Sit start at a shelf under the left-central roof, use shelf crimps to dyno up to a good edge, then work left through slopers to a tricky direct mantle over the top. Butch.

ARRAN - *The Mushroom*   NS 026 387

This giant red sandstone monolith lies in Merkland wood in the National Trust grounds to Brodick Castle. It used to be hidden by the rhododendrons until cleared recently for path-making. Now it is easily accessible, lying twenty metres from the road. It's still easy to miss however, so from Brodick head north along the coast road past the brewery and the castle entrance. Continue past an entrance signed 'Merkland Wood Walks' until a gravel layby on the right 1km later. Park or leave the bikes here, walk north up the road for 100m and hop the wall on the left. Bash through the vegetation to the Mushroom under the pines.

Claire Youdale on the Mushroom

Mushroom projects...

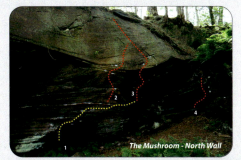

The Mushroom - North Wall

The Fern Boulder

The rock is a juggy, laterally banded old red sandstone, with steep jug-hauling through roofs. It is also highball so many problems are safer as traverses and jump-offs at lip jugs. The north east wall has the best rock, the wee 'Fern Boulder' opposite the Mushroom is excellent and there are some hard projects to go through the various roofs and caves. Needs dry conditions, but is quite cool even in high summer.

The Mushroom - North Wall

1. **Cave Traverse** Font 6b+ *
Start low on the left side of the left cave, crank up to a juggy rail and contine right mostly footless until a finish up problem 3 can be made.

2. **Highballer** Font 6b
A juggy start between the caves leads to a hard pull through to jugs above the lip… jump off or gain crimps and get established (and scared) on the headwall.

3. **Rock Lobster** Font 6b **
Pull on just left of the right cave to find good edges under the roof, heel-toe left to allow a long reach over the lip to a good hidden hold, pull further to jugs and rock on to the headwall or jump off.

4. **Third Cave** Font 6a
Climb out of the dank cave to ramps on the right.

The Fern Boulder
Just opposite the Mushroom is a short wall with good rock.

1. **Left Arête** Font 6b+
Climb the left arête from a sit start without using the big jug up and right.

2. **Petit Tiroir** Font 6a *
From good sidepulls just right of the left arête, slap up to a sloping ramp, match this and traverse to the far right to a rock-over at jugs.

3. **The Hole** Font 5
From sharp central jugs, sit start and pull up through an inset pocket, then traverse left to the finishing jugs on the left arête.

4. **Eliminator** Font 7a+ *
From jugs under the right roof, gain an eliminate crimp on the lip, then power left to the inset hole, traverse left to finish.

5. **Fern Traverse** Font 5+ **
From jugs under the right roof, monkey left along good slopers and jugs to finish at problem 1.

187

Thankyou to all the boulderers and people who helped build this guide.

Sandra Spence
Colin Lambton
Lee Robinson
Lisa Wastling
Pete Murray
Sara Hunt
Tim Morozzo
Adrian Crofton
Richie Betts
Ian Taylor
Dave MacLeod
Michael Tweedley
Tim Rankin
Kev Howett
Alan Cassidy
Allan Wallace
Andrew Marshall
Andy Nisbet
Angus Murray
Ben Litster
Chris Adams
Chris Fryer
Chris Graham
Claire Youdale
Criag Henderson
Dave Cuthbertson
Jo George
David Jaberoo
Dave Redpath

Dave Wheeler
Dominic Kehoe
Dominic Ward
Graham Foster
Guy Robertson
Fraser Harle
Iain MacDonald
James Sutton
Kirsty McBirnie
Graham McBirnie
Mark Robson
Richard McGhee
Michael Lee
Neil Shepherd
Neil Morrison
Niall McNair
Pete Hill
Peter Roy
Steve Richardson
Scott Muir
Sean Culpan
Steven Ireland
Stuart Stronach
Tom Kirkpatrick
Tim Carruthers
Tim Palmer
Tom Charles-Edwards
Tony Simpson

Please check out the websites for these climbers:

Dave MacLeod   www.davemacleod.com
Dave Redpath   www.scottishclimbs.com
Tim Rankin   www.transition-extreme.com
Dave Cuthbertson   www.cubbyimages.com
Kev Howett   www.mountaineering-scotland.org.uk
Scott Muir   www.extreme-dream.com
Tim Morozzo   www.morozzo.co.uk
Lee Robinson   www.betaguides.com
Nick Carter   www.alphamountaineering.co.uk
Colin Lambton   www.creaghdhu.org.uk

188

Front Cover: Angus Murray on the Bloodstone Arete, Rhiconich.

Back Cover: John Watson on Sky Pilot, Glen Nevis.